1247

THE CHOSEN PRIMATE

· THE ·
CHOSEN
PRIMATE

HUMAN NATURE AND CULTURAL DIVERSITY

ADAM KUPER

HARVARD UNIVERSITY PRESS
CAMBRIDGE, MASSACHUSETTS
LONDON, ENGLAND
1994

Library of Congress Cataloging-in-Publication Data

Kuper, Adam.
The chosen primate : human nature and cultural diversity /
Adam Kuper.
p.   cm.
Includes index.
ISBN 0-674-12825-7
1. Anthropology.   2. Man.   3. Culture.   I. Title.
GN25.K87   1994
301—dc20   93-31770
CIP

Designed by Gwen Frankfeldt

For Jessica, Simon, Jeremy, and Hannah

PREFACE

Although in principle all anthropologists are Darwinians and concern themselves with the history and diversity of the human species, in practice each of us spends most of our time working on some particular aspect of culture, language, prehistory, or human biology. Yet we were drawn into anthropology because of the grand issues, and we are sustained by the hope that in the end our investigations, however obsessive and minute, will tie in with a larger argument. Accordingly, we are sensitive to theoretical shifts in any branch of the human sciences. From time to time new findings challenge old certainties, or an insubordinate scientist strips the wrappings from a venerable mummy and finds that it has turned to dust. Periodically a shock wave passes through the anthropological community in response to intellectual shifts in other disciplines. After each quake, a few prophets will proclaim that at last the truth is within our grasp.

In the eighties, two radical movements spread rapidly. One claimed that modern genetics would at last provide a material basis for the understanding of human behavior. The human sciences would now become a branch of biology. The other argued that, on the contrary, the modernist project of the human sciences is now finally played out. The great organizing narratives of human history were myths, produced by specific cultures in particular moods, whose time has passed. Nietzsche proclaimed over a century ago that God was dead. His heirs now insist that Science, too, is dead. No science can fully explain what moves us. There are no certainties, at least where human beings are concerned; no indisputable facts in search of theoretical explanation; no theories that can do justice to the play of human consciousness (except, of course, for the theory that says there can be no theory).

Both views—inevitably caricatured in this summary—represented extreme restatements of the oldest and most central debates in the human sciences. Are human beings so different from other animals that they require a special science all to themselves—a science, perhaps, that breaks with the classical methods and ambitions of the positivists? Could such a study ever yield insights as powerful and certain as those of other sciences?

Between 1985 and 1993 I served as editor of *Current Anthropology*, an international, interdisciplinary anthropological journal that is one of the main arenas for theoretical debates in the field. I was plunged into a series of interlinked conversations on the history of the species and on human cultural diversity, becoming a sort of ethnographer of anthropology.

It was a period of intellectual ferment. Theoretical debate was alive and well, and the issues were more complex than the radicals of either party would readily concede. The arguments were fresh and urgent. The papers I read spilled over with evidence and ideas that demanded a fundamental rethinking of some of the central questions in the anthropological tradition.

I immediately began to look around for a book that would review the state of play for me, but I could not find one. There are good textbooks in particular fields, but few modern syntheses; and there are far too many prophets about, each possessed by a Big Idea.

Isaiah Berlin, in his essay on Tolstoy's view of history, quotes the Greek poet Archilochus, who wrote: "The fox knows many things, but the hedgehog knows one big thing." Prophets are hedgehogs, prickly and myopic. They make poor companions and terrible guides. In the end I chose to write my own book, and to make it a fox's book. It will inevitably disappoint hedgehogs, but I am afraid that it will also irritate a lot of foxes. I am only a would-be fox, who knows a few little things. But that is perhaps in the nature of foxes.

I have written this book for anyone who wants to engage in the current debates about human origins, human nature, and human diversity. It is written in particular for my children, all of whom are now at university and wrestling with some of the problems discussed here; and for Jessica, as part of a conversation that has continued now for more than a quarter of a century.

I owe a great deal to my editor at Harvard University Press, Michael Fisher, and even more to Horace Freeland Judson, who wrote reams of wise, learned, and critical notes on an earlier draft, pushed me through the writer's pain barrier, and finally made me produce a much better book.

CONTENTS

ILLUSTRATIONS

And although in civil society man surrenders some of the advantages that belong to the state of nature, he gains in return far greater ones; his faculties are so exercised and developed, his mind is so enlarged, his sentiments so ennobled, and his whole spirit so elevated that . . . he should constantly bless the happy hour that lifted him for ever from the state of nature and from a narrow, stupid animal made a creature of intelligence and a man.

Jean-Jacques Rousseau, *The Social Contract*

What a chance it has been . . . that has made a man—any monkey probably might, with such chances be made intellectual, but almost certainly not made into man.

Charles Darwin, *Notebooks on the Transmutation of Species*

· 1 ·

ALL DARWINIANS NOW?

We are all Darwinians now. Darwin's is the one great Victorian theory that still commands assent from almost all who understand it. And it has survived and prospered for good Darwinian reasons. Tested again and again by new discoveries and observations, in competition with other theories, it has proved its fitness. Specialists debate technical side-issues, express sophisticated reservations, propose refinements, but virtually all natural and social scientists are Darwinians now, and with good reason. I take that as read.

The question I pose is a minor one in the broad context of Darwinian theory, yet perhaps no question is of greater consequence for our understanding of ourselves. Darwin was right about human origins, but is there a Darwinian account of human nature? Is there a Darwinian explanation for all the ways of life that *Homo sapiens* has tried out over the past hundred and fifty millennia? Can Darwinian theory help us to comprehend what we are doing here?

Almost from the first, Darwin was convinced that his theory would have profound philosophical implications. "Origin of man now proved," he wrote in a notebook in 1838. "Metaphysic must flourish.—He who understands baboon would do more toward metaphysics than Locke." He had resolved the problems of human origins, and biologists would now be able to settle the great questions about human destiny that had baffled the wisest of the English philosophers. But even good Darwinians may hesitate to go along with that.

The question of human origins was never at the top of Darwin's own agenda. He completed his five-year voyage on the *Beagle* in 1836, and between 1837 and 1839 he wrote 900 pages of notes that effectively set out his theory of general evolution. Though sure he was right, he was tormented with anxiety about the reception that awaited him when he published. He concealed his ideas for as long as possible even from his wife, out of respect for her religious sentiments. He wrote to one of the few colleagues he entrusted with his secret, "I am almost convinced (quite contrary to the opinion I started with) that species are not (it is like confessing to a murder) immutable." And he knew that his theory of human origins would strike even some of his respected colleagues as the greatest heresy of all.

Darwin delayed publication for two decades, breaking cover only when he was threatened with the loss of priority. In 1858 a young naturalist, Alfred Russel Wallace, sent him a letter from Borneo, enclosing a statement on natural selection that he asked Darwin to publish on his behalf. Darwin was now forced into the open. He arranged for the simultaneous publication of Wallace's statement and extracts from his own work, and then prepared a long summary of his findings, which was published under the title *The Origin of Species* in 1859.

He now explained the processes of evolutionary change, and asserted the common origin of all life: "Probably all the organic beings which have ever lived on this earth have descended from some one primordial form, into which life was first breathed." However, he skirted the specific and dangerous question of human origins, and tried to postpone the scandal that loomed so inexorably. He was too prudent—and too courtly—to wish to shock his contemporaries out of their most sensitive convictions. But clearly the issue could not be evaded for long.

Some of his friends urged him on, and one in particular, Thomas Henry Huxley, would brook no compromise. A skull and skeletons of gorillas had been discovered in West Africa in 1847 by an American Episcopalian missionary with the apposite name of Thomas Savage. These were exhibited in London, and, like other English anatomists, Huxley had been greatly impressed by the resemblances to humans. In 1855 Wombwell's traveling menagerie acquired the first gorilla to be seen alive in Europe, and toured with it, generating great popular excitement. The clergy and the scientific conservatives were troubled by the very human appearance and behavior of the creature, but one leading anatomist, Richard Owen, announced in 1857 that the brain of humans was completely different from that of the apes. Human beings, he concluded, were as different from apes as apes were from the platypus.

The Darwinians could not decently remain silent. On March 16, 1858, Huxley confronted his students at the Royal Institution with skeletons of man, the gorilla, and the monkey *Cynocephalus*. "Now I am quite sure," he told them, "that if we had these three creatures fossilized or preserved in spirits for comparison and were quite unprejudiced judges we should all at once admit that there is very little [he then added 'if any,' but deleted it] greater interval *as animals* between the *Gorilla* & the *Man* than exists between the *Gorilla* & the *Cynocephalus*." He elaborated the argument in his book *Evidences as to Man's Place in Nature,* which appeared in 1863.

"Hurrah the Monkey Book has come!" Darwin exulted when his copy of Huxley's book arrived at his home, Down House, in a Kentish village. But only in 1871, with the publication of *The Descent of Man,* did he abandon all public equivocation. Now at last he asserted that the same processes of gradual change, of descent with modification, accounted for the development of all species, including human beings. We are not specially created, but are "descended from some lowly organised form"—a conclusion, Darwin conceded, that "will, I regret to think, be highly distasteful to many."

What was this "lowly organised form" from which human beings stem? A study of our embryological structure clearly indicated that we are "descended from a hairy, tailed quadruped, probably arboreal in its habits, and an inhabitant of the Old World." If we are not exactly descended from the monkeys, we certainly share a common ancestor with them.

TWELVE decades after Darwin published that hypothesis, some crucial questions remain to be settled. There is still no complete account of human genesis. We have assembled only partial genealogies of our ancestors, and these are as yet only provisionally dated. Nor will the remaining uncertainties be resolved when someone, somewhere turns up a crucial fossil, the teasingly elusive missing link. There are conceptual problems too. How are we to fix the line that demarcates humans from other hominids? Was the defining moment reached when the average size of the brain passed a certain point, or when articulate language became general, or perhaps when tools began to be used to make other tools?

Nevertheless, the essential point, the primate origin of humanity, has been abundantly supported, most recently by the discovery that humans and chimpanzees are identical in 98.4 percent of their DNA nucleotide sequences and in 99.6 percent of their amino-acid sequences. But this conclusion provides only a starting-point for inquiries into the natural history of human beings. What does the knowledge of our close kinship with other primates tell us about our own nature?

In the final sentence of *The Descent of Man*, Darwin gave his answer, in measured but telling phrases.

> We must, however, acknowledge, as it seems to me, that man with all his noble qualities, with sympathy which feels for the most debased, with benevolence which extends not only to other men but to the humblest living creature, with his god-like intellect which has penetrated into the movements and constitutions of the solar system—with all these exalted powers—Man still bears in his bodily frame the indelible stamp of his lowly origin.

This seems unequivocal, yet read a second time the passage suggests two quite different possibilities. The first is that human beings must be regarded as just another primate species. Darwin was not disposed to deny that human beings are very unusual animals. Yet although he insisted upon the "high standard of our intellectual powers and moral disposition," he pointed out that many other animals could reason, learn, communicate, and make plans. They might even behave as moral creatures, displaying sympathy and contributing to the welfare of others. Darwin concluded that all animals which exhibit these qualities inherited them from a common ancestor, although in each species their development had followed a different route. Human behavior is therefore a modification of the habits of other apes. Darwin showed the way in which this insight could be exploited in his pioneering study, *The Expression of the Emotions in Man and Animals*, published in 1872, a year after *The Descent of Man*.

Yet Darwin's conclusion can also be read to suggest that the stamp of our primate origins clearly marks our bodily frame, but is less evident in those "noble qualities" and "exalted powers" that distinguish humans from other primates. The Darwinian story of human origins may accordingly be read as an account of divergence from the ancestral line, a great move, as one wit suggested, from tree-house to white house.

The theme of this narrative is change. One line of apes developed proto-human attributes, notably a larger brain and a bipedal gait. A series of successively more advanced hominid types evolved from this ancestral species. At last the capacity for language evolved, and from then on a series of cultural advances punctuated human history, culminating in a way of life very different from that of other primates.

Both these views have always had their proponents. Their debates shade off into another equally passionate argument, between those who prefer to understand human beings in terms of biological and inherited capacities and instincts, and those who emphasize the unique role of learning—of nurture—in molding human behavior. At the extreme, two parties, the biological and the cultural, contest the Darwinian heritage. They propose irreconcilable images of human beings.

The biological party would favor a primate model of humanity (nicely satirized in W. S. Gilbert's couplet, "Darwinian man, though well-behaved / Is really but a monkey shaved"). Members of this party have written most of the recent scientific blockbusters, suggesting that we are ready to see ourselves as the "naked ape" of Desmond Morris's famous phrase (despite our notorious concern not only with clothes but also with fashion), or as the "third chimpanzee," which is how Jared Diamond's recent best-selling book portrayed *Homo sapiens.* For these writers, the human animal is just another primate. In the past two decades, the pacemakers of the biological party have been a rampant radical faction, the sociobiologists, who have been inspired by the great advances in human genetics.

The other party—rather unfashionable at present—does not, of course, deny the common primate ancestry of humanity, but it points out that our primate origins did not determine the particular course taken by human evolution. We turned out differently from the great

African apes, although we share a common ancestor with them. Culture is a uniquely human achievement, and it is simply perverse to deny the distinctiveness and significance of the cultural factor in human history. The culture school has its contemporary radicals too, the ultra-relativists, who emphasize the uniqueness of every culture and the power of cultures to shape the mind. Drawing on the French philosophers of postmodernism, they deny the very possibility of a generalizing science of human consciousness.

The biological party argues that there is a universal human nature, genetically transmitted, largely shared with other primates, and with proven evolutionary advantages. Human culture is just a more sophisticated version of chimpanzee culture; it follows the grain of our biological needs and instincts. Human beings wear their culture lightly.

Their opponents emphasize human adaptability, the great differences in customs and institutions between communities, the autonomous trajectories of cultural development, the cumulative value of the human cultural heritage. They remind us that because we know something about ourselves, we can also think about changing our ways. That may even be the truest measure of our uniqueness.

The biological party points to the fact that for perhaps ninety-nine percent of their history human beings lived by foraging, under conditions not very different from those of other primate species. The recent history of humans may appear to break free from this established pattern, but they warn that any rupture with nature may have a terrible, perhaps terminal cost. The culture school denies that we are the unimproved heirs of a primate-forager Adam, and claims that cultural development has transformed our destiny. Culture introduced specifically human risks but also offered opportunities remote from the experiences of our primate cousins.

Apart, perhaps, from dissident postmodernists, Darwin is claimed as a patron by all factions of both parties; but he is also a hero to those who are impatient with the old arguments, who prefer to emphasize the interplay of cultural and biological factors in human history.

In reconstructing the process of human evolution, Darwin introduced a feedback loop from culture to nature, suggesting that the development of the brain permitted the invention of language and of tools, which in turn stimulated the further development of the brain. This implies that biological and cultural factors interact, and that neither is static. We are, for example, considerably larger than even our medieval ancestors, because we are better fed and healthier. For similar reasons, more of us survive infancy, we can expect to live very much longer, and there are a great many more of us. Biological constraints may be changed by cultural innovations even in our day—indeed, perhaps more radically and quickly now than ever before. We have recently started to tinker with our genetic endowment itself.

It could in any case be argued that the classic disputes between the grand old parties are foreign to Darwinian thinking. The Darwinian is not concerned with essences or with absolute differences between species, but rather with the processes of evolutionary change. These processes—as Darwin was the first to recognize—go on in populations. That was itself a revolutionary proposition.

The great dogma of biology well into the nineteenth century was that species were fixed and eternal, each occupying a set place in an orderly schema, rather like the elements in the periodic table of the chemists. In the year 1800, at the age of fifty-five, a much-maligned French biologist, Jean-Baptiste de Lamarck, abandoned the traditional, static typologies of species and reached the conclusion that species could undergo transformation. He wrote that over a lengthy period of time, "individuals, originally belonging to one species, become at length transformed into a new species distinct from the first."

Species did not merely change, they progressed. The direction of change was toward increasing complexity, and Lamarck was convinced that each new model delivered greater efficiency. No species died out, defeated. Each moved on to something a little better.

The ultimate mechanism was obscure, but God-given. Changes in the environment somehow obliged organisms to develop new tricks, and these were passed on to their offspring. This notion that traits acquired in one generation could be passed on to the next was shared by most biologists in the nineteenth and early twentieth centuries, including, at times, Darwin himself; but it has come to be regarded as the most characteristic error of Lamarck.

Like many revolutionary thinkers, Lamarck crystallized ideas that were already in the air. One of many predecessors was Darwin's own grandfather, Erasmus Darwin, a country doctor, who in 1794 had published a speculative volume, *Zoonomia,* in which he insisted on the universal existence of a "faculty of continuing to improve" and endorsed the notion that acquired characteristics could be inherited. He had the motto *E conchis omnia,* "Everything from shells," painted on his carriage door until the clergy persuaded him to remove it; and he wrote triumphant verses on evolution.

But Lamarck was the major evolutionary thinker of his day, and although his theories were dramatically denounced in a funeral oration by the greatest of his French contemporaries, Georges Cuvier, and subjected to a further scathing critique by the English geologist Charles Lyell, his ideas were widely diffused in the following generations. Lyell's critique was, in fact, strikingly counterproductive. It had the effect of converting to Lamarckism both the social philosopher Herbert Spencer and an enterprising publisher, the autodidact Robert Chambers, who in 1844 issued anonymously a popular Lamarckian book on evolution, *Vestiges of the Natural History of Creation,* which went through eleven editions between 1844 and 1860, when Darwin's *Origin* undermined it. Chambers's book brought evolutionist thinking to the attention of many, including A. R. Wallace, who was inspired by Darwin's journal of his voyage in the *Beagle* to travel to Borneo and put Chambers's ideas to the test, a venture that led him to the independent discovery of natural selection.

Yet, although evolutionism was in the air in the first half of the nineteenth century, Darwin's theory broke with all its precursors. He called Lamarck's book "veritable rubbish" and added, "I got not a fact or idea from it." "Heaven forfend me," he once wrote piously, "from Lamarck's nonsense of a 'tendency to progression,' 'adaptations from the slow willing of animals,' etc.!" He repudiated Lamarck's faith in progressive improvement, insisting that history had no such convenient design, and that local populations and even whole species did indeed sometimes become extinct. He also rejected Lamarck's notion that all changes in physical form and behavior were somehow designed to serve particular goals.

Darwin explained the mechanisms of biological evolution in *The*

Origin of Species. Every organism has unique features. These unique individuals compete for survival. On the whole, those that survive do so because they have characteristics that give them an edge over their rivals in a shared environment. These traits are passed on to their descendants. Gradually, the favorable characteristics become more common in a breeding population. Over a number of generations, changes may accumulate to produce a population radically different from the original ancestral population: as different as human beings are from the arboreal apes, our ancestors.

These insights shifted the attention of naturalists from species to local, inbreeding populations of biologically variable individuals. Variations are thrown up continually, but they are produced at random and their fate is governed by chance circumstances, the most significant being immediate, local environmental pressures. Change is gradual and takes place in a series of small, faltering, unpredictable steps. Any progress, any success, is purely local. It is measured against temporary and particular circumstances. Each local history is unique. In contrast to the movements of the planets or atomic particles, biological events do not follow predictable paths. Natural selection, grumbled Sir John Herschel, the astronomer and physicist, is the law of higgledy-piggledy.

Darwin triumphed, and Lamarckism persists only in the form of a dreadful warning, paraded before the wondering eyes of impressionable students. It stands, today, for the false theories that ruled before Darwinism. It is a bundle of exploded propositions: that organisms are intrinsically bound to improve themselves, that evolutionary progress realizes the plans of a creator, and (most notoriously) that acquired characters may be inherited.

Yet despite the power of Darwin's theory, it had one great flaw. Precisely how modifications arose and were passed on remained mysterious. Contemporaries were aware that Darwin did not have a satisfactory theory to explain how traits were transmitted from one generation to the next. Darwin recognized this himself, and felt the lack acutely. He attempted to formulate a theory of heredity in *The Variation of Animals and Plants under Domestication,* the longest book he published in his lifetime, two mighty volumes that appeared in 1867, between *The Origin of Species* and *The Descent of Man.*

There, in the last chapters, most uneasily, he proposed what he termed the "provisional hypothesis of pangenesis," a theory invoking the action of invisible "gemmules" that blended in the germ plasm to produce inheritance and variations. Though Darwin's gemmules were perhaps not altogether unlike what we know as genes, he speculated that they circulate about the body and receive the imprint of new experiences, and so transmit acquired characters to the next generation. (On this point, at least, Darwin had not entirely freed himself from Lamarckian assumptions.)

The weakness of his theory of heredity was recognized by some of his closest associates. It represented a grave handicap to Darwinian theory, and Darwin's vulnerability on this point was one of the main causes for what Thomas Huxley's grandson, the biologist Julian Huxley, was to call "the eclipse of Darwinism," the period from the turn of the century until the 1930s when his theory lost its position as the central orthodoxy of biology.

In fact, an alternative and, as it turned out, correct theory of heredity was broached in Darwin's lifetime. Published by an Augustinian monk, Gregor Mendel, in 1865, it lay buried in the *Proceedings* of a learned society in Brno, a provincial city now in the Czech Republic, then the capital of a province of the Austrian Empire. By the time Mendel's writings were rediscovered at the turn of the century, others had reached the same fundamental conclusions: that heredity is transmitted in particles which are passed unchanged to the next generation. The offspring inherits some traits from each of its parents. Darwin was wrong to believe that characteristics inherited from each parent blended together, and that the use and disuse of traits affected their genetic transmission.

The great evolutionary synthesis of the 1930s and 1940s brought Darwinian theory and Mendelian genetics together in a new, unified theory. Nevertheless, it was genetics that proved to be the most dynamic field in evolutionary biology. For over a generation now, following the discovery in 1953 of the structure of DNA, the most spectacular advances in human biology have been scored by molecular geneticists. The mechanics of genetic transmission have been uncovered, and the processes that cause mutations are now understood.

It is obviously tempting to suppose that this research program will eventually deliver new certainties about the roots of human behavior. Even the agencies and processes of cultural evolution may be genetically encoded, and genetics may rewrite all the other human sciences. Modern genetics also offers more precise ways to intervene in the transmission of inherited traits, and new projects of human engineering will no doubt be mooted if, indeed, genes that program complex patterns of behavior in humans can be identified.

This would represent a triumph for the biological party, but the cultural party objects that cultural traits are too readily taken up and dropped, too variable between populations, to be the products of a basically universal genetic endowment. Moreover, cultural traits are not transmitted by physical inheritance. They are learned, and not only from direct ancestors. Learning is also a rapid and cumulative process, and the rate of cultural change is quite different from the gradual, unplanned, and largely unsupervised drift of biological evolution. We are shaped by a dual system of inheritance, by genes and by learning, and these processes may follow different courses and produce quite different results.

G ENETICS has answered the questions that baffled Darwin about the genesis of mutations and the transmission of traits from one generation to the next. It has also yielded powerful evidence to support his theory of common descent. Virtually the same genetic code is used by almost every form of life. Even some organisms that lack a structured cell nucleus, including forms of bacteria and algae, have the same genetic code as plants and animals. Yet geneticists still use Darwin's theory of natural selection to explain why some modifications become established in a population and others do not.

Evolution is caused by descent with modification, in a famous phrase of Darwin. But not all genetic mutations produce useful modifications. Although modifications are thrown up constantly, only exceptional new features become established in a population. Variations become established if they increase an individual's chance of surviving and procreating. "This preservation of favourable variations and the rejection of injurious variations," Darwin wrote, "I call natural selection."

In his autobiography, Darwin recorded that the theory of natural selection occurred to him in October 1838, when he "happened to read for amusement Malthus on *Population*, and being well prepared to appreciate the struggle for existence which everywhere goes on from long continued observation of the habits of animals and plants, it at once struck me that under these circumstances favourable variations would tend to be preserved and unfavourable ones to be destroyed. The result of this would be the formation of new species."

The theory of common descent, which has been called the first Darwinian revolution, was rapidly accepted by the scientific community. In contrast, the theory of natural selection, the second Darwinian revolution, was resisted by many, including even such close allies of Darwin as Thomas Huxley. Indeed, the rise of genetics in the early twentieth century fed doubts about the significance and efficacy of natural selection. The Mendelians argued that evolution was caused by a series of mutations that occurred by chance, and that selection was a minor factor in determining the direction of change.

It was only when the evolutionary synthesis reunited the advocates of Mendel and those of Darwin that the central role of natural selection was generally accepted. Ever since, it has been the central pillar of evolutionary thinking, surviving the next great revolution in genetics, the discovery of the structure of DNA. Francis Crick—who, with James Watson, made that discovery—accepts what he calls "two fair criticisms" of natural selection: that we still cannot calculate the rate at which it operates, and that the mechanisms it uses are still imperfectly understood—"we may not yet know all the gadgetry that has been evolved to make natural selection work more efficiently. There may still be surprises for us in the tricks that are used to make for smoother and more rapid evolution . . . But leaving these reservations aside," concludes Crick, "the process is powerful, versatile, and very important."

Natural selection explains that success breeds success. It fosters and rewards new ways of competing and so encourages diversity and specialization. Our intellect and moral consciousness may have reached a level unmatched by any other creature, but the spectacular development of these qualities in humans was the result of natural

DARWIN with his eldest son, William, 1842.   Charles Darwin (1809–1882) joined HMS *Beagle* in 1831 as a naturalist and circumnavigated the world in a journey that lasted five years, making systematic observations that provided him with the basis for many years of analysis and provoked his first ideas on evolution. In 1839 he married his cousin Emma Wedgwood, after drawing up a note of arguments for and against marriage. ("Constant companion, (& friend in old age) who will feel interested in one, – object to be beloved & played with. – better than a dog anyhow. – Home, & someone to take care of house – Charms of music & female chit-chat. – These things good for one's health. – *but terrible loss of time.*") The rest of his life was spent largely in a family home in the country, cushioned by a substantial private income and, in time, by the great sales of his books. He invested shrewdly and became a rich man. Though he was troubled by constant ill health, he worked immensely hard in his library and his makeshift laboratory, and maintained close friendships with some of the great scientists of the age. He was devoted to his family, and perhaps the greatest sadness of his life was the early death of his beloved daughter, Anne.

selection, just like a cheetah's unequaled speed over the ground or an albatross's unique range in flight.

The notion of competition and selection was current before Darwin, but he gave these ideas a distinctive twist. He did adopt Herbert Spencer's summary phrase "the survival of the fittest" to describe the effect of natural selection, but his understanding of selection was very different from Spencer's. Spencer believed that whole species were pitted in competition with each other in the struggle for survival. Social Darwinists in the twentieth century argued that races and nations were like natural species, and were inevitably engaged in a natural struggle for domination, from which the fittest would emerge triumphant.

This was very largely a perversion of Darwinian thought. One of Darwin's decisive insights was that selective pressures operate on individuals. Modern biologists generally agree that selection does not operate at the level of a species or a community. What is called "group selection" has become a term of more or less polite derision. Some would go further and argue that selection operates most powerfully on the individual gene or set of genes rather than on the individual organism.

But Darwin is a slippery ally on this crucial issue, for when it came to human beings he sometimes flirted with something very like group selection. When treating what he termed the "moral qualities" that distinguish human beings, he argued that their yield was social rather than individual. Being a good citizen might have a high cost for the individual, but it benefits the community.

It must not be forgotten that although a high standard of morality gives but a slight or no advantage to each individual man and his children over the other men of the same tribe, yet that an increase in the number of well-endowed men and an advancement in the standard of morality will certainly give an immense advantage to one tribe over another. A tribe including many members who, from possessing in a high degree the spirit of patriotism, fidelity, obedience, courage, and sympathy, were always ready to aid one another, and to sacrifice themselves for the common good, would be victorious over most other tribes; and this would be natural selection.

On this argument, it is the tribe that adapts, as a community, rather than the tribespeople as individuals. Darwin is quite explicit: natural selection operates upon a human community through its institutions—its beliefs, modes of organization, technologies—in a word (though a word notoriously resistant to clear definition), its culture. If that is true, then it may signify a great difference between human populations and others.

One might say that by and large human beings adapt to an environment culturally, as communities, rather than biologically, as individuals—but the very terms of such an apparently innocuous statement would be open to question. The implication is that cultural adaptations establish themselves in essentially the same way as biological adaptations. Natural selection rules, even in the field of human cultural history.

This may turn out to be correct, but it is possible that natural selection does not apply to cultural innovations, or, at least, not in the same way that it applies to biological changes. Cultural instruments may even block natural selection. We can and do protect the weakly, assist those who cannot support themselves, erect defenses against the challenges of nature. Cultural skills allow us to make ourselves at home in the most inhospitable places without any physical adaptation. Darwin cited with approval an observation by the other original theorist of natural selection, Alfred Russel Wallace: "Man, after he had partially acquired those intellectual and moral faculties which distinguish him from the lower animals, would have been but little liable to bodily modifications through natural selection or any other means." Perhaps natural selection loosened its grip on us as we began to exercise our new skills.

THE celebrated immunologist Peter Medawar reached the conclusion that cultural development is so very different from biological evolution that it cannot be explained in Darwinian terms. As an alternative, he proposed that we might look again at the failed, pre-Darwinian theory of evolution that has been named after Lamarck.

Medawar had nothing to say in favor of this Lamarckian package of ideas in biology itself. Indeed, he scornfully pointed out that it is just the type of evolutionary thinking that appeals to scientifically naive optimists, who dream of a purposeful and progressive evolution. And yet he suggested that Lamarckism might be granted a place in science. Lamarck was right, by accident, but about culture.

"Apart from being mediated through non-genetic channels," Medawar wrote in 1977, "cultural inheritance is categorically distinguished from biological inheritance by being Lamarckian in character; that is to say, by the fact that what is learned in one generation may become part of the inheritance of the next." Acquired cultural characteristics are indeed passed along to our descendants, and cultural change is purposive, just as Lamarck imagined biological change to be.

Perhaps Medawar was simply trying to bounce biologists out of their lazy and arrogant conviction that one day the Darwinian program will surely sort out the social sciences (if that hasn't happened already). Perhaps, though, he really did believe that only biology can deliver secure advances in our understanding of human nature and human history, and that even the bad biology of Lamarck may be preferable to the best that social scientists can offer.

This is certainly not a view that appeals to social scientists. They are less inclined than the biologists to suppose that theories about human history must be drawn from biological theory. They are certainly not best pleased to be offered the leavings of biology. It is true that the most famous human scientists of the nineteenth century, Spencer, Marx, and Freud, were all Lamarckians, but modern social scientists must acknowledge the Darwinian victory over Lamarck. If Darwinism cannot solve all their problems, are they condemned to scavenge the fossils of a discredited version of evolutionary theory? We might be better advised to consider theories that were honed specifically for the explanation of cultural history (not forgetting the possibility that human history has no pattern at all, but is just "one damn thing after another," a view which—in some moods—Darwin might have found attractive).

Darwin was curious about the Fuegians, the Maoris, and other native peoples he came across on his voyages. He kept up to date with the investigations of anthropologists and psychologists, and read with interest the sociological theories of Comte and Spencer. His close associates, Lubbock and Galton, devoted themselves to the nascent social sciences. Today cultural anthropologists, archaeologists, and psychologists are engaged in every modern Darwinian argument about human nature. The Darwinian questions about human beings probably cannot be solved by biologists alone, but this does not mean that there are no Darwinian answers to them.

Yet even the most committed will concede that there is still no Darwinian consensus on the natural history of human beings. Moreover, some of the most urgent questions may never be susceptible to scientific resolution. Moral, political, even theological uncertainties linger on. What follows, in terms of practical politics, if we accept a Darwinian view of human beings? An old complaint is that Darwin regarded us as animals; but there is a more sophisticated concern, that Darwin saw us as the inhabitants of the Victorian British Empire. Darwin himself never doubted that his biological theories had political implications. His most recent biographers point out that Darwin's entries in his notebooks "make plain that competition, free trade, imperialism, racial extermination, and sexual inequality were written into the equation from the start."

We may shrug that off. Scientific genius does not provide a warrant for the political views of this particular Victorian Whig gentleman; the enduring Darwinian message can be salvaged from the discourse of his day. Perhaps so, but it is well to bear in mind that any persuasive theory about human nature is bound to become the basis for policies—about child-rearing, social mobility, educational selection, immigration, even war and peace; and such policies may underwrite radical programs of social engineering. In the twentieth century, Darwin's name has been used to justify virtually every political position on the spectrum, which suggests that his theory does not necessarily sanction any particular social philosophy. Yet it can scarcely be doubted that Darwinian programs in the human sciences have political consequences. The very terms in which a research project is formulated may convey a political message.

We are also uneasily aware that even the most reliable scientific findings will not necessarily benefit us, and that the hubris of theorists can have terrible consequences. Academic theories about nature and nurture, race and culture found a terrible application in the Nazi death camps. Writers on social evolution paved the way for Lenin's "engineers of the human soul," who constructed the Soviet gulags and operated the purges of Stalin and of Mao that killed many millions. Even in liberal modern societies, theories about mental health and personality find troubling expression in archipelagos of prisons and asylums. We must understand evolution while remaining skeptical about progress.

IN this book I explore the great questions about human origins, human history, and human nature, sketch the investigations they have inspired, and review the answers currently on offer in the human sciences. There are often no sure answers, and it is essential to appreciate why this is so, to grasp the difficulties, to maintain a sophisticated skepticism.

I shall review the debates on human origins, on the history of human culture, on genes and intelligence, on the nature of the differences between males and females, on incest, marriage, and the family, on the foundations of human politics, and on the prospects for the future of the species. At almost every turn it will be necessary to treat the political implications of particular theories, but the scientific arguments have an integrity and coherence that command respect despite the wrenching experiences of the modern world. These debates are the record left by some of the most powerful thinkers of the past hundred and fifty years who have turned their minds to the special destiny of our species.

· 2 ·

TO BEGIN AT THE BEGINNING

What makes the human species different from other primates? The Swedish botanist and explorer Carl Linnaeus pioneered the systematic classification of natural species. He named the genus *Homo* in 1735, and classified it alongside apes and monkeys, which he called "Simia," in a family that he named *Anthropomorpha*. Curiously enough, Linnaeus distinguished the members of this family particularly by the form of the teeth. He also insisted that they were all quadrupeds—including humans. Man, as Linnaeus summed him up, "has a mouth made like that of other quadrupeds, and finally four feet, on two of which he goes, and [he] uses the other two for prehensive purposes."

In 1776 the German anatomist Johann Friedrich Blumenbach protested that humans were bipeds, and he placed them in a separate class, the Bimana, or two-handed. Blumenbach insisted that there was a great gulf between humans and other animals, of which bipedalism was a sign. Linnaeus, in contrast, believed that the differences between people and simians were not great. "Indeed," he admitted, "to speak the truth, as a natural historian according to the principles of science, up to the present time I have not been able to discover any character by which man can be distinguished from the ape."

When a colleague remonstrated with him for situating the human species among the *Anthropomorphi,* he replied: "It matters little to me what name we use; but I demand of you, and of the whole world, that you show me a generic character—one that is according to generally accepted principles of classification, by which to distinguish between Man and Ape. I myself most assuredly know of none. I wish someone would indicate one to me. But, if I had called man an ape, or vice versa, I should have fallen under the ban of all the ecclesiastics. It may be that as a naturalist I ought to have done so."

Linnaeus thought that species were fixed. He rejected the vulgar notion that the human races were significantly different from one another, and therefore assumed that the genus *Homo* had always contained only one species, *Homo sapiens,* the modern human type.

Today, two extinct species—*Homo habilis* and *Homo erectus*—are classified as *Homo,* alongside *Homo sapiens.* They are ancestral to modern humans. It is likely that *Homo sapiens* evolved from *Homo erectus,* which evolved from *Homo habilis.* The identification of these ancestral human species makes it even harder to meet Linnaeus's challenge and to identify one generic principle that would mark off *Homo.* Moreover, Linnaeus only had to worry about the similarities between humans and apes, while we have to accommodate a further extinct genus of near-humans in our debates: *Australopithecus,* which was discovered in 1924. *Australopithecus* was the ancestor of the genus *Homo,* but the boundary line that divides the one from the other is still uncertainly demarcated. Some problematic specimens might be put in either category.

Perhaps the boundary must be moved. It would not be the first time that this has happened. Every time a new species was recognized as *Homo,* the very definition of *Homo* had to be changed to accommodate it. This may seem paradoxical, even somewhat unnerving, but similar uncertainties are inherent in the whole project of evolutionary biology. Every population is changing, and must be transitional between an earlier and a later type. A system of classification has to be devised that captures fluid, diverging characteristics. The old-style definitions of Linnaean biology, which were supposed to fix the unchanging essence of a species, simply became obsolete once evolutionary theory was understood.

What, then, makes us human? Various changes in morphology marked off the human lineage from other primates. Those most commonly cited are the switch to bipedalism, which is associated with the specialization of the hand; changes in the shape and function of the jaw and teeth; and increases in brain size. There are also specifically human skills, notably, perhaps, hunting (which is rare among other primates), tool-making, and language.

Although some purists would prefer to consider morphology and behavior separately, changes in behavior and morphology are usually tied together in evolutionary narratives. Consider one familiar example. Bipedalism is said to have freed the hands for tool use, which enabled humans to hunt stronger and faster animals. As the hominid diet changed, the jaws and teeth went through various adaptations. The cleverer proto-humans must have enjoyed an advantage as toolmakers and hunters. Consequently there would have been selection for higher cranial capacity, which eventually made possible the development of language. And so such narratives go on, constructing human history from a plausible mix of natural and cultural forces.

However complex the narratives they spun, most theorists have assumed that one particular element in the makeup of humans drove the evolutionary process. Linnaeus speculated that the peculiarly human attribute might prove to be the ability to reason: he was, after all, an eighteenth-century man. Darwin naturalized reason. He was particularly impressed by the size of the human brain, and argued that the exceptional growth of the brain in humans had caused the intellectual and moral development that ensured human success.

In a special note contributed as an appendix to chapter 7 of *The Descent of Man*, Huxley compared the brain of humans and that of other primates, and established their structural similarity. The main difference was one of size and, presumably, complexity. "As the various mental faculties gradually developed the brain would almost certainly become larger," Darwin wrote. "No one, I presume, doubts that the large proportion which the size of man's brain bears to his body, compared to the same proportion in the gorilla or orang, is closely connected with his higher mental powers."

Following Darwin and Huxley, cranial capacity became a defining trait of the genus *Homo*. The somewhat dubious assumption was that cranial capacity provided a surrogate for a measure of brain size, and, what was perhaps even more questionable, that brain size would indicate brain power. The volume and weight of the human brain, relative to body size, are some three times greater than might be expected in a primate. The cerebral cortex accounts for three-quarters of total brain weight in humans, which is, again, a uniquely high proportion. Moreover, the development of human cranial capacity is a dramatic feature of the evolutionary story.

But what cranial capacity did a primate have to achieve before it

HUXLEY lecturing on the gorilla. Thomas Henry Huxley (1825–1895), "Darwin's Bulldog," the son of a schoolteacher, was trained as a doctor and, like Darwin, sailed the world at an early age, traveling to the South Seas on HMS *Rattlesnake.* He was an early adherent of Darwin, and in 1860 he confronted one of the clerical enemies of evolutionary theory, Bishop Samuel Wilberforce, at a famous meeting of the British Association for the Advancement of Science. Wilberforce inquired with heavy irony whether Huxley was descended from an ape on his grandmother's or grandfather's side of the family. "If then, said I [as Huxley later told the story], the question is put to me would I rather have a miserable ape for a grandfather or a man highly endowed by nature and possessed of great means & influence & yet who employs these faculties & that influence for the mere purpose of introducing ridicule into a grave scientific discussion I unhesitatingly affirm my preference for the ape." His book *Evidence as to Man's Place in Nature* (1863) was a major early statement of the relationship between humans and other primates.

qualified as *Homo?* Wilfred Le Gros Clark, the great English anatomist, suggested in 1964 that a cranial capacity of 900 to about 2,000 milliliters was required. (One teaspoon holds 6 ml.) This was already a concession. The reason Le Gros Clark was prepared to go down so low was that he wanted to incorporate *Homo erectus* in the genus *Homo.* He did not wish to go any lower, however, because he wanted to exclude another species, now known as *Homo habilis,* which Louis Leakey and two colleagues had named in the same year, and which they claimed belonged to the genus *Homo* despite a brain size that ranged from below 600 ml. to about 800 ml. (*Australopithecus* had brain volumes ranging from 375 ml. to about 485 ml. In *Homo habilis,* the mean volume was about 750 ml. From *Homo erectus* on there was a gradual growth of brain volume from some 800 ml. to the average of modern *Homo sapiens,* which is about 1,400 ml.)

There were similar problems with other defining features. Bipedalism, to take another instance, turned out not be an absolute state. "Two legs bad, four legs good," chanted the animals in Orwell's *Animal Farm.* The australopithecines, however, were a mixture of good and bad. Sometimes they walked upright, sometimes they lurched along bent over like apes; and they may have spent a lot of their time in the trees.

Almost half a century ago, Ernst Mayr was insisting that the genus *Homo* cannot be defined and delimited on a purely morphological basis. All a morphologist could rightly say was that *Homo* is characterized by upright posture, and that this new posture freed the "anterior extremity" to take on new functions, "which, in turn, have stimulated brain evolution." That is an extract from a story rather than a definition.

Behavioral criteria pose similar problems. It might be argued that to qualify as a human an animal must have certain skills: most obviously, it should make tools and speak a proper language. As it turns out, these skills do not provide unambiguous criteria for the definition of humans.

A recent orthodoxy held that human speech evolved early, and that some primates have proto-language skills. Today, opinion is swinging back to the older view that human speech is unique. Even chimpanzees can be taught only to respond to simple commands, and their signaling system is undeveloped. According to some authorities, however, early hominids were not much better equipped to communicate complex messages. A physical anthropologist, Jeffrey Laitman, compared the vocal tracts of early humans and other primates and came to the conclusion that australopithecines "undoubtedly had some sort of communication system, probably slightly more advanced than that of the living apes, but they could not speak the way we do today." Even *Homo erectus* probably could not speak in the modern human style: "Their vocal abilities were probably somewhat intermediate between those of the australopithecines and modern humans." There is some evidence to suggest that even archaic *Homo sapiens* lacked the physical equipment to speak modern languages. If that is true, then *Homo* cannot be defined as a language-using creature.

Tool-making is also an ambiguous criterion. Chimpanzees make rudimentary tools, but distinctively human tool-making—including the use of tools to make other tools—is a very recent business, no more than 2 million years old. It started long after the human lineage had split off from other primates. Consequently, effective hunting must have become possible only in relatively recent times.

In short, the morphological criteria are inconclusive, and there is no obvious behavioral criterion that marks off all species of *Homo*. The fundamental problems of definition that plagued Linnaeus have still not been resolved. In 1992 Bernard Wood of Liverpool University complained wearily in the journal *Nature* that the task of hominid paleontologists "would be greatly eased if agreement could be reached about criteria for including material into the genus *Homo*."

THERE are also problems with the evidence, the real things—the stones and bones—which we must somehow sort into these slippery, makeshift categories.

How can we ascertain what our human ancestors looked like, and how they behaved? One option is to compare living humans and other primates, making deductions about the characteristics of their common ancestors. This is the comparative method, favored by Darwin and Huxley. In recent years a new comparative method has been developed, which uses samples of DNA from different species in order to establish relationships and to suggest genealogical links.

The alternative is to make deductions from the fossil record, but the record is, inevitably, a patchy one. The only part of the body that is at all likely to survive for any length of time is the skeleton, but even bones and teeth do not usually last very long after death. Scavengers gnaw at bones and scatter them. Those that escape the scavengers are bleached by the sun, or worn away by the rain and the wind. Only quite exceptional conditions lead to their preservation. Volcanic soils help to protect alkaline materials. So do limestone caves and fissures, and consequently some of the most famous fossil sites are caves.

A series of accidents is therefore required to preserve fossils. Other accidents must then follow before they are found and identified. The absolute number of ancient human fossils out there is probably not very great, and if ancient fossils are found, they are likely to be fragmentary. As a rule, only fragments of skulls or jaws, or a few teeth, are recovered. It takes stupendous luck to turn up a complete cranium, let alone a complete skeleton. "The fossil man game is like being an astronaut," says Don Johanson, no mean time-traveler himself. "Actually finding the fossils is only for the very few, and when you're a graduate student in Chicago the prospects seem as far away as Jupiter."

Once fossils are found, another set of problems must be solved. There are still no unequivocal methods for dating very ancient fossils. Measures of genetic association are available, but the rate of genetic change is still a matter of contention. Beyond some 40,000 years the well-established radiocarbon dating technique is unreliable. Geological associations are helpful, but these are often confused by later disturbances. Human paleontologists have often been misled by what they call "intrusive burials": bones that for one reason or another get mixed up with rocks and fossils of another period.

After a fossil has been found and dated, its classification may give rise to arguments. Some ancient species of apes and humans have been described on the basis of a handful of teeth and bone fragments, whose dating is problematic. Given a small sample, it may be impossible to tell how great the differences are between males and females of a single species. If a fossil is uncovered that deviates on some measures from the tentative picture that has been built up of species x, some scientists will be tempted to suppose that a further species has been found, while others will redraw the parameters of x.

Finally, classification is not enough. The goal is to fit the various species of humans and proto-humans into a genealogy. To make matters more complicated, there were almost certainly several lines of hominid evolution, one leading to *Homo sapiens,* others to closely related species that became extinct.

These difficulties might induce caution, even despair, but the field has always attracted bold, combative optimists. Fossil hunters are often visionaries, mavericks, publicists—independent operators with great faith in their own intuitions. Some exhibit proprietorial pride in the fossils they discover, and persuade themselves that they have unique insights into their characters. The excitement of discovery spills over into great expectations for the significance of particular fossils.

The pioneers liked to play Sherlock Holmes, using the few fossil clues at their disposal to reconstruct ancient murder mysteries. These murderers were also routinely suspected of eating their victims. Yet putting the wilder speculations aside, even the most persuasive theories often rest on slender fossil evidence. It is not easy to choose between competing views, particularly when they are propounded with passion by charismatic figures. Stubbornness, wishful thinking, competitiveness have all played a role in the great debates. But then human paleontologists are not the only people who find it hard to take the unexpected on board, and there is good cause to be carried away by the promise of a new theory. The stakes are very high.

IN 1856, workmen in a limestone quarry in the Neander valley near Düsseldorf in Germany discovered some curious fossils. These were identified by Hermann Schaaffhausen, Professor of Anatomy at the University of Bonn, as ancient human remains. He concluded that they represented a barbarous race that had roamed northwestern Europe before the Roman Empire, and he speculated that their repulsive aspect and flashing eyes must have given the first Roman soldiers to penetrate the region rather a nasty shock.

Charles Lyell, the geologist, ordered a plaster cast of the specimens and studied the animal bones that had been found in association with the remains. He concluded that they were very much more ancient than Schaaffhausen had supposed. But although Lyell was a mentor of Darwin, with whom he remained in regular contact, he was reluctant to accept the view that human beings had evolved relatively recently. He identified the fossils as belonging to an extinct species of ape.

Huxley, one of the first Darwinians, was impressed rather by the cranial capacity of the Neanderthals, which fell within the modern human range. This feature persuaded him that the Neanderthals were humans rather than apes. Nevertheless, he judged that they were not directly ancestral to modern humans, since the Neanderthal skull shape was very different from that of living populations.

Other fossils of a similar nature were soon discovered, but the experts could not agree on their interpretation. Some anatomists, like Marcellin Boule in Paris and Grafton Elliot Smith in London, argued that the Neanderthals were quite without the distinctive physical traits of *Homo sapiens,* and so should be excluded from the human lineage. Other leading scholars maintained that the Neanderthals represented diseased and decadent human beings—their bones horribly distorted from rickets, arthritis, and head injuries, according to Rudolf Virchow of Berlin University, a strong critic of Darwinian theory.

In time two incompatible theories crystallized on the Neanderthal question. Gradualists believed that the Neanderthals were immediate ancestors of modern Europeans. Catastrophists argued (as Huxley had done) that the Neanderthals represented a fairly recent "Praesapiens" human which had lived in Europe, become extinct, and left no issue. There was one point, however, on which agreement was soon reached: the Neanderthals were not ancient apelike protohumans who would represent at once the first generation of humanity and the last link with the apes. They had perished long before the Roman legionaries penetrated northern Europe, but nevertheless they had lived too recently, and were too similar to modern humans, to qualify as the elusive "missing link."

The leading Continental advocate of Darwinian theory, Ernst Haeckel, initiated a tradition of research that aimed to identify the missing link between apes and humans, a creature he called *Pithecanthropus* ("Ape-man"). He speculated that it would walk semi-erect but lack the power of speech.

Darwin and Huxley had identified the African apes as the species closest to humans, and Darwin thought it likely that human beings had also evolved in Africa. ("It is therefore probable that Africa was formerly inhabited by extinct apes closely allied to the gorilla and chimpanzee," Darwin wrote, "and as these two species are now man's nearest allies, it is somewhat more probable that our early progenitors lived on the African continent than elsewhere.") Haeckel, however, judged that human evolution began in the East, where the orangutan and gibbon of the Indonesian archipelago might prove to be yet closer kin to ourselves than the African apes.

Inspired by these speculations, a young Dutch doctor, Eugene Dubois, signed up with the colonial army and proceeded to Sumatra. Reports that a curious skull had been found there took him to Java in 1891, but the skulls he was shown were clearly modern. Then he found his own specimens: a skull that appeared to be primitive, in association with a femur which was like that of a modern human. He concluded that he had found an erect but apelike creature, and in 1894 he announced that he had identified the missing link, which he called *Pithecanthropus erectus* ("the erect ape-man").

It was not certain that the skull and femur did indeed belong to the same specimen, or even that they dated from the same period, for the stratigraphy was complex. At the time, however, experts were more concerned that the skullcap seemed more modern than Dubois allowed.

Cheated of his triumph, Dubois retreated in dudgeon to a series of Dutch museums, where he held minor appointments, taking his fossils with him. Eventually, in 1923, he permitted British and American authorities to examine his finds, which they identified as belonging not to an ape or an ape-man, but rather to an archaic but definitely human type. This judgment was vindicated when in 1929 W. C. Pei discovered a skullcap in the Zhoukoudian cave near Peking that closely resembled the Javanese specimens, but was clearly human. Further specimens were uncovered in the following decade. All are less than a million years old, and all are unequivocally human. They are now identified as archaic *Homo sapiens*, or as representatives of another, extinct, species of *Homo, Homo erectus*.

The search for more ancient ancestors continued elsewhere. On December 18, 1912, it was announced to a packed meeting of the Geological Society in London that remarkable early human remains had been found in a gravel pit at Piltdown, in Sussex. Their discoverer was a local solicitor, Charles Dawson. An amateur, Dawson had taken them to Arthur Smith Woodward, the Keeper of Geology at the Museum of Natural History in London. Woodward prepared a reconstruction of the skull and jaw, using the fragments of bone and teeth that Dawson had collected. Confronted with an apparently apelike jaw and a rather human skull, Woodward reached the dramatic conclusion that Dawson's specimen represented a direct ancestor of modern humans, older than the Neanderthals, who represented a degenerate offshoot. The expectant members of the Geological Society were told that nothing less than a new hominid genus had been identified. In a poetic flight rare among paleontologists, it was named *Eoanthropus dawsoni* ("the dawn man of Dawson").

Arthur Keith, one of the leading British anatomists, conservator of the Museum of the Royal College of Surgeons, was one of the specialists who immediately turned his attention to the interpretation of the finds. The Piltdown creature, which he described as "a strange blend of man and ape," was a most portentous apparition. "At last, it seemed," so Keith recalled a decade later, "the missing form—the link which early followers of Darwin had searched for—had really been discovered."

Nevertheless, Keith was troubled by some aspects of Woodward's model. The Damon Company of Weymouth had made casts of the Piltdown specimens, and was offering them for sale at nine pounds and seventeen shillings for the set. Keith bought the casts and began to experiment with alternative reconstructions. Eventually he arrived

EXCAVATING PILTDOWN. This photograph, taken around 1913, a few months after the original discovery of the Piltdown remains, gives a general impression of the site. On the left is a laborer, Venus Hargreaves; in the middle is Arthur Smith Woodward, the Keeper of Geology at the British Museum (Natural History); and on the right Charles Dawson, a solicitor in Sussex and an amateur geologist and archaeologist. Dawson was almost certainly responsible for the Piltdown fraud, which was finally exposed only in 1953. The goose was named "Chipper," which might have been part of Dawson's joke.

at a fresh model of the head that minimized the apelike features of the jaw and increased the cranial capacity of the skull. His Piltdown Man was decidedly more human-looking than Woodward's.

Even if Keith's reconstruction was preferred to Woodward's (and there was much controversy over this issue), the creature was a very strange blend of man and ape, for while the cranial capacity and head shape of Piltdown Man were those of a modern human, its teeth and jaw were very like those of an ape. Apparently, therefore, very early hominids had highly developed brains. Creatures who were otherwise rather like apes had streaked ahead in intelligence. In short, human evolution was triggered by the expansion of the brain.

This was Keith's conclusion, and it was precisely what he had come to expect. He took the Darwinian view that human evolution was brain-led. It was brain power, above all, that chiefly distinguished humans from other primates, and their intellectual edge would have marked humans off from the very first. This view was shared by other Darwinians of the day. "It was not the adoption of the erect attitude that made Man from an Ape," Keith's rival, Grafton Elliot Smith, wrote in 1912, "but the gradual perfecting of the brain and the slow upbuilding of the mental structure, of which erectness of carriage is one of the incidental manifestations." Piltdown Man confirmed this interpretation. Moreover, a variety of implements were found in association with the fossils, suggesting that Piltdown Man was culturally sophisticated. Keith even guessed that he must surely have buried his dead.

A further theoretical consideration made the evidence from Piltdown doubly significant to Keith. Orthodox Darwinians in the early twentieth century believed that evolutionary changes took a very long time to be achieved. The dating of the Piltdown finds was therefore of crucial importance, and this was immediately a matter of controversy. Woodward was convinced that the site dated from the Pleistocene (and so was less than 1.7 million years old), but Keith preferred the view of the Belgian geologist Louis Rutot that it dated from the Pliocene, and so might be up to 5 million years old. Other fossils found in the same gravel pit included teeth of a mastodon, a stegodon, and a hippopotamus, all of which suggested that the Piltdown remains were very ancient.

Keith was convinced that humans had reached their present stage of evolutionary development in that remote period, as, indeed, had other mammals, including the wolf, the bear, and perhaps even the gibbon. Fully modern humans—people not very different from ourselves—had been around for at least 5 million years. Moreover, if advanced humans lived in the early Pliocene—some 5.5 millon years ago—then our human ancestors might have lived perhaps 20 million years earlier.

What then was to be made of the Neanderthals, or of Dubois's specimens? Keith was a recent convert to the view that two parallel human types had evolved in Europe, one leading to modern humans, the other—the Neanderthals—representing a branching line doomed to extinction. Similar branch-lines, leading to dead ends, could perhaps be traced at even earlier periods of hominid evolution. Ancient fossils that were clearly not very well endowed with intellectual capacity—fossils like Java and Peking Man—all represented evolutionary side-alleys, parallel hominid evolutionary tracks that had run into the sands. On the other hand, the true ancestral line of modern humans would stretch far back into antiquity—far beyond Java and Peking Man—but would have exhibited from the first a closer kinship to ourselves. Accordingly, Keith was gratified to find a Pliocene hominid with the signature of true humanity, great brain power.

Additional Piltdown fragments were reported in 1913 and 1915, collected by Dawson at sites close to the original Piltdown. The most significant were further fragments of a brain-case together with a tooth. (Dawson also turned up the tooth of an archaic rhinoceros.) These finds quieted some doubters, including the influential Parisian Marcellin Boule. Yet not every expert was satisfied, and as hominid fossils began to accumulate from other parts of the world, in the years following the discoveries at Piltdown, it was apparent that a number diverged from the Piltdown type, and from the expectations that Keith had raised. Keith might rail against their authenticity, or dispute their interpretation, as a last resort consigning them to evolutionary side-tracks on the path to extinction. Nevertheless, he

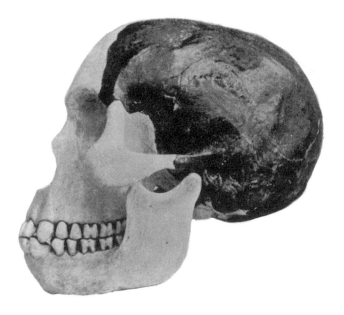

RECONSTRUCTING PILTDOWN MAN. "The reconstruction of the skull was also not without its difficulties," Frank Spencer writes in his authoritative study, *Piltdown: A Scientific Forgery* (1990). "From the nine cranial fragments it was possible to reconstruct four larger pieces of the original brain case, representing nearly the whole of the left side, and a considerable portion of the parietal region on the right side which articulated with a large fragment of the occiput. But, since the upper margins of the left and right parietals (with the accompanying sagittal suture) were missing, it was not immediately clear how they should be articulated. This was critical since their relative position ultimately determined the size of the cranial vault."

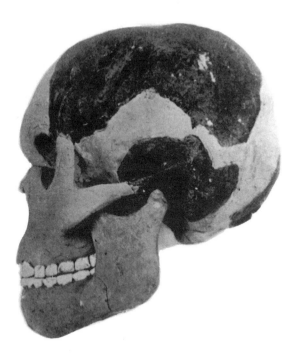

Arthur Smith Woodward's reconstruction is illustrated on the left, and is consistent with his view that the skull exhibited "a closer resemblance to the skulls of the truly ancestral mid-Tertiary apes than any fossil human skull hitherto found." Sir Arthur Keith, who was convinced of the great depth of the human lineage, rejected Woodward's model. He did not agree with Woodward that the very apelike canines belonged to the skull, and he proposed a far more human reconstruction (illustrated on the right). "The height of the brain chamber is increased by nearly half an inch," he commented. "The width and fullness of the top parts are enlarged. The brain capacity is augmented; the shape of the brain is changed. The anomalous conformation of the occipital bone, the extreme asymmetry of the lambdoidal suture, almost disappear, and all the points we are familiar with in human skulls . . . leap to the eye."

and his allies began to find themselves in increasingly lonely isolation; and a storm was brewing up in Africa.

DESPITE Darwin's deduction that human origins would be traced to Africa, the home of the gorilla and the chimpanzee, for a generation after his death all the important finds had been made in Europe and Asia. Then, in 1925, a young anatomist in South Africa, Raymond Dart, described a fossil hominid infant skull—the "Taung baby"—which had been discovered in a remote quarry in the northern Cape. He claimed that it represented an apelike human ancestor, and named it *Australopithecus africanus,* the "Southern ape."

But while Dubois had been told that his ape-man was really human, Dart's specimen was classified by the London scientists as a fossil ape. Leading the opposition was Sir Arthur Keith, the advocate of a large-brained ancestor, Piltdown Man. The comparatively recent Taung fossil, with its rather human jaw and apelike brain, was virtually a mirror image of Piltdown Man. "What was so unexpected about its structure?" asks Phillip Tobias, Dart's successor as Professor of Anatomy at the University of the Witwatersrand. "The short answer is that Taung was the first of the *small-brained hominids* to be found." It was above all because of its cranial capacity that Keith was not disposed to accept that the Taung specimen could possibly represent an ancestor of modern humans.

Like Dubois, Dart endured decades of isolation without ever doubting his initial intuition, but his case was helped by the discovery of more complete fossils in South African sites, thanks largely to the efforts of another isolated South African scholar, Robert Broom. Broom and other scientists eventually recovered some three hundred specimens of *Australopithecus* from one site alone, the Sterkfontein cave in the Transvaal. Yet for many lonely years Dart and Broom were treated as cranks, as they proclaimed their discoveries in scientific journals and even the popular press. It was only in the late 1940s that one of the leading British scientists in the field, Sir Wilfred Le Gros Clark, visited Dart and was persuaded that the African *Australopithecus* did indeed represent a remote but direct ancestor of *Homo.*

Reluctantly, even Sir Arthur Keith was obliged to agree, admitting in a letter to *Nature* that "Professor Dart was right and I was wrong."

But an even more humiliating setback awaited Keith. In 1953, the Wenner-Gren Foundation for Anthropological Research funded a conference in London to discuss the recently discovered African fossils. The assembled experts were taken on a tour of the Geological Department of the British Museum, and viewed the Piltdown remains. These had slipped from the forefront of anthropological debate, and many of the delegates had never examined them. The visit stimulated the doubts that many of them harbored, and in particular it stirred into action a young anatomist at Oxford, Joseph Weiner, who had taken his first degree at the University of the Witwatersrand Medical School under Dart.

Brought up as he was on *Australopithecus*, Weiner had been puzzled by Piltdown. Back in Oxford, he passed a sleepless night. "Thinking it all over again," he recalled later, "I realized with astonishment that while there were in fact only two possible 'natural' theories, i.e. that Piltdown Man was in fact the composite man-ape of Woodward's interpretation, or that two distinct creatures, fossil man and fossil ape, had been found side by side, neither of the 'natural' explanations was at all satisfactory." The alternative hypothesis was that the jaw and the cranium belonged to different creatures and had been brought together through human agency. By accident or design? An accident was plausible once, but it could hardly have happened twice. Clearly the possibility of fraud had to be faced, although, as Weiner somberly concluded, "the idea was repellent indeed."

Weiner persuaded LeGros Clark at Oxford University and Kenneth Oakley of the Museum of Natural History to help him subject the Piltdown specimens to a fresh, careful investigation. It was soon apparent that something was seriously awry. Tests proved that the teeth were rather recent, and much younger than the cranium. The cranium was found to have been artificially stained. The wear on the teeth was characteristic neither of humans nor of apes, and they showed signs of deliberate abrasion. Some of the stone implements had apparently been shaped with metal blades. In November 1953 the investigators announced that the fossils were forgeries: "It is now clear that the distinguished palaeontologists and archaeologists who took part in the excavations at Piltdown were the victims of a most elaborate and carefully prepared hoax."

Shocking though this might be, the demonstration did at least resolve a major theoretical problem. As the three men remarked, Piltdown Man had represented "a most awkward and perplexing element in the fossil record . . . entirely out of conformity both in its strange mixture of morphological characters and in its time sequence with all the palaeontological evidence of human evolution available from other parts of the world." A human lineage that stemmed from a small-brained, erect, Taung-like ancestor was now less problematic.

The only question that remained was, who had perpetrated the fraud? Dawson was an obvious suspect. Investigation revealed that his career as a local solicitor had not been free from scandal, and he had a reputation as a practical joker. Weiner decided that he was the culprit, and that he had acted alone. Yet the forgeries had required considerable scientific knowledge and technical skill, and so some suspected that Dawson had collaborated with an expert. A series of scientific detectives have tried to identify the evil genius behind Dawson. Stephen Jay Gould suspects the French priest and evolutionary theorist Teilhard de Chardin, who as a young man had participated in the early Piltdown excavations. Recent studies, however, have pointed the finger at Sir Arthur Keith. Perhaps he had been frustrated that evidence for his theory of human evolution was so slow to turn up.

APPARENTLY Darwin and Huxley had been right after all. The original proto-human beings were neighbors, and kin, to the African apes. For the next generation, the great source of fossil hominids was in Africa, above all eastern Africa, where the Leakey family made a remarkable series of discoveries.

Louis Leakey was born in 1903 in a mission station near Nairobi, where he learned Kikuyu, conceived a passion for collecting Stone Age tools, and grew up with a strong sense of loyalty to his African home. Education in an English public school and at Cambridge University seems only to have confirmed his sense of himself as a colonial outsider (although he did manage to persuade the university authorities that he should be allowed to offer Kikuyu to meet the modern language requirement). He made his career in East Africa, where he was based at the Nairobi Museum. His funding depended on his ability to inspire benefactors (notably the *National Geographic*). He loved to publish his discoveries and speculations in popular papers, and to demonstrate that an undeferential outsider could oblige those in the British establishment to rethink their view of the world.

His second wife, Mary Leakey, was descended from the father of British archaeology, John Frere (1740–1807), but she was more immediately the rebellious daughter of an artist, who had given her a cosmopolitan but wayward upbringing. Adrift on her own as a teenager in London, she had made herself into a good scientific draftsman and become a fervent amateur archaeologist. When she marched into Leakey's life at the age of twenty-two, smoking cigarettes, wearing trousers, beautiful, and devoted to his quest, she brought with her a further and incalculable gift: luck.

Their son, Richard Leakey, was to become—at first reluctantly— the third member of the family team. He showed all of Louis's talent for organization and publicity, and a similar determination; and something too of Louis's sense of himself as a gifted outsider struggling against the entrenched, prejudiced metropolitan specialists. (Richard, like Mary, lacked any formal training.) To all this was added the irreplaceable luck of Mary Leakey.

Louis's English training imbued him with the established view of human evolution. In particular, he was greatly influenced by the theories of Sir Arthur Keith. Evolution had been a long, gradual process, which began with the development of the brain. The earliest humans would have had large brains, and manufactured tools, though otherwise they would have resembled apes. They had lived very long ago, in the Miocene Age. There were, however, parallel lines of hominid evolution, and small-brained hominids, which did not make tools, could be relegated to branching lines. They were not direct ancestors of modern humans.

A promising find had been made close to Leakey's home, in Tanzania. Before World War I this country had been a German colony, and in 1911 a German scientific expedition had discovered the Olduvai Gorge, a small canyon, shaped like the letter Y, that stretches for some 25 kilometers on the edge of the Serengeti Plains. The Gorge is a dried-up lake bed, filled with sediments, and it had been inundated periodically with ash from nearby volcanoes. It was rich in fossils.

In 1913 a German team, led by Hans Reck of Berlin University, went to Olduvai, primarily to study volcanic formations. They established the great geological age of the deposits and also discovered more than 1,700 fossils, preserved by the volcanic ash.

One fossil aroused particular controversy. Reck's team had turned up a human skull and skeleton, which Reck named "Oldoway." It showed some of the characteristics of Piltdown Man: large-brained, but apparently with the body of an ape. On the basis of geological associations, Reck claimed that he had found the earliest human remains yet uncovered.

British scholars were skeptical, and when Leakey himself went to visit Reck in Berlin to examine the remains he came to the conclusion that they were not as old as Reck believed. Nevertheless, he was persuaded that Reck had found a human ancestor, and that therefore it must have been a tool-maker. Reck objected that he had searched thoroughly for stone implements, but in vain. Leakey bet him ten pounds that he would find tools. They mounted an expedition together in 1931, and Leakey immediately found what he was looking for. (He was, of course, familiar with the typical East African stone tools, which were made from volcanic lavas and quartz, while Reck expected to find only flint tools, of the European variety.)

It was perhaps unfortunate that Leakey won his bet, since his triumph inclined him to embrace Reck's find. Oldowan Man did, after all, now meet the full Piltdown specifications: very ancient, large-brained but otherwise rather apelike, and a tool-maker. Arthur Keith, who had at first rejected Reck's claims, now congratulated Reck and Leakey on their great discovery. That was, perhaps, the kiss of death.

Unlike Piltdown, Oldowan Man was no forgery, but the conclusions that Reck and Leakey had reached were quickly upset. Geologists established that the bones did not belong to the geological deposits in which they had been found: the skeleton had collapsed in a geological fault, ending up in a much older deposit.

Leakey was not unduly downcast by this setback, for he thought that he had found more ancient human remains in Kanam and Kanjera in western Kenya. Again, metropolitan scientists were dubious. One outspoken skeptic was Percy Boswell, Professor of Geology at Imperial College London, and Leakey boldly invited him to join an expedition he was mounting and see for himself. When they arrived at the sites, Leakey found that local people had apparently removed the iron pegs he had hammered in to mark the spot at which the finds were made. Boswell was unimpressed. In any case, the local stratigraphy was complex, and the context and thus the dating of any specimens would be doubtful. In his report for *Nature,* Boswell suggested that the Kenyan fossils should be placed in what he called a "suspense account."

Leakey's reputation was gravely damaged by these two fiascos, and although he continued to explore Olduvai (accompanied after 1935 by Mary), their luck turned only in 1959, when Mary found a large cranium, evidently associated with stone tools, and possibly 600,000 years old.

By any standard this was a significant find. Louis's ambition, however, was to establish the classic English vision of human evolution, and his first reaction was disappointment. The fossil looked like an australopithecine. So far as Leakey was concerned, australopithecines could not be direct ancestors of *Homo:* they were too recent and too small-brained, and they had not made tools. He was sure that they belonged to a branching line that led away from the main stem of human evolution.

But there was another way of looking at the find. If this creature had indeed made tools, then whatever it looked like at first—or even second—glance, it could not have been an australopithecine. Leakey persuaded himself that this was a better appreciation of Mary's specimen. Despite the grave warnings he received from his English mentors, he announced the discovery of a new genus, which he named for the ancient term for East Africa, Zinj, and his sponsor, Charles Boise. He claimed that *Zinjanthropus boisei* was the true ancestor of the human species.

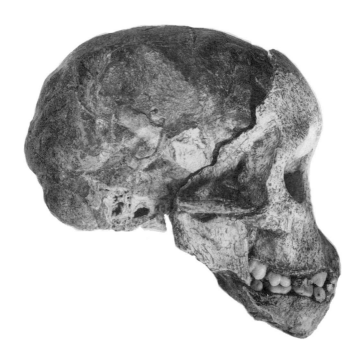

*A*USTRALOPITHECUS. *(Left)* The skull of a child found in limeworks near the village of Taung in the northern Cape, in South Africa, in November 1924 was analyzed by Raymond Dart and became the type specimen of *Australopithecus africanus.* The photograph shows the face and anterior part of the brain case, the upper teeth, part of the lower jaw and the lower teeth, and a fine natural endocranial cast. The date of the Taung fossil is still uncertain, but analysis of faunal remains from the site indicates that it is at least 2 million years old. *(Right)* This cranium, which became the type specimen of *Australopithecus (Zinjanthropus) boisei,* was discovered by Mary Leakey at Olduvai Gorge, in Tanzania, in July 1959. Louis Leakey suggested that it represented a new taxon, which he named *Zinjanthropus boisei.* It was later described and evaluated by P. V. Tobias, who showed that it was a

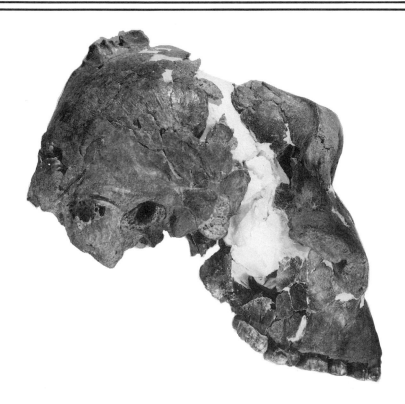

distinct species of the genus *Australopithecus*, closely related to the southern African "robust" australopithecine. Tobias wrote: "*A. boisei* represents the largest-toothed of all the early hominids, the premolars and molars being excessively expanded, especially in their width. However, the front teeth, the incisors and canines, are disproportionately small. The crest thrown up by the temporalis muscles of mastication is clearly shown on this specimen." Specimens of *A. boisei* found in East Africa date from between 2.2 and 1.4 million years ago.

This time the dénouement was less swift, but equally unkind. The fossils turned out to be even older than Leakey had thought—some 1.75 million years old—but Phillip Tobias, the anatomist who had succeeded Dart at the University of the Witwatersrand, decided after the most minute investigation that it was, after all, an australopithecine. The tools found nearby were not necessarily associated with the fossil at all.

It was a further setback, but the Leakey family had meanwhile discovered yet another candidate for an ancient human forebear. The discoverer was Louis Leakey's youngest son, Jonathan, only nineteen years old and just out of school. Wandering around Olduvai in May 1960, he came upon some bones and teeth that apparently belonged to a large-brained human creature. Geologists were on hand, and they fixed the date of the site at 1.7 million years old. A promising feature was that the fossils were associated with forty-eight stone artifacts.

Phillip Tobias was called in again by the Leakeys, and this time, after another prolonged investigation, and despite initial skepticism, he came down on Louis's side. Here at last was an ancient human tool-maker. In 1964, Leakey, Tobias, and a British anatomist, John Napier, announced the discovery of a new species of the genus *Homo,* which they named *Homo habilis.* It was the third species in the genus, joining *Homo sapiens* and *Homo erectus.* (Represented by Java and Peking Man, *Homo erectus* had been accepted thirty years earlier.)

Leakey was triumphant, but this *Homo habilis* was still too recent for his ultimate purposes. The account of human evolution to which Leakey remained loyal required a very ancient, large-brained ancestor. Leakey's quest was to find a human ancestor older than the australopithecines. And in 1967, once again, a member of his family seemed to have come up with the goods. Richard Leakey had made a promising find at a new site, Koobi Fora, near Lake Turkana in Kenya.

New dating methods were being tried out in California, and these at first yielded a date for the fossils of 3 million years old. There were grounds for supposing that it was *Homo:* its skull was thinner, higher, and rounder than the typical australopithecine skull, and it had a larger cranial capacity. Moreover, stone tools were associated with the finds.

Richard Leakey thought that he had found an earlier specimen of his father's Zinj, which now seemed to predate the australopithecines. Zinj might yet prove to be the true human ancestor. The austrolopithecines would be expunged from the human genealogy. The aging Louis was convinced that here, at last, was the vindication he had awaited. Thirty-six years after the debacle of his Kanam finds, he told a meeting at the Leakey Foundation in 1969, "We have proved I was right, which to me is very, very, very satisfying." He died only three years later, but by then these certainties had already ebbed away.

Richard Leakey had tried to buttress his intuition with the best scientific analysis he could command, but the experimental dating methods used for the Koobi Fora fossils soon proved to be unreliable. It took several years to establish a firm date, and then the Koobi Fora specimens turned out to be less than 2 million years old. The only question that remained was whether they should be classed as *Australopithecus* or *Homo habilis*.

By now the Leakey family had competition. Scientists flocked to what a young Leakey collaborator, Glynn Isaac, called the East African Klondike. Among the new wave was a young American, Donald Johanson.

Johanson's parents were immigrants. His father was a barber, his mother a cleaning-lady. His manner was confident, even brash, his ambition boundless. And in November 1974, taking part in an expedition at Hadar in Ethiopia, he and a colleague discovered the most complete hominid skeleton that had yet been found. The young men were euphoric. "There was a tape recorder in the camp," Johanson has recalled, "and a tape of the Beatles song 'Lucy in the Sky with Diamonds' went belting out into the night sky, and was played at full volume over and over again out of sheer exuberance." At some stage during the celebrations that evening, the new fossil was christened Lucy.

Lucy was important because she was virtually intact. This was the only complete skeleton that had been found of any fossil human older than the Neanderthals. She had died at the age of about 25, some 3.5 million years ago. She seemed human, for she walked erect, but she was an odd creature: her brain was in the same range as

A NCESTORS: Dart, Leakey, and the Taung skull. This photograph of Raymond Dart and Louis Leakey was taken in 1959 in Johannesburg, shortly after Mary Leakey's discovery of the type specimen of *Australopithecus boisei* at Olduvai Gorge. Dart is holding the skull of the Taung child, the type specimen of *Australopithecus africanus*, which had been discovered in 1924.

that of chimpanzees, she was only 36 inches high, and her hands hung down to her knees. If Lucy was an australopithecine, it was clear that these creatures were similar to apes. If Lucy had been caught alive, Glynn Isaac remarked, she would have been put in a zoo.

The Leakey family had to share the limelight now, but Mary Leakey was making intriguing discoveries in a new site, Laetoli in northern Tanzania. Her most astonishing find was made by accident in 1978–1979, when she discovered hominid footprints set as if in concrete, preserved in volcanic-ash layers, and dating to at least 3.6 million years ago. Analysis of the footprints provided firm proof that early hominids were fully bipedal.

But as the finds piled up they began to raise fresh questions. A rather diverse set of samples was accumulating within the broad category of *Australopithecus*. Should they be lumped together, or should different types of *Australopithecus* be distinguished? And how did this increasingly diverse group of specimens differ from *Homo habilis*?

Homo habilis was the object of much professional skepticism at first, and recent evidence suggests that it is not easy to distinguish *Homo habilis* from its close kin. The distinction between *Australopithecus* and *Homo habilis* depends largely on two features: an increased cranial capacity and a reduced tooth size. Brain capacity has traditionally been critical to the definition of the genus *Homo*, but although the cranial capacity of *Homo habilis* (which was, however, highly variable) could be significantly larger than that of *Australopithecus*, it did not fall within the accepted human range. Moreover, the extent of variation between fossils classified as *Homo habilis* turned out to be disturbingly great. In the end, the main evidence that a new evolutionary epoch had begun was not so much morphological as cultural. As its name—"Handyman"—suggests, *Homo habilis* was identified as the first tool-maker.

Ruminating on these uncertainties, Don Johanson teamed up with Tim White, another American scientist, who was working with Mary Leakey in Laetoli. In the summer of 1977, they put the Laetoli casts and the Hadar samples side by side on one table in Johanson's laboratory in Cleveland. "It was an uncanny experience," Johanson recalls. "One fact came bursting from the surface of the table: the two sets of fossils were startlingly alike."

But were they australopithecines? They seemed to be quite different from the South African specimens that were taken to define the type. Two South African varieties of australopithecines were already recognized, the robust and the gracile, though anthropologists did not agree which was the more ancient, and how each fitted into a human genealogy. Now a third variety was added, dubbed *Australopithecus afarensis*, after the region in Ethiopia where specimens were first discovered. White and Johanson suggested in 1981 that *afarensis* was the direct ancestor of *Homo habilis*, and also of a branching line that led to the other australopithecines.

This solution did not convince everyone, and some scientists began to suspect that among the fossils found in East and South Africa were representatives of yet more species of both *Australopithecus* and *Homo.* Was Lucy herself perhaps the representative of another species of *Homo?*

The questions were urgent, and there were spirited public debates between the two stars, Richard Leakey and Don Johanson. Nevertheless, by this stage much had become clearer. A new synthesis could tentatively be put together.

THE first traces of the primate order in the fossil record have been dated to some 60 million years ago. This suggests that primates evolved about 5 million years after the catastrophe that brought about the extinction of the dinosaurs and left the mammals with a decisive comparative advantage in the struggle for life.

The first fossil remnants of anthropoid apes are dated to some 30 million years ago. About 12 million years ago, the common ancestors of the hominids and their closest surviving relatives, the African apes, branched off from the other apes. The human lineage itself—the hominid family—became differentiated roughly 5 million years ago.

Unfortunately, this crucial period coincides with one of the longest modern gaps in the fossil record, which runs from some 4 to 8 million years ago. In consequence, there is still no direct evidence for the nature of the first hominids. We must rely largely on deductions based on the differences between hominids and other surviving primate species.

Until the hominid branch diverged, all primates were dominantly arboreal creatures, living on a mainly vegetarian diet. Living primates—and probably their ancestors—are remarkable for the dominance of vision over the sense of smell, their complex grasping and manipulative skills, and the possession of a brain that represents a significantly higher proportion of body weight than is the case for any other mammals. The apes (and humans) are further distinguished by a preference for fruit and plant food over leaves, their lack of tails, and their generally greater size than the monkeys.

The first distinctive feature of the human lineage to evolve was bipedalism, although the decisive nature of this break should not be exaggerated. Hominids remained well adapted to tree climbing for at least two million years. Nevertheless, all other primates preferred to use their forelimbs to help them move about. The apes generally practice "knuckle-walking," their forepaws bent inward as they brush across the ground. Hominids were the only primates that walked upright for much of the time.

The causes and consequences of the distinctively upright, two-legged human gait have been debated since Darwin. The immediate stimulus for bipedalism was probably the need to adapt to terrestrial living. There was a gradual decline in temperatures. In the tropical regions the forest retreated and savannah spread. Many forest creatures became extinct, including a number of species of ape. The first hominids prospered by adapting to life on the plains. The ability to walk on two legs gave them an edge in making this shift: it permitted them to move about in open country with less effort than the other apes, allowed them to see over the vegetation as they moved, and protected them to some extent from exposure to direct sunlight.

What then were the consequences of bipedalism? Darwin suggested that bipedalism left humans defenseless, and so stimulated the invention of tools and weapons, and that the survival of a bipedal tool-user in this new open environment would also have required the development of intelligence and of those "social qualities which lead him to give and receive aid from his fellow men." Several generations of scientists assumed that there was a close relationship between bipedalism and the development of a human brain, but it is now evident that bipedalism had developed by 4 million years ago, while the rapid evolution of the human brain began only some 2 million years ago. Quite possibly, then, bipedalism was important simply for itself: it enabled early hominids to operate more effectively in open country. Our main physical differences from other apes and from our own distant ancestors have to do with bipedalism, associated shifts in the pelvis and the upper skeleton, modifications of the teeth and jaw, and changes in cranial capacity.

In the 1950s and 1960s, anthropologists associated the shift to bipedalism with the change in dental structure that can be observed in early hominids. The apes have very large canines, relative to the molars, and when they bite the canines interlock. Human teeth are more even in size, the canines are small, and they wear at the tips rather than at their front and back surfaces, as do the teeth of the apes. As the shape of the teeth changed, so did the shape of the jaw. These modifications followed the adaptation to savannah life. They permitted hominids to chew more efficiently the coarse vegetable foods that they now gathered on the ground, and that made up the greater part of their diet.

These changes in range and diet must also have been associated with changes in behavior. Some anthropologists linked bipedalism and changes in dentition with the beginnings of tool use and hunting, but once again the dates do not fit. Even the most rudimentary tools came into regular use only around 2 million years ago.

In the 1970s and 1980s, exceptionally complete specimens of *Australopithecus* were described both by Richard and Mary Leakey and by Johanson and White. It became clear that the creature was morphologically and probably behaviorally very close to the apes. Moreover, these apelike hominid fossils were very recent: they could be dated to less than 4 million years ago.

The late date seemed more plausible when, also in the 1970s, geneticists tentatively proposed a new method of tracing human origins, which used DNA taken from living populations. They deduced that the divergence between the hominid line and closely related African apes occurred about 5 million years ago. This independent confirmation of the conclusions drawn from the African fossil record seemed to many to be decisive, though it soon turned out that genetic methods delivered less conclusive dates for our ancestors than had initially been hoped.

Another conclusion was also generally accepted at this time: that *Australopithecus* was the direct ancestor of *Homo*. The shift from *Australopithecus* to *Homo* is, however, poorly documented. There is another frustrating gap in the African fossil record for the period between 3 and 2 million years ago, which is precisely when the transition must have occurred. We cannot even be sure how many varieties of *Australopithecus* there were. Two species—*Australopithecus boisei* and *Australopithecus robustus*—were identified in the 1960s, but a third, *Australopithecus afarensis*, was added in the 1980s to accommodate the finds from Laetoli and Hadar. Today some scientists identify three, others four, and yet others five species. There is also a question as to which of these varieties developed into *Homo*.

Despite all the uncertainties, the overwhelming probability is that the first members of the genus *Homo* evolved from one of the varieties of *Australopithecus* in eastern Africa about 2.5 to 2 million years ago. The most striking feature of the new species was a marked increase in cranial capacity in comparison with *Australopithecus*.

This was a time when adaptive pressures increased. The polar ice cover expanded rapidly, and the trend to cooler and drier climates accelerated. The increase in hominid brain power may have been associated with the first development of tool use, which has also been traced back some 2 million years. At the same time, meat became a significant part of the human diet (with the consequence, it has been suggested, that many other African carnivores became extinct about 2 million years ago).

One plausible theory suggested that the increase in cranial capacity and the appearance of tools coincided with the appearance of a new hominid: perhaps, indeed, the first human being. This was what Louis Leakey, Tobias, and Napier were proposing in 1964 when they described *Homo habilis*. The furor that was caused by their daring proposal abated somewhat as it became evident that *Australopithecus* was on any measure very like an ape, and that there was therefore room for at least one other species between these creatures and *Homo erectus*. However, as more specimens of *Homo habilis* were identified and described, another problem became apparent. The specimens were remarkably variable. In 1987 Bernard Wood of Liverpool University inquired mockingly in *Nature*, "Who is the 'real' *Homo habilis?*"

Today some specialists are tempted to reclassify the *Homo habilis* specimens as local varieties of *Australopithecus* and *Homo erectus*. This would leave only two species of *Homo: Homo erectus* and *Homo sapiens*. Others—including Bernard Wood himself and Chris Stringer of London's Natural History Museum—take a very different view. They think it more likely that there are further species of *Homo* still to be identified. *Homo habilis*, perhaps, seems so variable because more than one species has been put into the same category.

Homo erectus evolved 1.8 or 1.7 million years ago. Whether the new hominid species evolved directly from *Homo habilis* or from another hominid contemporary, or even perhaps directly from one of the varieties of *Australopithecus*, is still uncertain. In any case, the earliest *Homo erectus* fossils have all been found in eastern and southern Africa, which was almost certainly once again the place of origin of a new hominid type. About one million years ago, at the start of the main Pleistocene ice age, representatives of *Homo erectus* dispersed to Asia, where they appear in the record most famously as Java Man and Peking Man. They also may have penetrated into Europe. *Homo erectus* was probably the only hominid species on earth for nearly a million years. There was no doubt considerable local variation, but what is most striking is the relative stability of *Homo erectus*, both biologically (as far as can be discovered from fossil remains) and in its behavior over this huge stretch of time.

Throughout its history and in every part of the world in which it has been found, *Homo erectus* is associated with a tool kit that is both restricted in range and monotonously uniform. Nevertheless, archaeologists were at first inclined to credit the creature with an advanced cultural repertoire. It was said to use fire, to hunt, to share food around a "home base": to behave, in fact, very much like modern hunter-gatherers such as the Bushmen of southern Africa. This was consistent with the view that human origins are very ancient, human evolution a slow process of gradual accretions.

In the 1970s, an attack on this orthodoxy was launched by a

brilliantly critical American archaeologist, Lewis Binford. Another charismatic, determined, populist figure, Binford is famously aggressive. He enters into a debate with colleagues, so it has been said, in the spirit of a longshoreman clearing out a bar. He has shown a talent for picking unorthodox ideas that turn out to be right; but sometimes what he has to say is accepted—or rejected—largely because Binford is fighting so hard for it.

Beginning with a radical reexamination of the animal bones associated with early *Homo,* Binford brought into question the hunting capability of *Homo erectus.* Soon he began to undermine each of the established claims for the cultural skills of early humans, and young scholars swarmed in to consolidate the work of destruction. By the mid-1980s it seemed that none of the familiar claims could stand up to critical scrutiny.

The implications were formidable. *Homo erectus* had very nearly a modern brain capacity, but apparently very little in the way of human culture to show for it. If human origins are taken to mean the beginnings of a recognizably human culture, then the first 3.5 million of the 4 million years of hominid evolution must be counted still as a period of pre-human history.

A HUMAN WAY
OF LIFE

No definition of humanity is adequate if it leaves out the ways in which people communicate, reflect, share experiences, order their lives, raise children, plan and execute political campaigns, and learn to make a living in particular environments. A morphological definition of *Homo* excludes too much that we need to know; it risks missing crucial turning points in human history just because these may not have left evident traces on the body. (*Homo habilis* would not have been identified if the tools he made had been left out of account.) Fossils do offer clues to behavior; for instance, changes in diet can be deduced from dentition. But although the fossil record may one day yield a complete genealogy of the human species, it will offer only an impoverished picture of how early humans lived.

Archaeology reads traces of life-styles in the implements that have survived (none more than 2 million years old), and from the debris of living floors. For comparatively recent periods—certainly for the past 40,000 years—these sources can provide rich pickings. For the more distant past they provide only rare, disputed glimpses of how people lived.

The other possible route into the past is by way of comparison, the method favored by Darwin. Darwin examined living species, compared them, and made deductions about their ancestors. It is tempting to use comparison to eke out the evidence from paleontology and archaeology. But which living populations afford clues to the lives of ancient humans and apes?

Modern primates are different in many ways from the species that were contemporaries of *Australopithecus*, but perhaps, if due care is exercised, gorillas, chimpanzees, and even baboons might serve as living stand-ins for extinct primate populations. They may even provide some indications of how the australopithecines ordered their existence.

African hunter-gatherer communities, which have been studied by ethnographers for a century, are now quite well understood. Some generalizations can be made about the foraging way of life, at least as it persists in the twentieth century. Perhaps this understanding can be drawn on to reconstruct the ways of the early human foragers, who lived for millions of years in the African plains before the evolution of modern humans.

This was the program that Sherwood Washburn, professor of anthropology at the University of California, Berkeley, proposed for American anthropology in the 1960s and 1970s. "The Pleistocene way of life can only be known by inference and speculation," Sherwood Washburn and C. S. Lancaster told the famous "Man the Hunter" Conference in Chicago in 1966. "Obviously speculations are based on much surer ground when the last few thousand years are under consideration. Ethnographic information is then directly relevant and the culture bearers are of our own species. As we go farther back in time, there is less evidence and the biological and cultural difference becomes progressively greater."

That was undeniably correct. But Washburn was not averse to risk-taking. And risks had to be taken, he urged, since "it was in those remote times that the human way took shape, and it is only through speculation that we may gain some insights into what the life of our ancestors may have been." And, indeed, that was also undeniable.

The son of a Congregationalist minister who became dean of the Episcopal Theological School in Cambridge, Massachusetts, Sherwood Washburn was educated at Groton and Harvard. Brilliant, assured, imaginative, Washburn is also, as he says, like his father, "a very good Protestant Episcopal-type speaker." He soon became a leading figure in American physical anthropology, making his career at the center of the action, at Harvard, Columbia, the University of Chicago, and Berkeley.

In 1948 Washburn followed other paleontological pilgrims to Johannesburg, to examine the australopithecines collected by Dart and

S HERWOOD WASHBURN was the architect of the studies made in the 1950s of African primates in the wild, and in the 1960s of the !Kung Bushman. A physical anthropologist, he argued that it was necessary to study the social organization of primates and hunter-gatherers in order to gain an understanding of the transition to a human way of life in eastern Africa in the distant past. Washburn insisted on the importance of hunting in the evolution of humans.

Broom. In 1955 he attended the first Pan African conference on prehistory, organized by J. Desmond Clark at Livingstone in what was then Northern Rhodesia (now Zambia). There the first substantial collection of the earliest human tools was examined and discussed. But Washburn was most fascinated by the baboons who lived close to the Victoria Falls Hotel, where he was lodged. As he became familiar with them he noted that each animal had a definite personality; and in a visit to the Wankie Game Reserve he began to get a sense of the way in which baboon troops were organized, with leaders who could coordinate defense against predators. Morphology would not explain this behavior; a social study was required.

Back in the United States, Washburn received a three-year Ford Foundation grant for "the study of the evolution of behavior." One of his priorities was to organize a field study of baboons in East Africa, and he selected as the fieldworker a social anthropologist, Irven DeVore, who had been his teaching assistant at the University of Chicago. It was a characteristically imaginative and unconventional decision.

"He chose me," DeVore recalls, "for the explicit reason that, in his opinion, primate studies had languished in no small part because previous studies had been undertaken by physical anthropologists and/or comparative psychologists whose methods and research agenda were too narrowly focused (locomotion, diet, etc.). He was also convinced that, since the training of such persons included little or no exposure to the analysis of complex social behavior, he should recruit a person whose orientation had been in that direction—in this case, a 'social anthropologist' like myself. It was apparent at the time, and has been a running joke between us ever since, that I had none of the usual training for primate studies (biology, anatomy, etc.), but his choice was a deliberate one." DeVore spent eleven months in Kenya, working mainly in the Nairobi National Park but also briefly together with Washburn at the Amboseli Reserve.

It soon became evident that baboons are organized in stable communities, but the size of their groups varies from a handful of individuals to populations of over a hundred. The main constraint on the size of a troop is probably the distribution of food resources in a group range. Baboons travel within a range of three miles each day

D<small>**EVORE**</small> studying baboons in Kenya.　　Irven DeVore was engaged by Sherwood Washburn to undertake a "social anthropological" study of baboon
troops in the wild. DeVore discovered that the baboons had a stable social
structure, "organized around the dominance hierarchy of adult males."

in search of food, returning at night to a sleeping place in the trees or steep cliffs. They rarely fight to defend the range, but it is not easy for experimenters to drive them beyond it. Their diet is varied, although almost exclusively vegetarian. They are flexible feeders, learning quickly from each other when fresh sources of food have been proven.

The stability of the communities particularly impressed the first field observers. "Baboon groups," concluded Irven DeVore and K. R. L. Hall, "are closed social systems. During all of the field investigations . . . we have seen only two baboons (both of them adult males) shift from one troop to another." Lone individuals were also extremely rare.

The baboon troop seemed at first sight to contain a disproportionate number of adult females, who apparently outnumbered adult males by a ratio of two or three to one. Were the males more at risk from predators, perhaps? DeVore showed that this problem was a false one. Females mature twice as quickly as males, a female reaching full size at five years, by which time she is breeding. Males attain full physical maturity only after seven to ten years. Mature females therefore outnumber mature males simply because they mature more quickly.

The mature males are much larger than the females, and differ above all in features that suit them for defense. They are notably aggressive and dominance-oriented, even when compared to other primates. The relatively small size of the females is not a disadvantage, since they rely on the males for defense against predators— and it may be an advantage, for them and indeed for the community, since they require less sustenance.

The size and aggression of the baboon males also have consequences for the internal structure of the troop, which "is organized around the dominance hierarchy of adult males." This dominance is not measured by control of food sources, since baboons forage individually and rarely compete for specific items. Dominance is displayed in the control of fertile females and in the ability to require shows of deference from other males. It is also apparent when a threat presents itself to the group, for females and infants cluster near the dominant male.

In the simplest case, one male is dominant, but there are instances in which a coalition of two or more males is found. Sometimes several individuals and pairs of males contest command. DeVore reported in detail on one group in Nairobi Park, numbering forty animals, including six adult males and about twice as many adult females. Three of the males were dominant: Curly, young but unusually aggressive; Humbert, older, with worn-down canines; and Gam, the largest and most powerful individual. While Gam could intimidate either of the other two males on its own, they habitually combined against him, forming a dominant alliance.

It was in this troop that DeVore observed two rare cases of animals changing groups. First, a subordinate adult male of a neighboring troop, whom DeVore called Lone, began to attach himself to Curly's troop. Initially he kept his distance; then he moved closer, engaging in several sharp fights with Curly and with Gam. Then Humbert disappeared. Soon his ally, Curly, was observed to be marginalized, and Gam and the new animal, Lone, emerged as the dominant alliance in the troop.

A matching hierarchy of females was less evident, although females did sometimes combine against rivals, and also occasionally against males. DeVore concluded that the key to baboon social organization was the dominance pattern among adult males, which "usually ensures stability and comparative peacefulness within the group, maximum protection for mothers with infants, and the highest probability that offspring will be fathered by the most dominant males." The group structure was flexible, varying in size and composition, probably in response to environmental opportunities.

DeVore's pioneering study was swiftly followed by others. Perhaps the most interesting ones dealt with chimpanzees and gorillas, the apes most closely related to humans. The differences in social organization between these species, and even within species, proved to be unexpectedly great. In 1962–1963 a group of specialists led by Washburn and David Hamburg gathered for a year at the Center for Advanced Study in the Behavioral Sciences in Stanford, California, and their meetings led to the production of a landmark collection of essays, *Primate Behavior: Field Studies of Monkeys and Apes*, edited by Irven DeVore. For the first time, a set of authoritative studies of primate behavior in the wild was available.

For those interested in human evolution, the data on the African apes were particularly significant. Gorilla groups were fairly cohesive units, like baboon troops, but the bands were much smaller, typically including from two to thirty individuals. A group might contain only two adults, one male and one female, although some included several adult males and females. Reporting on mountain gorillas in Zaire, George Schaller concluded that most bands were dominated by a single silverbacked male, who was the leader of the group and its main defender. Other males were peripheral.

Chimpanzees formed communities of sixty to eighty individuals, but in contrast to baboons and gorillas, these communities were not stable, often splitting into parties of several males together, females, and infants together, or males, females, and infants. Individuals moved freely between ranges, and dominance was not clearly expressed within the troop, except that males were dominant over females.

Copulation could be initiated by males or females, and Jane Goodall reported that chimpanzees could be very promiscuous. A female might copulate with several males in quick succession: "during one of these occasions seven males mounted one female, one after the other (one of them twice), with less than two minutes between each of the first five copulations."

Gorillas are almost entirely herbivorous, and the diet of chimpanzees, like that of baboons, is mainly vegetarian. However, there were reports of occasional meat-eating by chimpanzees. Jane Goodall described one successful hunt that she observed at the Gombe Stream Chimpanzee Reserve in Tanzania. Two adolescent male chimpanzees collaborated to catch and break the neck of a red colobus monkey. A large male quickly arrived to take the bulk of the meat, the rest being snatched up by other chimpanzees. "On the other occasions when I saw meat-eating," Goodall reported, "the prey was initially in the possession of a mature male. Each time the other chimpanzees in the group sat close to him, holding out their hands with the begging gesture."

THE way of life of the East African baboons and apes was becoming clearer. What of the Pleistocene hominids? In an ideal world, Washburn would now have dispatched students to study the social life of animals more or less equivalent to *Australopithecus* or *Homo erectus;* but these hominid varieties have been extinct for millions of years. There were no living equivalents. It was necessary to jump ahead and seek stand-ins for the role of the Upper Paleolithic human beings who replaced them in eastern Africa.

Darwin himself had no doubt that contemporary "savages" could play such a part. He recalled:

> The astonishment which I felt on first seeing a party of Fuegians on a wild and broken shore will never be forgotten by me, for the reflection at once rushed into my mind—such were our ancestors. These men were absolutely naked and bedaubed with paint, their long hair was tangled, their mouths frothed with excitement, and their expression was wild, startled, and distrustful. They possessed hardly any arts, and like wild animals lived on what they could catch; they had no government, and were merciless to every one not of their own small tribe.

With his standard Victorian prejudices about so-called savages, Darwin was grossly unfair to the Fuegians; though no doubt the Fuegians would have been equally appalled to learn that the Anglo-Saxons had the effrontery to claim kinship to them, yet nevertheless practiced slavery and mechanized warfare, flogged women in public, sent their children away from home in early childhood, and believed that their god had been born to a virgin.

Darwin confessed that he would prefer to claim a loyal gorilla as his ultimate progenitor, yet whatever his preferences might have been, he did not doubt that the Fuegians lived in much the same way as his own distant ancestors had lived. Washburn, similarly, thought that the African hunters might be taken to represent surviving practitioners of a very early human way of life. Of course, people such as the Kalahari Bushmen or the Pygmies of the central African rain forest had their own history, their long-established peculiarities, their own identity; nevertheless, making a living with their poor implements in an inhospitable terrain, they might recapitulate in crucial ways the lives of our distant ancestors.

The times were propitious for such a study. "In the early 1960s," recalls Richard Lee, then a Berkeley graduate student working with Washburn and DeVore, "the anthropological world was excited by the new data pouring in from field studies of nonhuman primates and from the Leakeys' discoveries of ancient living floors associated with fossil man."

Another Berkeley anthropologist, J. Desmond Clark, had been collaborating with the Leakey family in the study of early human sites, and he urged that observations of campsite behavior of contemporary African hunter-gatherers be used to provide guidelines for the interpretation of early human remains. More boldly yet, Washburn suggested that field studies of contemporary African hunter-gatherers might help us to understand the ways in which early humans had made a living and adapted to environmental pressures.

This project was entrusted to DeVore and Lee, who elected the Kalahari Bushmen to represent the first humans in the plains of eastern Africa. In 1963, they initiated a comparative study of Bushmen hunter-gatherers in the Kalahari. The objective was to study the social adaptation of Bushmen bands, in much the same way as DeVore had studied the social adaptations of baboons in East Africa. A comparison between the two studies might then help to pinpoint the ways in which the first bands of humans differed from their primate cousins and neighbors, thus perhaps identifying what had happened in the transition to human society. "My hunch," Lee recalled, "was that research on contemporary hunter-gatherer groups—subject to critical safeguards—could provide a basis for models of the evolution of human behavior."

Lee fixed on a remote community of Bushmen who lived in a semi-desert environment in the Kalahari, on the Botswana-Namibia border. These were the !Kung. (The Kalahari languages are remarkable for the range of click consonants they employ. The ! stands for a popping sound rather like a cork being pulled from a wine bottle. It is made by pulling the tip of the tongue sharply away from the front of the palate.)

Lee soon found that the !Kung did rather well for themselves, despite the poor resources at their disposal, and without tools beyond digging-sticks, ostrich eggshell water containers, skin clothes and bags, and simple bows and arrows. Adults were working the equiva-

THE FUEGIANS. Writing in 1835 to his sister Caroline, Darwin listed "the three most interesting spectacles I have beheld since leaving England – a Fuegian savage – Tropical Vegetation – & the ruins of Concepcion – ."

Tierra del Fuego had been discovered by Magellan in 1520, but the visit of the *Beagle* was in connection with the first proper survey, carried out by the British Admiralty between 1826 and 1836. The native peoples—the Ona, Yahgan, and Alacaluf Indians—were related to Indian groups that occupied the whole Chilean archipelago down to Cape Horn. Living largely on fish and shellfish, hunting in a small way, traveling by canoe, these communities were very small, scattered, and vulnerable. After the discovery of gold and the intrusion of sheep farmers in the 1880s, the area came under the control of Chile and Argentina. The Ona are now extinct, and only a handful of survivors remain from the other populations.

A small party of Fuegians had been taken to England by FitzRoy, the captain of the *Beagle*, and had swiftly absorbed the language and customs. When the *Beagle* returned the Fuegians to their homes, Darwin commented: "They have far too much sense not to see the vast superiority of civilized over uncivilized habits." However, when the ship returned some months later they found that Darwin's special friend, Jemmy Button, was reconciled to Fuegian

life and had no desire to return to England. "I hope & have little doubt that he will be as happy as if he had never left the country," Darwin now wrote. He concluded that the Fuegians did not lack intelligence; their conservatism had a social cause. "The perfect equality of all the inhabitants will for many years prevent their civilization."

RICHARD LEE and the author in the Kalahari, 1963. Washburn and De-Vore planned a study of contemporary African hunter-gatherers to illuminate the findings of archaeologists on early African populations, and to discover the way in which people made a living from foraging, using simple technologies, in marginal African environments. Richard Lee was engaged to carry out fieldwork among the !Kung of the Kalahari desert. In the summer of 1963 he and DeVore made their first exploratory visit. I was about to begin fieldwork in the Kalahari too, and hitched a lift with them. DeVore is behind the camera. On the left of the photograph is Richard Lee, in the middle the interpreter who accompanied this first expedition, Enoch Tabiso, a man of San descent living in Zambia. I am on the right, holding a baby baboon that DeVore had found near the body of its mother, who had been killed by a leopard.

lent of two or two and a half days a week, and yet their diet was more than adequate by most established standards. This contradicted the expectations of many anthropologists, who had believed that hunter-gatherers lived a marginal existence. Lee was not surprised, however. As he pointed out, such a stable way of life could hardly have persisted for thousands of generations unless it had been efficient.

The main reason the !Kung enjoyed a comfortable existence was that they lived largely on vegetable foods, and a great variety of plant foods were available to them. One resource above all gave them security: the mongongo nut, which was abundantly available throughout the year, easy to gather, and at once tasty and nutritious. But if the mongongo nut was their staple, it was only one of 105 species of edible plants available in the area. Even in the worst of seasons, starvation was unlikely. "Some foods are adversely affected by drought," Lee explained, "but others are drought-resistant; some foods are damaged by heavy rainfall; but other foods (like tsama melon) actually thrive on it."

Both men and women gathered plant foods—the women more frequently than the men—but only the men hunted. Hunting was in some ways a paradoxical activity: risky, time-consuming, costly in terms of energy expended, it was less obviously rewarding than gathering; and vegetable foods in fact provided the bulk of the diet. For much of the year, only some 20 percent of the diet was provided by the hunters. Nevertheless, meat was much prized, and in peak seasons the hunt might provide up to 90 percent of the food eaten, when each person in the camp could be consuming an average of more than 2 kilograms of meat a day. Over the year a !Kung Bushman would get 30 to 40 percent of his or her calories from meat.

Although women did more of the gathering than the men, men worked somewhat more than women (a ratio of about four to three), even taking into account the fact that much of the child care and domestic work was done by women. The division of labor between the sexes was not, however, mirrored in different standards of consumption. The basic unit of consumption was the family, but all the members of the camp could share the meat that a successful hunter brought in. Even the pile of plant foods outside a family's shelter would be shared with visitors squatting beside the hearth. The campsite was home to an open, hospitable community of families.

O N the most optimistic assumptions, the next step in Washburn's agenda would be to compare the !Kung with baboons or chimpanzees or gorillas. Such a comparison would highlight the differences between primates and even low-tech human beings. It might then be possible to treat these differences as indications of the social changes that had occurred in the transition to humanity.

Yet there are obvious objections to such a superficially attractive move. Even if we treat contemporary primates as stand-ins for the primate contemporaries of early humans (and some specialists were reluctant to do so), and even if we are further inclined to take a deep breath and agree that Bushmen may for some purposes be very roughly equated with late paleolithic hunters (and there are strong reasons to hesitate at this point), this would still leave us with a huge gap to fill between our australopithecine ancestors, some five million years back, and our paleolithic forebears, who would have lived a mere two hundred thousand or so years ago. There remains the dark age, lasting some four million years, when the East African savannah was dominated by ape-men or man-apes for whom there are no remotely plausible contemporary equivalents. Moreover, the way of life of these proto-humans can only be dimly perceived by archaeologists, since there are very few really ancient hominid sites, and the deposits are meager and hard to interpret. Nevertheless, Washburn favored speculation, at least at this stage of the game.

Spurred on by Washburn, Richard Lee and Irven DeVore organized a symposium on their return from the Kalahari. It was held in 1966 at the University of Chicago, and it bore the Washburn-inspired title, "Man the Hunter." Lee's data on how the !Kung made a living provided the most notable fresh material for the participants in the symposium to chew over, and in a famous intervention the anthropologist Marshall Sahlins suggested that the !Kung were a living refutation of the classic image of the hard-up hunter-gatherer. The !Kung were not rich in worldly goods, but they achieved an enviable standard of living on the basis of very little work. From a Zen—or hippie—point of view they represented, he said, "the original affluent society." This suggestive notion was apparently corroborated by impressionistic descriptions supplied by other participants, who had made field studies in Australia, East Africa, and Alaska.

Washburn fastened particularly on the importance of hunting. He had long been convinced that hunting was the specialization that most sharply differentiated humans from other primates. Technically and intellectually, the invention of hunting was the crucial move in the transition to humanity. For most of the existence of the genus *Homo*, hunting had been a major activity. If—as then seemed plausible—even *Australopithecus* was a great hunter (rather than—as we now believe—mainly a plant-gatherer with a sideline in scavenging), then, by Washburn's calculations, human beings had been hunters for 99 percent of their history.

In perhaps the most influential contribution to this crucial symposium, Washburn and Lancaster asked what "general characteristics of man" could be "attributed to the hunting way of life." Success in hunting required some technological specialization, even if this was not remarkable by the comparatively sophisticated standards of the late Pleistocene. It also demanded planning, scouting over areas far beyond the limited range of other primates, and cooperation between hunters. This complex set of operations could evolve only as part of a division of labor. If men were to spend long periods hunting large mammals (and in all modern societies of hunter-gatherers, as among the !Kung, men did most or all of the hunting), then women had to gather the daily bread, as it were, and look after the infants. Adults would also have to share their food, as did the adult !Kung.

Hunting therefore implied various social arrangements. "It involves divisions of labour between male and female, sharing according to custom, cooperation among males, planning, knowledge of many species and large areas, and technical skill." A home base had to be maintained, where food could be shared. This would serve also for cooking, and cooking allowed the exploitation of seeds. Taken together, these considerations suggested a daring conclusion: "When males hunt and females gather, the results are shared and given to the young, and the habitual sharing between a male, a female, and their offspring becomes the basis for the human family."

Washburn's "Man the Hunter" soon provoked the emergence of his alter ego, "Woman the Gatherer." Her advocates pointed to the striking fact that among most so-called hunter-gatherers (including the !Kung), foraging for plant food was the main basis of subsistence. Women did most of this plant-gathering, also usually preparing the plant food for consumption.

Adrienne Zihlman took up a suggestion of Richard Lee, that a carrying-bag rather than a weapon was the first human implement, freeing women to carry infants as they worked, and allowing them to transport food to a base-camp. Females were, on this scenario, pioneers of a more advanced sociability in which the mother-infant unit provided for itself without help from males.

This evocation of a liberated female gatherer supporting a community of vegetarians that marginalized adult men was naturally attractive to some, but there were patently a number of difficulties with it. An obvious hurdle was the baboon society model, in which males dominated and organized females. Chimpanzees, however, were very different. A chimpanzee baseline made sense given the close genetic relationship between chimpanzees and humans, and it provided support for a scenario in which a woman could provision her offspring and keep males peripheral. Chimpanzee females enjoyed relative independence, forming strong bonds with their infants but otherwise ranging quite freely without being subordinated in a stable relationship to particular males. Japanese studies of pygmy chimpanzees begun in the Zaire River Basin in 1973 turned up a system in which male bonding and aggression were lacking, and young males had close relationships with their mothers. Cooperation and peaceful coexistence were the norm, and copulation was remarkably frequent, taking place as often as eleven times a day. The pygmy chimpanzees made love, not war, and suggested an attractive baseline for early hominid social practices.

But the arguments were not simply about what primate model should be preferred for the reconstruction of early human societies. A more serious difficulty for the proponents of Woman the Gatherer was the fact that no specialized female-gatherer economies had ever been reported. The earliest human campsites revealed evidence of meat-eating. This led another Berkeley colleague of Washburn's, the archaeologist Glynn Isaac, to propose an evolutionary scenario that allowed for a more balanced participation of males and females.

Isaac specialized in the early human record in eastern Africa. Taking Lee's account of the !Kung division of labor as his point of reference, he suggested that neither male hunting nor female gathering dominated the subsistence of early hominids. Rather, males and females shared food with each other and with the young, in a common home base that was dedicated to social interchange and commensality. The development of a home base was itself a major evolutionary breakthrough, distinguishing hominids from other primates.

Food-sharing was evidently linked to investment in hunting, since hunting is only occasionally successful but will bring relatively large quantities of rapidly decaying food into the camp from time to time. It made sense to share these windfalls, which would otherwise largely go to waste. Moreover, if the hunter's gift of meat was normally reciprocated, it amounted to an investment in the future success of other hunters. And not only meat would be shared: with her carrying-sack the female gatherer could bring home more plant food than she needed for herself and her infant. The consequence, Isaacs suggested, would be a division of labor by age and sex along the lines reported by Lee for the !Kung: women would specialize in gathering, men in hunting, and the proceeds would be shared in a communal home base.

These daring scenarios multiplied and became weapons in a new academic war of the sexes. The anthropologist Lionel Tiger fastened on Washburn's image of "bonding" male hunters and used it to fashion a macho view of human social behavior. He managed to incense some feminists to such an extent that he sometimes needed protection when he came to lecture on university campuses.

It was all very exciting, but the stories that were being told increasingly struck skeptical readers as imaginative constructs with clear ideological purposes. Their authors sometimes took a cavalier attitude to the fossil record. Lewis Binford also brought into question the evidence for early hunting and cast doubt on whether home bases were represented in the early paleolithic sites in eastern Africa. He argued persuasively that hominids continued to rely largely upon foraging and scavenging for a long time before hunting became at all significant.

A young Boston-based physical anthropologist, Misia Landau, told her colleagues that they were simply constructing narratives on the lines of Kipling's how-the-elephant-got-his-trunk. "I now see," Washburn confessed in 1983, "that what I was really doing was trying to assemble information for making a consistent story of human evolution and supporting it with facts wherever possible."

A LS O in the 1980s, just as the market for paleolithic reconstructions was being undermined by inflation and debased coinage, a "revisionist" critique of the !Kung model began to gain ground. The stable end-point on which all these imaginative narratives had converged now began to dissolve as well.

The essence of the revisionist case is that the evolutionists were too quick to treat the !Kung as stand-ins for late paleolithic hunters. Archaeological evidence came to light which showed that Kalahari hunter-gatherers had been in intimate contact with pastoral groups for perhaps a thousand years. For some two centuries they have been a part of an integrated southern African economy that bound together Portuguese, Dutch, Bantu-speakers, and Bushmen (or "San") in complex relationships of exchange. Thus it has been many centuries since the ancestors of the present !Kung were (in a phrase of Sahlins) "hunters in a world of hunters," and perhaps they are not practitioners of a prehistoric adaptation.

At the original "Man the Hunter" conference, Claude Lévi-Strauss, the great French social anthropologist, had cautioned against using modern hunter-gatherer peoples as stand-ins for a paleolithic way of life. Ethnographies of living hunter-gatherers might, he suggested, be describing "devolved descendants of richer contemporary cultures."

This was essentially the view taken by the leading !Kung revisionist, Edwin Wilmsen. He argued that the culture of the Kalahari "San" is a culture of poverty, an adaptation to marginality, powerlessness, and exploitation. They have been driven to live as they do by Bantu-speaking pastoralists, who have subordinated them, expropriated them, driven them to the margins of their country. They do not represent aboriginal hunter-gatherers any more than contemporary gypsies working in a fair or a market in Europe can serve as a reliable guide to ancient nomadic civilizations.

A rather different critique of the !Kung paradigm was advanced by anthropologists such as Alan Barnard, George Silberbauer, and Jiro Tanaka, who have studied other Kalahari Bushman groups. These ethnographers acknowledged that Bushman groups had long-term contacts with other peoples, but they were still inclined to regard communities like the !Kung as representing a traditional foraging adaptation which might have considerable historical depth. This did not necessarily mean, however, that the !Kung are typical even of Kalahari Bushmen, let alone prototypical hunter-gatherers. These anthropologists described the different adaptations that various "Bushman" or "San" communities have made to local ecological circumstances, emphasizing the variety of cultural traditions represented in the Kalahari. Whereas Wilmsen downplays the cultural particularity of various "San" groups, representing the "San" as an underclass in a Marxist sense, Barnard and Silberbauer stress the variety exhibited by traditional foraging cultures.

Yet even if they are not prototypes, the !Kung do have much in common with other Bushmen, and indeed with other hunter-gatherers. Many small-scale populations of foragers live rather comfortably, even in apparently unpromising environments. The division between male hunting and female (together with some male) gathering is also very general. Another common feature is the emphasis on sharing. Finally, the social organization is remarkably similar in many hunter-gatherer societies: there are small local communities, a fluid band organization, no fixed leaders, and everywhere men and women form enduring associations in nuclear family units.

There is another general feature of great significance. As Wilmsen correctly pointed out, modern foraging bands do not live in isolation—but then it seems that they never did. Even hunters in a world of hunters found themselves in a differentiated social environment. John Yellen, an archaeologist who worked with Lee among the !Kung, points out that even before the spread of agriculture and pastoralism to southern Africa (about the time of Christ), small communities of hunter-gatherers were exchanging locally variable resources over large distances.

Archaeological studies of foragers generally turn up regional differences in technology. This is unsurprising, given ecological variations. Particular foraging traditions were based upon the local mix of food sources and the raw materials conveniently available. Variation, in turn, leads ineluctably to borrowing and exchange. The evidence is clear, even for very ancient times. The first artistic tradition, the Upper Paleolithic rock paintings of Europe, shows evidence of cultural interaction. Stylistic influences can be traced from the Atlantic to the Urals.

The !Kung are therefore perhaps most representative of hunter-gatherers in general precisely because they are different from their neighbors, and yet engage in complex relations of exchange with them. Any model of early human sociability must leave room for this open trading life, which was crucial for the survival of each community. There may not have been a single, fixed type of paleolithic hunter-gathering community, but one can, perhaps, discern a broader system of exchange relationship that made possible the particular adaptation of local communities. Variation, with its concomitants, communication and exchange, underlay the earliest human adaptations.

WHILE the revisionist critique was being launched against the Man-the-Hunter orthodoxies of the sixties and seventies, the primatologists had not been idle. DeVore's 1965 volume, *Primate Behavior,* had been able to draw on studies of only some dozen species of primates. By the mid-eighties, when a new generation of students produced a comparable volume, *Primate Societies,* good data were available on such matters as group composition, ranging, feeding, and social organization for more than a hundred species. The diversity of behavior between species was now more apparent than ever. Variations had also been documented in the organization and behavior of populations of the same species living in different environments.

Perhaps most important of all, longitudinal studies had revealed changes in social organization over time.

The young generation of primatologists corrected the "classical" model of the sixties on several crucial points. DeVore had described baboon social groupings as closed, bounded organizations. With the advantage of in-depth field studies that proceeded for years and even decades at permanent field stations in eastern Africa, the new generation had learned that primate social groups were, on the contrary, open and permeable. During his year in the field, DeVore had noted two transfers of male baboons between troops. Longitudinal studies revealed that in all primate species, members transfer on maturation. In most species it is the males who move, and there are some astonishing accounts of their adventures, which feature encounters with predators and even scarier episodes. Japanese students reported one male macaque leaving his group and traveling 17 kilometers through urban Kyoto to join a group at the other side of the city.

This pattern of male migration is familiar to students of animal behavior. The general mammalian pattern is that members of one sex stay in the natal group while members of the other sex move out. In almost all cases it is the females who remain, the males who move. Those primate species—the majority—in which males move and females stay put are behaving in the normal fashion of vertebrates.

There is a classic evolutionary explanation for the common pattern, an argument based on considerations of fitness. Its initial premise is that the migration of one sex reduces the chances of inbreeding. This is advantageous, and so one would expect out-migration. Obviously only members of one sex need move to avoid incest.

The second premise is that the success of females in breeding depends very largely on their diet. Finding a male to impregnate them occasionally is less problematic. The success of males in leaving offspring depends on access to females. Since they do not carry the fetus their diet is less crucial to reproduction, and males generally "invest" little in their offspring. This suggests that females will do better to stay within an environment that is familiar, since studies have shown that this is usually safer and pays off in the feeding stakes. Males will then move to find females with whom to breed. Moreover, migration puts the individual at higher risk from predators, and therefore species in which only the males have to move will in general reproduce more efficiently.

Given these starting assumptions, it is clear that males should move to find females with whom to breed, while females should remain settled in their home range. How then does one explain the cases of gorillas and chimpanzees?

Among gorillas, almost alone among group-living primates, both males and females migrate. Females may migrate more than once, and the impulse to move seems to be an attraction to an out-group male. Usually each grouping has only one silverback, accompanied by several females and their immature offspring. Males move out as they mature because they are not acceptable to the dominant silverback. Solitary adult males make up some 10 percent of gorilla populations, and these males may detach females from a silverback, or occasionally succeed in driving an aging silverback from his females and taking his place. Among chimpanzees, the males generally remain in their natal group while all females transfer as adolescents, and sometimes move again to a third or even a fourth troop.

Related males who live together are more likely to cooperate and less likely to fight each other. In consequence, populations in which the home team is based on a core of related males may be more effective in defending their females. On the other hand, where females remain at home, female bonding and cooperation flourish, and that may have all sorts of advantages in fostering infants. There is no obvious reason why the advantages of male bonding should tip the balance in favor of female migration among a few apes and monkeys, but not among the large majority of primate species. The question is particularly puzzling when closely related species diverge—for example, gelada baboons are male-dispersing while hamadryas baboons are female-dispersing.

One thing, however, is clear: the African apes provide most of the handful of cases of primate species in which females rather than males migrate to join new groups as they mature. Is this perhaps a clue to the evolutionary history of humans? Or is the human pattern quite different in some crucial fashion, even from that of chimpanzees and gorillas?

A challenging hypothesis on this question was offered in a landmark paper published in *Current Anthropology* in 1991 by a team of primatologists: Lars Rodseth, Richard Wrangham, Alisa Harrigan, and Barbara Smuts. What, they ask, is distinctive about human social organization when humans are set against the whole range of primate variations?

One evident human peculiarity is that whether or not males or females—or both—move away from their parents on maturity, they retain lifelong ties to their close relatives. Among other primates it is only the stay-at-homes who sustain ties with other stay-at-home kin (and these are of the same sex as themselves). Among humans, even those who marry out keep up ties with their parents and siblings. ("In fact, with the possible exceptions of bottlenosed dolphins and killer whales," the authors write, with the manic pedantry of zoologists, "the maintenance of consanguineal relationships by both males and females seems to be uniquely human.")

Humans also tend to form more stable mating partnerships than most other primates, though there are some more consistently monogamous species. The really unusual aspect of the human tendency to monogamy is that it is combined with membership in a wider community. Among other primates, there seems to be a necessary choice. Either the social unit is based on a monogamous couple (as among gibbons or orangutans), in which case they live in isolation; or else there is a community, and that is dominated by a male who monopolizes resident females (as among gorillas) or by a group of males who share access to females (as among chimpanzees and baboons). If there is a community, then monogamy is absent—except among human beings. Only humans combine two forms of organization: the stable married pair and the band. This dual system must be connected to the fact that humans, uniquely, sustain relationships with children of both sexes even after they mature.

The human mating pattern must also have something to do with gender roles. Among all primates, including humans, males who live together cooperate against males from other communities. This cooperation includes aggression and collaborative defense. Neverthe-less, in hunter-gatherer bands physical dominance is not enough to make a leader. Occasionally bands may even be led by a woman. In other primate species, migrating females seldom cooperate with the females they encounter in their new home. Human females are differ-ent. Uniquely among primates, they rarely join in a collective show of force, but they do cooperate for other purposes, even with female non-relatives. Males and females also specialize more in their forag-ing work than is the case among other primates, and in consequence they have more elaborate arrangements for sharing food with their partners, with children, and even with non-relatives.

The primatologists suggest that all these characteristic features are entailed by one distinctive aspect of human sociability. Uniquely among the primates, human beings have "the capacity to sustain relationships in absentia." Significant relationships can be kept up beyond the boundaries of the local group. What they term "the release from proximity" also has a time dimension: it is a release from a social life bound by immediate returns and the necessity for continual reinforcement.

Only humans have made this escape from the closed circle of the band because they alone have other crucial, specifically human skills, above all the capacity for symbolic communication. It is this that allows human beings to talk about other times and places and to develop rituals, which reinforce a sense that even people who are in fact separated for long periods belong together. Exchange relation-ships among humans can be based on the assurance that children will remember their parents after they have grown up and married, and that they will maintain ties with siblings; that gifts will be re-called, and returned one day. The argument, in short, is that the development of language, and with it social memory, permitted the "uncoupling of relationships from spatial proximity" whereby "social evolution as a *human* affair was launched upon its career."

· 4 ·

THE EVOLUTION
OF CULTURE

The lineaments of a distinctively human way of life may be roughly discernible, but it is not easy to date that epoch-making "escape from proximity" which ushered in human society. However, it seems increasingly likely that the most momentous changes occurred only after the evolution of *Homo sapiens*. They may even have begun later still, after anatomically modern humans replaced the early varieties of *Homo sapiens*. Some contemporary anthropologists argue that only at that point did cultural evolution—or cultural change—become an independent and decisive element in the human story. "Prior to the emergence of modern people," writes Richard Klein of the University of Chicago, "the human form and human behavior evolved together slowly, hand in hand. Afterward, fundamental evolutionary change in body form ceased, while behavioral (cultural) evolution accelerated dramatically."

The most ancient specimens of *Homo sapiens* (broadly defined) have been dated to some half a million years ago. These specimens are distinguished from *Homo erectus* by larger cranial capacities or a somewhat more modern skull shape, or both, but the differences are not great. Typings are often a matter of dispute, and Richard Klein concludes that "there is no basis for arguing that the evolution of early *Homo sapiens* . . . was a particularly important event. Future discoveries may in fact show that it was not an event at all and that what we now call early *Homo sapiens* is really an amalgam of several distinct species, evolving along separate trajectories in different regions."

The best-known variety of early *Homo sapiens* are the Neanderthals, but they appeared at a relatively late stage. The Neanderthals are, indeed, one of the most modern populations to be classified as "archaic" *Homo sapiens*. They occupied sites in Europe and the Middle East. The date of their emergence in the region is still uncertain, but they lived there until 45,000 or 30,000 years ago.

European prehistory is the best documented in the world. In 1865 a young friend and neighbor of Charles Darwin, John Lubbock, published an early synthesis, *Pre-historic Times*. Lubbock drew heavily on theories that had been advanced by Scandinavian archaeologists, and he took over their division of European prehistory into a succession of stages, each characterized by a type of technology and a mode of production. The first of these was the Stone Age, which Lubbock divided into the Paleolithic, or Old Stone Age, and the Neolithic, or New Stone Age. Later writers introduced further, perhaps equally important, distinctions between what they called the Lower, Middle, and the Upper Paleolithic.

The Neanderthal remains are associated particularly with the European Middle Paleolithic cultures that are called Mousterian. Until recently, these cultures had been rather highly rated. The Neanderthals were said to have been great hunters, to have manipulated symbols and buried their dead. The romantic myth of a Neanderthal cave-bear cult inspired a popular novel and a film. If the African *Australopithecus* was represented as Hobbesian man by Dart and Leakey, the European Neanderthals were sometimes described almost as proto-Frenchmen, enjoying their hunting, cooking their food, and pious, in a rather ritualistic way.

Not true, according to a new generation of archaeologists. An iconoclastic review published in 1987 by two American archaeologists, Philip Chase and Harold Dibble, examined and dismissed most of the claims that had been made for Neanderthal "culture," concluding that even at this stage of human history the records confront us with the remains of a "paleoculture" which "differed significantly in nature from modern culture."

The Neanderthal diet was little different from that of very ancient *Homo sapiens*. According to Lewis Binford, Neanderthals were probably not armed to hunt with much success, being largely dependent, like their hominid ancestors, on foraging for plant foods and perhaps scavenging carcasses which had died naturally, or which had been killed by other predators. (There is evidence, though, that the elephant and rhinoceros were hunted by driving them to their death over a cliff.)

Neanderthals may not even have been able to make fire, though there is evidence of controlled fire use from a much earlier stage of human history; and the hearth does not seem to have become a focus of activity. The Neanderthals did not perform rituals and did not bury their dead. Their tool-kit changed little over the millennia, and they did not make tools with several parts, such as hafted spears or harpoons, and rarely used bone, antler, or ivory as materials. There is little to suggest the distinctive modern human tendency to impose form—revealed in the archaeological record as stylistic traditions—and there are few hints of the diversity and dynamism that are characteristic of later human cultures.

Europe's Middle Paleolithic cultures were not a Neanderthal monopoly: some fully modern humans also plied Mousterian trades. However, virtually all the Upper Paleolithic cultures (the Aurignacian cultures) are associated uniquely with fully modern humans, the Cro-Magnon people. The only exception known to date is the site of Saint-Césaire in France, where in 1979 a Neanderthal skeleton was found associated with industries of an Upper Paleolithic type.

The transition from the Middle to the Upper Paleolithic is dated at about 40,000 to 30,000 years ago, depending on the precise region. (In the Middle East, the transition is dated to 47,000–40,000 years ago.) In the Upper Paleolithic, a variety of new tools were developed from different raw materials. Materials were sometimes transported over considerable distances. There were flint mines and flint-processing workshops. The production of art, jewelry, and musical instruments flourished. Ritual practices were elaborated. More animal species were exploited. In northern Europe, reindeer hunting developed in a fashion that suggests incipient domestication. In other areas, technical advances allowed people to hunt birds and to exploit the resources of seas and lakes. Some hunter-gatherers in the central Russian plain began to form relatively large and settled communities. They made a considerable investment in art and decoration, and distinctions of wealth began to appear. A few communities of foragers developed storage techniques. Long-distance trade was institutionalized.

A long-established tradition in European archaeology emphasizes continuities. This is in line with gradualist Darwinian ideas about evolution. Yet in the 1980s a number of specialists began to suggest that the cultural changes between the Middle and the Upper Paleolithic were truly revolutionary.

According to Lewis Binford, this was the most profound break in human history. In 1989, he made the radical claim that "culture"—modern human cultural life, quite distinct from anything found among other primates—began effectively with the arrival of a new population in Europe and the transition to the Upper Paleolithic:

> Among the remarkable changes in the content of the archaeological record across the threshold represented by the appearance of fully modern groups in many regions are the elaboration of burial; art; personal ornaments; new materials, such as bone, antler, and soft stone; long distance movement and/or circulation of goods; and increased variation in site size, duration, and content . . . Many of these new archaeological features directly inform us about something organizationally quite new: the presence of language . . . In short, they signal the appearance of culture.

Binford's suggestion that the great spurt of cultural creativity some 45,000 years ago corresponded to the development of language is certainly plausible. All animals communicate, and other primates have quite complex codes. Apes can be taught to respond to simple linguistic messages, and even to imitate fixed formulas. But human language is qualitatively different—infinitely flexible, self-reflective, creative. It seems inconceivable that the peoples of the Upper Paleolithic lived in the style they did without the benefit of language. Equally, it seems unlikely that people with fully developed languages would have been as culturally sterile as the Neanderthals. Indeed, according to Philip Lieberman the Neanderthals would not have been physically capable of making the range of sounds necessary for modern human speech.

There are, in short, good grounds for the radical view that the start of the Upper Paleolithic—between 45,000 and 30,000 years ago—

marks the emergence of modern human cultures in the European archeological record. Richard Klein voiced the modern consensus of many sober archaeologists when he wrote that the transition to the Upper Paleolithic "signals the most fundamental change in human behaviour that the archeological record may ever reveal, barring only the primeval development of those human traits that made archeology possible"—by which he meant the making of the first stone tools, 2 million years ago.

It could indeed be argued—as two American archaeologists, J. M. Lindly and G. A. Clark, pointed out in a paper published in 1990—that the general adoption of symbolic behavior in Europe might reasonably be dated not to 35,000 years ago but only to 25,000–20,000 years ago. For example, all but three of the seventy-four well-documented European Paleolithic burials actually date from this late period, as do most of the famous late Paleolithic artistic creations. There are faint indications of cultural development in the Middle Paleolithic, and a fresh start seems to have been made in the early Upper Paleolithic, but the first widespread cultural markers appear in the record only with the transition to the Late Paleolithic, becoming commonplace only in sites less than 25,000 years old.

IF the transition from "paleoculture" to "culture" in Europe took place so much later and was so much sharper than had been supposed, what is the explanation for it? An economical answer is that the new culture was introduced by a different population, one quite distinct from the Neanderthals. At this point the debate becomes entwined with another, more explosive controversy, which concerns the origin of anatomically modern human beings, indistinguishable from ourselves.

Since the discovery of the Neanderthal fossils in a cave in Germany in 1856, the relationship of the Neanderthals to modern humans has been the subject of intense speculation. Quite recently there was a swing to the view that they were physically very like modern human beings. Cleaned up and properly clothed, it was flippantly suggested, a Neanderthal could pass without exciting remark on the New York subway (though perhaps this would not represent a spectacularly difficult test). Accordingly, there was strong support for the view that the Neanderthals were the direct ancestors of modern Europeans.

In the 1960s a modified thesis became popular: some Neanderthals may have developed in a modern direction, probably in the Near East. Skeletons found in Israel in the caves of Skhul and Qafzeh were initially thought to date to some 120,000 years ago, and were interpreted as representing a type intermediate between the Neanderthals and modern humans. Elements of these populations had then moved, or moved back, into Europe.

Today, however, this view is no longer widely accepted. Specialists are now generally more impressed by the differences between Neanderthals and modern humans. Relative to modern humans, the Neanderthals were squat and more powerfully built, their heads flatter and wider, with heavy brows and large teeth. The infants were larger than modern children, suggesting an accelerated rate of maturation, and, as adults, early senescence. These features may represent physiological adaptations to extreme cold, which allowed the Neanderthals to survive despite their crude cave homes, limited control of fire, and flimsy clothing. Not only did they develop these specialized adaptations: the Neanderthals also preserved features associated with more primitive varieties of *Homo.* All in all, these features suggest that they were too specialized to have evolved over a few tens of thousands of years into modern humans.

This suggests that Thomas Huxley was right, and that the Neanderthals had been displaced by a more advanced population. As W. W. Howells reformulated this view in 1967, the European "cave Neanderthals came to a relatively quick end, and their place was taken by a different kind of man, who was entirely like ourselves."

Three further lines of argument support this conclusion. To begin with, a solid archaeological case now indicates that the transition between the Middle and Upper Paleolithic in Europe—between the Mousterian industry of the Neanderthals and the Aurignacian industry that succeeded it—was rapid and sharp. It seems unlikely that the Aurignacian industry grew slowly and haphazardly out of the Mousterian tradition. More likely, it was introduced as a working system by an immigrant population. And with one exception, all the

Aurignacian sites are associated with fossils of anatomically modern humans, the so-called Cro-Magnon people. (Further east, the comparable Gravettian cultures are also associated with modern human fossils.)

A second line of argument has developed as the fossils have been more securely and precisely dated. Modern humans may have evolved only between 200,000 and 100,000 years ago. Some of the oldest fossils, dating from 115,000 to 74,000 years ago, have been discovered in caves at the Klasies River Mouth in South Africa. The skeletons found in the Skhul and Qafzeh caves in Israel have now been firmly dated to the later Mousterian, some 40,000 years ago, and are identified as modern humans, though they retained some archaic features. They may have been the direct ancestors of the first anatomically fully modern humans in Europe, the Cro-Magnons, who date from about 35,000 to 10,000 years ago.

The Neanderthals survived—sometimes in close proximity to these modern populations—up to a little over 30,000 years ago. Most fossils for this period in Europe and the Near East are unambiguously either modern or Neanderthal: the identification of a few specimens as intermediate in type is disputed. The fact that the distinction between the two populations persisted so clearly for several thousand years points to a gradual displacement rather than a long-term merging of the populations.

The third line of argument is based on modern genetic techniques, which include the analysis of mitochondrial DNA from modern populations. These are thought to give a measure of divergence between groups, and (more controversially) an indication of the time scale over which the divergence occurred. This line of evidence has led several independent investigators to the conclusion that all living human beings are descended from African ancestors (the "African Eve" of some writers), who lived within the last 200,000 years.

On this view, then, Africa would have been the ancestral home of the modern humans who immigrated to the Near East and then to Europe. They also radiated eastward from the Near East, and reached Siberia in the north and Australia in the south almost at the same time as they colonized the inhospitable western marches of a glacial,

A NEANDERTHAL WOMAN. This reconstruction, by the Natural History Museum in London, is based on measurements taken from a skeleton found at Tabun in Israel. Originally dated to some 41,000 years ago, it is now thought to be perhaps 110,000 years old. Until recently, it was thought that the European and Near Eastern Neanderthals emerged about 130,000 years ago and survived until a little over 30,000 years ago, living for many generations in close proximity to modern humans. Discoveries made in 1992 indicate that their history is a longer one than had been supposed: they may have inhabited Europe half a million years ago. There are still debates about possible interbreeding and cultural exchange between Neanderthals and their modern human neighbors, but it seems more likely that they were an isolated and separate population which became extinct, and that they should not be considered ancestors of modern Europeans.

forested Europe. They were not descended from the Neanderthals. Some physical anthropologists are convinced that they were so different that interbreeding must have been rare and difficult.

These lines of evidence all suggest that the cultural naissance of the European Upper Paleolithic followed the arrival there of fully modern humans. Most probably they originated in Africa and arrived in Europe by way of the Near East. There are critics who argue for a more gradual transition, and who protest against the "dehumanization" of the Neanderthals. They point to the evidence for cultural diffusion between Neanderthals and other populations, and to the fact that the Mousterian cultures of the Neanderthals were not static. They also try to identify mixed, miscegenating populations.

The argument is by no means settled, and recent finds may oblige all concerned to think again. In July 1992 Spanish investigators turned up three important fossil hominids in the depths of a Middle Pleistocene cave site in northern Spain. The fossils date back some 300,000 years. Given these dates, the initial assumption was that they would turn out to be specimens of *Homo erectus*. Perhaps at last they would prove what many believed, that *Homo erectus* had penetrated Western Europe. But as Chris Stringer of London's Natural History Museum reported in *Nature* in April 1993, the affinities of the fossils are, rather, with the Neanderthals. This pushes the history of the Neanderthals back to perhaps half a million years ago, upsetting the established estimate that they emerged only some 130,000 years ago. The interpretation of these rich remains also forced a reassessment of the few fragmentary Central European fossils that represented the best evidence for a *Homo erectus* presence in Europe. "The Neanderthal lineage seems to have its roots deep in the Middle Pleistocene," Stringer concluded. And this suggested a radical speculation: "For those such as myself, who believe the Neanderthal lineage was distinct from our own, this would mean that the origin of the *H. sapiens* clade was similarly ancient."

The debate on Neanderthal origins is clearly starting up afresh, and as Stringer points out, it will have repercussions for the problem of modern human origins. The argument about how the history of the Neanderthals came to an end is also still open, although the thesis that they were rapidly displaced by modern humans, who enjoyed the advantages of a dynamic culture, is strongly supported.

But even if the rapid displacement thesis holds, this does not imply that a full-fledged human culture was brought to Europe by the first immigrant populations of modern *Homo sapiens*. Indeed, this cannot be correct, for a simple but extremely significant reason. Modern humans lived without this distinctive culture for perhaps two-thirds of their history, or even longer.

The first fossils of modern humans in Europe are not associated with modern cultural deposits but with Mousterian artifacts. In Africa, where the oldest specimens of modern humanity have been found, they are also associated with relatively crude technologies. The oldest modern human fossils, South African specimens from the Klasies River Mouth complex of caves and the Border Cave, are all associated with Middle Stone Age artifacts. The cultural life of these populations was perhaps more advanced than that represented by the Middle Paleolithic in Europe, but it was not equivalent to the high culture of the Upper Paleolithic. (In Africa there was apparently a swift but late transition to cultures that correspond closely to the last phase of the European Upper Paleolithic. The oldest of these, all from East Africa, date back some 20,000 years.)

The most plausible current view is that modern humans lived alongside Neanderthals for approximately 10,000 years in some places in Europe and the Near East. For a long time they lived in a similar style. Then the Aurignacian culture appeared, but it spread only among modern human populations. Not only that: its appearance in Europe coincided with the extinction of the Neanderthals.

Their new cultural resources evidently gave modern humans a decisive local advantage, and the Neanderthals could not copy their methods. Perhaps their cultural equipment allowed modern human populations to survive an ecological crisis in which the Neanderthals perished. Perhaps their new hunting methods cut a swath through the countryside that robbed the Neanderthals of their niche. Perhaps there were skirmishes between local populations of Neanderthals and modern humans, the Neanderthals being pushed back inexorably to less and less viable territories. In any case, the cultures of the European Upper Paleolithic provided their only exponents, representatives of modern *Homo sapiens*, with a decisive advantage over their competitors.

THE hiatus between the evolution of modern humans and the development of culture leads to a conclusion that is of pivotal importance for this book. Physical evolution and cultural development did not march hand in hand. The physical capacity for culture had been in place for millennia before modern human culture began its explosive development. Even the paleo-culture of our ancient ancestors may have had its own history, distinct at least in part from the history of biological change. Perhaps we should even rethink the established view that the first use of tools, some two million years ago, signaled the evolution of a new species, *Homo habilis*. Certainly the biological evidence for this speciation event is not conclusive.

In any case, the flowering of human culture in the Upper Paleolithic was not associated with major biological changes in the human population. The Neanderthals and their African and Asian contemporaries had a cranial capacity equivalent to that of modern humans, although there is some speculation that the brain of archaic *Homo sapiens* may have been structured differently from our own. Fully modern humans indistinguishable from ourselves appear in the fossil record at least 60,000 years before the development of a full-blown human culture. The physical basis for modern human speech may have evolved only with the first *Homo sapiens*, but 2,000 further generations were to pass before the first unambiguous evidence that attests to the existence of symbolic communication, the subtle and varied art of the Upper Paleolithic.

If by culture we mean learned, adaptable symbolic behavior, based on a full-fledged language, associated with technical inventiveness, a complex of skills that in turn depends on a capacity to organize exchange relationships between communities, then culture made a tardy entrance in the human story. But once cultural development got into its stride, it operated at a rate quite foreign to the slow, blind mutations of biological evolution. The outstanding characteristic of cultural history is its accelerating pace of change. Begun some 45,000 years ago, the revolutionary development of modern human cultures spurted 25,000 to 20,000 years ago, when the gains of the Upper Paleolithic were disseminated and consolidated. This was a time of quick inventiveness and rapid diffusion, great migrations, local cultural differentiation, marvelous artistic creativity. Only then, perhaps, did recognizably human cultures spread to all human populations.

A choice presents itself, therefore, between two contrasting views of the human condition. The biological measure draws attention to continuity with other primates; the cultural measure, however, shows a sharp break at the start of the Upper Paleolithic. The biological evolution of modern *Homo sapiens* made possible the development of modern cultural behavior; but that followed only after a period of conception that lasted for tens of thousands of years, with the beginning of the last Ice Age perhaps providing the impetus for great innovations.

Each of these two contrasting views has its own particular scales and poses distinctive questions. The biological history of the human species is measured in hundreds of thousands of years, and is programmed, perhaps, in our genes. It is Darwinian, in scale and also in method, its subject the origin of species, its distinctive preoccupation the continuities and discontinuities between humans and other primates. Accordingly, it pays particular attention to what is uniform in human performance, to stable elements of a general human nature, rather than to the particular processes of local history.

There clearly are elements of a common human nature. The languages of all modern human beings have a great deal in common, and are easily learned. The thought processes of people everywhere take familiar forms, though the content of the thought is culturally variable, and the respect granted to one form of logic over another will alter from one context to another. Because of these uniformities, we can generally understand what other people are up to. The near-universality of the family suggests that even our institutions are not infinitely variable. The convention of reciprocity underlies a great many human interactions in every known society. These human universals may have a common source. If this is not in our genes, it may lie in the conditions of human social life, and in the dispositions that make it possible.

The cultural history of the species has a shorter time scale than biological history, records rapid changes, and reveals far greater variations. It is measured in mere millennia, and is the work of our own hands and minds. Those who write cultural history tend to believe that the very nature of human beings is to adapt and learn, to transform their habits and behavior. Compared to any animal that has to rely mainly upon biological adaptation, humans are astonishingly flexible. It is cultural development that has made human beings so successful in the classic evolutionary terms: populating the whole world and expanding at a rate hitherto unknown for such a slow-breeding mammal.

Though cultural development must surely respect some—still uncertain—biological constraints, human beings have already transformed the physical conditions of human life. The basic condition of human existence is that people are in communication with each other, a communication that shapes their consciousness and their social experience. In recent generations the conditions of this communication have been changing decisively, and human nature has changed with it.

It is this second history that the French historian Ferdinand Braudel termed the history of the long term, by which he meant a history of those profound changes that may take tens of generations to accomplish, against the background of a very slowly changing landscape. Long-term adaptations at the level of village and household persist for centuries, despite political revolutions and religious movements which may appear, in the palaces at least, to be of far greater consequence. Deeply rooted cultural formulas survive technical change.

Braudel distinguished this history of the long term from the history of events, narratives that chart the vicissitudes of particular communities over the course of a few generations, and that typically pay particular attention to political and economic fluctuations. If this history of events were measured on the second hand of a clock, the minute hand would measure cultural and social history over the long term, and the hour hand would record the unfolding of our destiny as a species. A great deal of confusion has resulted from failing to distinguish between these different histories, the processes that they describe, and the forces that move them.

W AS there a second watershed in modern human cultural history after the first great moment, the Upper Paleolithic? Archaeologists call the period that followed the European Upper Paleolithic the Mesolithic. Some 10,000 years ago, new and sophisticated tools begin to show up in the archaeological record: bone fish spears and fish hooks in Scandinavia, needles, transverse arrowheads, and flake-axes. Mesolithic people exploited a far greater variety of plants and animals than their predecessors had done.

At about the same time, an even greater technological change was beginning in the Near East, with the domestication of animals and plants. To describe this new way of life, archaeologists use the term introduced by John Lubbock in 1865: they call it the Neolithic, or New Stone Age.

There is a well-established view that the technological innovations of the Neolithic ushered in a second great cultural revolution. Ever since V. Gordon Childe published *The Dawn of European Civilization* in 1925, as a recent reviewer remarks, "the Neolithic has been perceived as a package, linking the introduction of novel food resources (caprines, cereals) and new technology (ceramics, polished stone) with new economic practices (agriculture and animal husbandry) and, by implication, with new social and ideological relations." Pottery also began to be produced, perhaps first in Africa, nowhere with greater sophistication than in China. Wherever the technique was learned, people could store their food and drink more easily and could cook in new ways, escaping the monotony of roasted foods.

The neatness of this Neolithic package is, however, much disputed. The dynamism of European societies in the Mesolithic was duplicated elsewhere, certainly in the Near East. The introduction of agriculture and pastoralism in the Near East 10,000 years ago was not a sudden and revolutionary event. Nor did the new technologies immediately displace the old. Techniques of animal domestication and food production spread piecemeal (or were independently invented) over a period of some 7,000 years, and husbandry was frequently combined with foraging. Agriculture spread to northern Europe only 6,000 years ago, and to much of Africa and America only in the past 2,000 years.

Childe assumed that what he called the "Neolithic Revolution" began with the domestication of plants and animals; that farming obliged people to establish settled communities; and that these village peoples, producing food in a more efficient way, yielded a surplus which in turn led to the development of towns, and more elaborate and differentiated political systems.

Yet these great changes did not necessarily follow the introduction of agriculture. There were settled communities in the Mesolithic with populations much larger than modern bands of foragers (and larger than some pastoralist communities too). Complexity in social organization may even have prepared the way for agricultural innovation, rather than following as a consequence of the new technologies. Population pressure may have built up too, and population growth could have been a stimulus for technical innovation. (It is too simple to regard population growth simply as a result of a more stable food supply.)

In some places the development of agriculture had rapid and far-reaching consequences, but these were not always of enduring importance. Occasionally a political class emerged on the backs of the local peasantry, even establishing a precarious influence over a larger region. Yet the cities and states that began to emerge on the scene some six thousand years ago were concentrated at first in the Near East, and they were generally unstable, sometimes vanishing with little trace, leaving in their wake scattered, small-scale communities. Such fragile and modest societies were prevalent in most parts of the world until two thousand years ago, and in some large regions—including most of Africa and the Americas—until a thousand years ago.

The illusion of a "Neolithic Revolution" comes perhaps from paying too much attention to the wonders of an Uruk or a Babylon, or to Mohenjo Daro in the Indus Valley, or to Monte Albán in Central America. Yet the elaborate cultures of the Near East remained exceptional for thousands of years after the first flowering of Uruk or Jericho. The writers of the Book of Genesis were living in one of the most sophisticated regions in the world, even by the standards of the next two thousand years.

On one significant measure, the evidence for a revolution is slight. Foragers always live in small, scattered, mobile populations, for they must sustain a symbiosis with a natural population of animals and plants. Communities of agriculturalists and pastoralists, on the other hand, were relatively large and compact. They could expand at the expense of foragers, despite the fact that foraging was more efficient than early agriculture on some measures. (Measured by labor input, foraging probably produced more food than agriculture, though perhaps less reliably. Small, nomadic bands were also less exposed to the ravages of disease.) Yet even though the agriculturalists spread, world population growth was modest overall until very recent times. When the domestication of plants and animals began to be taken up by more and more human populations, some ten thousand years ago, the total human population was probably only some 10 million— the size of a small country today, or of a single great city. Although agricultural economies stimulated population growth, even four thousand years ago the world population was only some 100 million, less than half the population of the United States today.

The "Neolithic Revolution," then, turns out to be less sharp, in many places less real, than had once been thought. If there has been a second revolution in human affairs to compare with the first emergence of a complete human culture in the Late Paleolithic, it may have happened within the past five centuries. This revolution is normally defined by the accumulation of successive changes—a cultural revolution in Europe, beginning with an opening to the rich and complex civilizations of the Islamic world, and culminating in the Renaissance; the European expansion; the development of science and then of industrial technologies; the spread of a capitalist economy; and the creation of the nation-state. Its origins are in early modern Europe, its full development and global spread a very recent matter. Columbus did not only discover a new world; his voyage marked the beginnings of whole new world order.

Five hundred years ago, the history of the human population began to come together again into a single process, for the first time since the origin of modern humans. After a history of dispersal and differentiation that lasted perhaps a quarter of a million years, there is once more something approaching a single world economy, culture, and political system. We are all beginning to talk the same language.

Perhaps the most evident and yet extraordinary consequence of this modern revolution is demographic. More people are probably alive today than lived in the whole of human history up to 1900. This staggering, exponential growth continues. The world population, still only some 100 million when the Book of Genesis was written, was 5 billion in 1990. It is expected to top 6 billion in 2000, and 8 billion by 2025.

THE Lamarckians in the social sciences—and above all, Karl Marx—divided history into several great epochs, each carrying within it the embryo of its successor. The movement from one historical stage to the next was progressive, and it was driven by a single compelling mechanism—the development of rationality, or technology, or social differentiation. On this view, social change is generated by some internal force: each stage of the history of a society secretes seeds of growth, which inevitably leads to the next, higher stage. The theorist of the "Neolithic Revolution," V. Gordon Childe, was a Marxist, and he argued for such a break in history, initiated by the new farming technologies, which led to the emergence of class-based societies.

The Marxists claimed that their world history, one of progress punctuated by revolutions, was evolutionist; but it was evolutionist, if at all, only in a Lamarckian sense. The same could be said of the schemas favored by the Victorian anthropologists. Their reconstructions of the spiritual and social history of humanity were necessarily even more speculative, resting mainly on the simple assumption that the farther back one went in time the more different people must have been—on every possible count—from the Victorian English middle classes.

This bogus evolutionism presented itself as a theory of history; but it was a quack theory about a history that did not happen. Until recently there was no world history, and therefore, it follows, no world revolutions. Modern humans quickly scattered and diversified. Local conditions, interactions, and accidents led to the development of distinctive cultural traditions.

Where great cultural changes have been well documented, they are often the consequence of borrowings, or migration, or conquest. No society is isolated enough to have its own history. Significant changes are typically initiated in the spaces between cultures and societies. Communities are unstable; but as long as they survive it is through communication. Trade and exchange are the lifeblood of every known human community, but trade may lead to local specialization and diversification. It seldom imposes a single way of life.

"I believe in no fixed law of development," Darwin emphasized. Evolutionary changes do not follow set paths. Variation is random. Although the chances of variation are subjected to the iron necessity of selection, the local conditions that govern selective advantage are themselves unpredictable.

There is no reason to doubt that the same is true of human history. Today no serious evolutionist would dream of constructing a series of "stages" through which all societies pass in the course of their history. Human history until a few centuries ago is best told as a story of diversification and local adaptation, of exchanges and collisions.

Accepting this conclusion, anthropologists have found themselves engaged in a new debate. Where their predecessors competed to write a single evolutionary history of all humanity, they argue rather about the factors that shape the very different local histories of a very diverse humankind. And in these debates, once again, the biological and cultural parties are pitted against each other. The issue is selection. Do cultural innovations succeed or fail because of their biological consequences? Or has our capacity for culture freed us to a significant degree from the tyranny of natural selection?

The so-called functionalist anthropologists in the 1930s took the rather simple-minded view that any custom that became fixed in a population must be adaptive: either it directly helped people to survive and rear children, or it sustained other customs that had these happy effects. The differences between cultures were of secondary importance. All served the same goals.

A more sophisticated functionalism developed in the fifties and sixties, trading as "ecological anthropology" or "cultural materialism." The basic argument was, however, much the same. Customary practices could be explained in terms of their practical payoff. A culture is a machine that allows a population to adapt to an environment, or to adapt an environment, in part at least, to its own requirements. Institutionalized forms of behavior—most of them, most of the time—promote survival and procreative success under particular local conditions. Technologies, of course, but also, more surprisingly, some rituals, turn out to be ways of acting directly upon the environment. These directly adaptive tools and strategies in turn determine other aspects of social life.

The new functionalists went to work on apparently irrational customs. Their aim was to show that even the most unlikely rules and procedures can be explained in utilitarian terms. Flourishing as they did in America in the fifties and sixties, when the educated middle class pioneered jogging and diet plans, these theorists were particularly interested in the ways in which customs affect health. Favorite cases were the Hindu taboo on beef, or the Jewish taboo on pork; or, in spectacular contrast, New Guinean rituals that involve the mass slaughter of pigs instead of a prudent, steady culling.

Marvin Harris of the University of Florida has argued, for example, that pigs were sources of disease in ancient times in Middle Eastern conditions, and that camels had to be reserved for transport. Accordingly, communities that instituted taboos on eating pigs and camels would survive and prosper. More omnivorous tribes would succumb to disease and debility, falling easy prey to people who were thriving on a kosher diet. In India, the argument went, oxen were required to pull carts and ploughs, cows to give milk, and cattle generally to provide cow dung, which was an essential cheap fuel. A taboo on beef-eating protected these resources.

One problem with rationalizations of this sort is that they do not seem to apply widely enough to be convincing. Harris argues that pigs are poorly adapted to the heat of the Middle East, yet there is evidence that pig-rearing was widespread in the region in ancient times—witness the Gadarene swine. There may have been good reasons for nomads in the region to eschew pig-rearing, but why did the taboo persist when the Israelites settled down to a farming life? Why was it adopted by Muhammad? And why has it been respected by Jews and Muslims for many centuries, wherever they found themselves? Similarly, if a ban on killing cows had such satisfactory consequences in India, why was it not adopted by the Muslim invaders of the subcontinent? They seemed to manage there perfectly well without it, frequently defeating and subjecting the more ecologically sound Hindus.

Moreover, it is surely odd that if these practices had such satisfactory effects, the ancient Hebrews and Hindus did not say as much. Modern apologists sometimes do put forward utilitarian explanations for ancient customs, but the ancients seem to have been quite ignorant that their rules had such practical payoffs. On the contrary, they formulated complex and obscure reasons for their practices, or more commonly just laid down the law without presuming to explain the reasons for divine injunctions. "Whatever parts the hoof and is cloven-footed and chews the cud among animals, you may eat," says Leviticus. This is a very roundabout way of proscribing camels and pigs, particularly if you think that abstinence will do you good. It is also evident that quite damaging taboos or prescriptions sometimes survive over the generations. Americans only belatedly came to realize that their favorite twentieth-century diet of steak and eggs gave them the world's highest rate of cardiac disease.

Even the most sophisticated functionalist speculations provoke two sets of objections. First, there is a general difficulty with explanations that claim that the reason for a practice is to be found in the benefits it delivers. With a little ingenuity, one can identify some utility in any custom. Even such repulsive practices as the killing of twins, the ritual immolation of widows, or the draconian regulation of labor benefit some people. However, virtually any custom might also have deleterious consequences—social, psychological, or ecological. Furthermore, since ecological circumstances are rarely static, fixed patterns of behavior are bound to lose their effectiveness. The functionalist is too easily satisfied if he believes that a custom is explained, once and for all, when it is shown to have some good, objective consequences.

The second objection is that the functionalists spend all their energy guessing at the unconscious, ecological consequences of customs and pay no attention to the meaning of the customs for the people who practice them. But there is a logic in our conception of the world, and we tend, moreover, to adhere to this logic even if there is a price to pay for our stubbornness. We may even glory in our oddities, just because they mark us off from others.

Roy Rappaport of the University of Michigan, once a leading functionalist, has come to accept that cultural practices may have their own nonutilitarian imperatives. He now argues that we must analyze cultural practices at two distinct levels of abstraction, to discover both what they mean to the people who practice them, and also what consequences they may have for the community in its natural setting. Cultural practices may have no adaptive function; indeed, Rappaport is prepared to accept that they may even "come to be at odds with the creatures who bear them and with the ecological systems in which they are set." To the degree that this is correct, cultural history must be significantly different from biological evolution.

D ARWIN'S theory rocked the Victorians because it swept aside the biblical story of human origins. Accident and natural causation replaced the story of creation and eroded the conviction that history reflected some divine plan. And in the place of a human being formed in the image of God, Darwin gave us a human animal bearing the stamp of a primate ancestry.

In virtually every culture there is a myth of origin, which defines a view of humankind. The Darwinian revolution did not provide an unambiguous and certain new myth of origin, but it initiated the great modern debate about how we appear in evolutionary perspective. We may focus on our remote origins, and see ourselves as just another primate, sharing a great deal in common with our distant kin. If we focus on the cultural efflorescence of the Upper Paleolithic, we are defining ourselves as cultural creatures. This is, of course, the choice of the cultural party in the human sciences.

But in the hands of either party, this obsession with origins can be misleading. Human beings today live very differently from even their ancestors of a thousand years ago. We should not then expect to learn very much about our present nature from a study of remote ancestors scratching a living some forty thousand years ago, let alone from the primates who were contemporary with *Australopithecus* some four or five million years ago. If ultimate origins are supposed to explain the essence of what we are, we might just as well go back to the first insects that spread over the world, or forward to the origins of capitalism.

There is no obvious point of origin that fixed what human beings were to be. In very many ways, we are not what we were. As we become more like each other, we become more different from all the people who have lived before. We may now be converging with each other, but in the process we are distancing ourselves with unprecedented rapidity from even our recent ancestors.

· 5 ·

CULTIVATING
THE SPECIES

There are no neutral theories about human beings. Each carries a charge that can ignite a political program. Theories of human evolution are particularly potent, for they suggest that it might be possible to steer progress, to help change along.

That was the sense in which Marx understood Darwin, reading him through Lamarckian spectacles. He sent Darwin a copy of *Das Kapital,* inscribed from a "sincere admirer." Darwin did not read it through, recognizing that the tenor of Marx's thought was "so different" from his own, but he wrote to Marx that both of them would contribute to "the extension of knowledge" and "in the long run . . . add to the happiness of mankind."

Darwin's ideas were also plundered by some conservatives, who were inclined to believe that current social arrangements were natural, that races were as different as natural species, and that imperial politics reflected the law of natural selection (if not, indeed, the will of God). When race became the great political issue of the day, during the American Civil War, Darwin and his close associates united in the Ethnological Society to oppose the racist ideologists of the Anthropological Society. The creed of the latter was that the human races had evolved independently and were differentially endowed. Slavery was a proper expression of natural differences, no more objectionable in principle than the exploitation of animals belonging to other species.

This thesis had influential support, and in the next generation Sir Arthur Keith was inclined to revive it. Darwin, however, was uncompromising in his opposition. The human species was one, and it had evolved in a single process. Slavery was an abomination—"the destruction of Slavery would be well worth a dozen years war."

In addition to his visceral hatred of slavery, Darwin was ambivalent about British colonialism, politically liberal in domestic matters, and skeptical about some of the speculations of loyal Darwinian anthropologists; but the racial thinking of the day persisted even in Darwinian circles, and it survived as an important strand of Darwinian thinking after Darwin's death.

In a long, cool treatment of the human races in *The Descent of Man*, Darwin insisted that racial differences were generally insignificant and did not reflect a long process of natural selection. Yet he did allow that there might be differences in intellectual ability between the races (and, indeed, between men and women). The anthropologists with whom he was most closely associated—Lubbock and E. B. Tylor—had no doubt that higher cultures were associated with more advanced races, whose members had larger and more effective brains.

Darwin did not believe that racial differences caused cultural differences in a simple and straightforward way. Rather, he thought, cultural evolution stimulated the development of the brain, and the specialization of the brain allowed further cultural development. The upshot was that the most culturally advanced populations also had the most intelligent citizenry. Even within the most civilized populations, some Darwinians believed, there were primitive holdouts in the slums of the large cities and the backward rural villages. At the other extreme, the educated middle classes constituted a population that was at once culturally and cranially privileged.

Darwin also did not doubt that confrontations between racial groups would be regulated by natural selection, with victory going to the more advanced. The other original theorist of natural selection, Alfred Wallace, told a meeting of the Ethnological Society that the struggle for survival "leads to the inevitable extinction of all those low and mentally undeveloped populations with which the Europeans come into contact." Darwin concurred, recalling that in New Zealand he had been told that the Maoris were "dying out like their own native rat."

In this chapter I shall tell two cautionary tales about this now discredited legacy. The first is the story of eugenics, the second the story of intelligence testing. They are linked historically. Eugenics was a program for breeding superior human populations. Intelligence testing was used to prove that the highest but somewhat abstract human qualities were inherited, and could be bred. Later this became the issue that crystallized debates about nature and nurture, inheritance and learning. At every turn, these debates were also about race, and this gave them their great political salience.

W HE N human beings act to alter the genetic makeup of a population of plants or animals, the process is termed domestication. A breeder selects for reproduction those individuals that have the qualities he is looking for—dogs that are stronger or braver than most, cows that produce more milk than others, strains of corn that are more resistant to drought or more easily harvested.

Darwin himself was closely attentive to the effects of domestication, seeing the efforts of Britain's plant and animal breeders as experiments in evolution that mimicked the effects of natural selection. Chapter 1 of *The Origin of Species* was entitled "Variation under Domestication," and immediately after completing his *Origin*, Darwin began work on a book that was published in 1868 under the title *The Variation of Animals and Plants under Domestication.*

He pointed out some of the general consequences that follow from domestication. Protected from predators, and shielded from competition for food, varieties of animals can be reared that would never have survived the rigors of natural selection. A domesticated population becomes dependent on human participation in order to breed and survive. This results in great changes in the seasonal biology of animals. Domestic animals are capable of reproducing throughout the year, unlike animals in the wild, which typically reproduce only in particular seasons.

Domestication also brings swift and radical changes, since only controlled breeding is permitted. And because domesticated species are bred for highly specialized qualities, they quickly become differentiated from each other and from wild species. Lyell was astonished when Darwin reported to him that the English pigeon fanciers had developed fifteen varieties of the common pigeon which were equivalent to "three good genera and about fifteen good species." Darwin could show that even the red corpuscles of the various breeds were differently shaped.

But what of human beings themselves? We are, Darwin once wrote, an "eminently *domesticated* animal." Certainly we have been progressively cushioned from the direct action of natural selection. Directly or indirectly, our social arrangements influence our breeding activity. (The anthropologists in Darwin's circle believed that one of the great social innovations of early humans was the institution of the incest taboo.) Yet according to Darwin himself, we are still inclined to give sexual selection its head.

Darwin regarded sexual selection as a mechanism that operated alongside natural selection, accounting for the many ways in which males differed from females. At one stage he put it almost on a par with natural selection. The subtitle of *The Descent of Man* was *Selection in Relation to Sex*, and Part II, which dealt with sexual selection, took up half of the entire book.

The central premise of the theory of sexual selection was that in all species males pursued females with more enthusiasm than discrimination, while females, who could propagate relatively less often than males, exercised care in selecting partners. Among humans, men select women for beauty and also the promise of fidelity, while women choose men for the promise of security and support. The upshot is much the same as among any other species: men are more muscular, competitive, larger, and (Darwin thought) more intelligent; women more caring, gentle, reliable.

These features might be adaptive, but further secondary features— such as relative hairiness—reflected nothing more significant than local aesthetic preferences. These were important in mating, but they had no evolutionary payoff. Tastes in beauty were random, varying from one population to another for no particular reason. Perhaps these local fashions might eventually account for racial differences, but they were not functionally significant. The principles by which mates were chosen were, in an evolutionary perspective, frivolous. "Man scans with scrupulous care the character and pedigree of his horses, cattle, and dogs before he matches them," Darwin complained, "but when he comes to his own marriage he rarely, or never, takes any such care. He is impelled by nearly the same motives as the lower animals."

A. R. Wallace, who had independently discovered the principle of natural selection, was scornful of the idea of sexual selection. How could Darwin believe that the European aristocracy was distinguished by its beauty? Wallace insisted that they were simply richer and better fed, better dressed, and better looked after. He was convinced that natural selection explained all the variations that Darwin attributed to sexual selection. Nevertheless, he agreed with Darwin that after a certain stage of development, natural selection no longer governed the fate of humans. Humanity had indeed become a semi-domesticated species, and this provided an opportunity to introduce rational planning. Moral improvement, cooperation, civilized arrangements would see us through from now on. For his part, Darwin regarded Wallace's socialist dreams of progress as utopian. To the contrary, he felt, our escape—however incompletely achieved—from natural selection came at a great cost, and the risks grew as we became more skilled in protecting the weak from natural execution.

> Vaccination has preserved thousands, who from a weak constitution would formerly have succumbed to small-pox. Thus the weak members of civilised societies propagate their kind. No one who has attended to the breeding of domestic animals will doubt that this must be highly injurious to the race of man. It is surprising how soon a want of care, or care wrongly directed, leads to the degeneration of a domestic race; but excepting in the case of man himself, hardly any one is so ignorant as to allow his worst animals to breed.

Medical advances represented a paradoxical danger to the future of more sophisticated populations, but other cultural arrangements also undermined natural selection and weakened the stock. Primogeniture, Darwin worried, was preserving the aristocratic houses of Britain but destroying natural selection. Even the Puritan virtues might be counterproductive. He noted that the frugal and careful marry late, while the morally weak and reckless are great breeders. This might presage the degeneration of a great nation.

A former fellow-student from his days at Edinburgh University,

William Greg, the son of a Manchester cotton king, came to a gloomy conclusion that Darwin quoted: "The careless, squalid, unaspiring Irishman multiplies like rabbits: the frugal, foreseeing, self-respecting, ambitious Scot, stern in his morality, spiritual in his faith, sagacious and disciplined in his intelligence, passes his best years in struggle and in celibacy, marries late, and leaves few behind him." If a population started off with "a thousand Saxons and a thousand Celts," it would end up with a mob of Celts confronting a handful of Saxons. The Saxons would monopolize property, power, and intellect, but they would be outbred by the careless Celts. "In the eternal 'struggle for existence,' it would be the inferior and *less* favoured race that had prevailed—and prevailed by virtue not of its good qualities but of its faults."

Darwin noted that this process was subject to an element of self-regulation: "the intemperate suffer from a high rate of mortality, and the extremely profligate leave few offspring." He also admitted that there was a good moral reason for the protection of the unfit, arising from what he identified as an instinct of sympathy. Nevertheless, he favored a policy that would inhibit "the weaker and inferior members of society" from propagating readily, and encourage the valuable members of society to be fruitful and multiply.

Such concerns about fitness struck very close to home. Darwin's research on cross-fertilization in plants persuaded him that out-breeding was best, but his own marriage with a first cousin had spawned sickly children, several of whom had died young. Should he intervene to arrange marriages for his children? Hardly! As a true liberal, he was also reluctant to see the theory of evolution become an applied science for the breeding of superior human beings. He doubted, in any case, that it was practical politics. But he was troubled.

Had he been given to fantasies about breeding human beings, how would Darwin have identified the fittest, most desirable strain in a human population? His account of human evolution was, in essence, a story of the specialization of one organ: the human brain. "Of the high importance of the intellectual faculties there can be no doubt," wrote Darwin, "for man mainly owes to them his predominant position in the world." Precisely what he meant by the "intellectual faculties" is not easy to pin down, and he frequently wrote yet more broadly of the "intellectual and moral faculties," invoking a range of attributes from reason to the selfless conduct of a true gentleman. But although he defined these faculties rather vaguely, he was sure that they had a precise physical location in the brain.

The evolution of the brain was the result of natural selection. Darwin took it for granted that intellectual faculties, like other biological traits, vary between individuals. These faculties were biologically grounded in the brain, and they were passed on through inheritance. He speculated that "in the rudest state of society, the individuals who were the most sagacious, who invented and used the best weapons or traps, and who were best able to defend themselves, would rear the greatest number of offspring." Under natural conditions, therefore, the good qualities would spread among the population. But domestication eroded the force of natural selection, and sexual selection frittered away the gains of evolution. Perhaps there was a case for artificial selection, and if so it should favor "the intellectual and moral faculties."

IF Darwin hesitated to make evolution an applied science for humanity, his young cousin Francis Galton leapt in. Born in 1822, Galton was a grandson, on his mother's side, of Erasmus Darwin. His father, a successful banker, was the son of an armaments manufacturer. The family was prosperous. After studying mathematics at Cambridge, Galton spent several years traveling in the Middle East and Africa, publishing in 1855 a best-selling book entitled *The Art of Travel; or, Shifts and Contrivances available in Wild Countries.*

A restless, curious, iconoclastic young man, Galton was obsessed with the application of science to human affairs—not only evolutionary theory, but also mathematics. He was a pioneer of statistics, inventing the theory of regression and correlation. In an ingenious paper he attempted to measure the efficacy of prayer by statistical tests, concentrating on prayers for rain and prayers for the health of the royal family. (The results went against prayer.) He also invented fingerprinting to help the police. Ultimately he combined his passionate interest in evolutionary theory, statistics, and policy, producing a series of statistical studies of human heredity that were intended to provide a basis for human progress by way of artificial selection.

In 1865, Galton published articles on "Hereditary Talent and Character" in *Macmillan's Magazine*, which he expanded into a book, *Hereditary Genius*, published in 1869. In a chapter entitled "The Comparative Worth of Different Races," Galton argued that each race was adapted to its environment, and thus was fit by evolutionary criteria. There were, however, significant differences between the races in the qualities associated with civilization. The white race showed itself superior by throwing up more eminent men of science than other races. This gave them an edge in competition, but they must not carelessly let this superiority slip—as the ancient Greeks had done, he argued, through intermarrying with inferior groups. On the contrary, the evolutionary advantage must be fostered.

On Galton's theory, competition between the races was won by the population that produced the most men of genius. He never made clear what he meant by race, but he certainly assumed that this rule applied both to relations between "white" and "black" races in imperial situations, and to conflicts between the different European nations, which he also called races.

Could scientists offer some guidance for the production of men of genius to serve the race? Galton researched genealogies of British intellectuals, and reached two conclusions. First, exceptional intellectual ability constituted a coherent set of skills. Indeed, the gifted were well-packaged in every way. "There is a prevalent belief," he wrote, "that men of genius are unhealthy, puny beings—all brain and no muscle—weak-sighted, and generally of poor constitutions." This was completely mistaken: "The youths who became judges, bishops, statesmen and leaders of progress in England could have furnished formidable athletic teams in their time." He reminded his readers that in the very first boat race between Oxford and Cambridge, four future bishops were among the crews. "It is the second and third-rate students who are usually weakly." His second conclusion was that this admirable package of qualities tended to run in families.

This notion had not occurred to Darwin, but then Darwin had a very modest estimate of his own intellect. "I have no great quickness

FRANCIS GALTON (1822–1911), like Charles Darwin a grandson of Erasmus Darwin, inherited a comfortable fortune and—like Darwin and Huxley—spent several years as a young man exploring, in Galton's case in Africa. His book *Hereditary Genius* (1869) defined genius as "an ability that was exceptionally high and at the same time inborn," thus introducing the debate about the definition and heritability of intelligence. He was also the founder of eugenics, the movement that advocated controlled breeding of human beings in order to improve the intellectual and moral quality of populations.

of apprehension or wit which is so remarkable in some clever men, for instance Huxley," he wrote in his *Autobiography* (which was not meant for publication). "My power to follow a long and purely abstract train of thought is very limited . . . My memory is extensive, yet hazy . . . I have a fair share of invention and of common sense or judgment, such as every fairly successful lawyer or doctor must have, but not I believe in any higher degree." The only features in which he judged himself to be "superior to the common run of men" were sharpness of observation, independence of mind, industry, and his great love for his subject.

This complex assessment of his own "mental faculties" might well have made Darwin wary of one-dimensional and omnibus notions of "intelligence," but he was impressed by Galton's ideas. "You have made a convert of an opponent in one sense," Darwin wrote to his cousin, "for I have always maintained that, excepting fools, men did not differ much in intellect, only in zeal and hard work."

Galton was sure that the gifted were conveniently listed in books of reference such as the *Dictionary of Men of the Time*. But was there not some intrinsic mark of their superiority? The classic notion was that mental qualities were reflected in the shape and size of the skull. In Italy Cesare Lombroso, a professor of psychiatry at the University of Pavia, had come to what he thought was a Darwinian improvement on the ancient science of phrenology. Some individuals, he felt, represented a throwback to primitive races of humanity, and these would naturally turn to crime in modern societies. The Italian state beheaded the most violent criminals, and the governor of the local prison was good enough to allow Lombroso to measure the severed heads, which seemed to conform with his expectations.

Galton was critical of Lombroso but not, initially, of phrenology. He believed for some time that large-headed people like himself were outstandingly intelligent. He collected a sample of superior head measurements and reported that "Mr. Gladstone was amusingly insistent about the size of his head, saying that hatters often told him that he had an Aberdeenshire head—'a fact which you may be sure I do not forget to tell my Scotch constituents.'"

Unfortunately, there were limits to these simple extrapolations from head shape. Galton had his own head assessed by a phrenologist, who told him that he was not fond enough of the midnight lamp to be fitted for any of the learned professions. This was initially discouraging on a personal level, but even worse, it turned out to be ludicrously inaccurate.

Not only did he lack a way to measure intelligence; Galton also had no clear theory of heredity. He fancied that the "gemmules" postulated by Darwin as the agents of heredity might be carried in the blood. In 1870 he carried out a series of blood transfusions between black and white rabbits, without, however, managing to breed black offspring from white parents. Most discouraging of all, his own studies of the distribution of physical properties in populations indicated that extreme qualities were not necessarily transmitted to offspring: instead, there was a tendency toward what he called "regression to the mean."

Galton frankly stated these difficulties, but he remained convinced that intelligence was inherited, and that the nation was recklessly squandering its most precious resources. Spain, Galton argued, had gone into decline because of the counter-eugenic policy followed by the Holy Inquisition, which had selected the freest and boldest men for destruction. But he noted that even in the absence of persecution, gifted individuals did not necessarily rate high on the true measure of evolutionary success: propagation. Some of the most eminent geniuses had left no children at all. (Galton was childless himself.)

Galton's theoretical difficulties were apparently resolved by a young man who became his protégé. Karl Pearson was a mathematician—and a socialist—who in 1884 had taken a position at the nonconformist metropolitan institution, University College London. He was a member of a radical and feminist circle that included the South African novelist Olive Schreiner and a pioneering advocate of birth control, Amy Besant. These sympathies inclined him to favor Galton's proposals for social engineering.

Pearson and his colleagues doubted that the "gemmules" of Darwin and Galton would come to light (and British Darwinians were to remain skeptical about Mendelian genetics for much longer than their American counterparts). He preferred to experiment with mathematical models that would account for the operation of heredity. Working in tandem with the Professor of Zoology at University College

KARL PEARSON (1857–1936) was a mathematician and pioneer statistician who applied statistics to the problems of heredity and evolution that Galton had broached and made further contributions to the study of intelligence. In 1911 he became the first Galton Professor of Eugenics at University College London.

London, Walter Weldon, he eventually reached the conclusion that what Galton had called regression to the mean—the tendency of a population to remain within an established range of variation—was not an absolute, fixed constraint. If breeding was controlled, selection could work within a few generations to modify the incidence of traits within a whole population.

Pearson then went on to pioneer the systematic study of intelligence. He asked teachers to assess the intellectual capacity of children in their classes, and compared the scores of siblings with those of unrelated children. He also took physical measurements. His conclusion was that siblings were likely to be similarly endowed intellectually, just as they were likely to be of similar height and coloring.

Galton was delighted; at last his program had a proper theoretical basis. He proceeded at once to give it political form. Britain should institute a positive breeding policy, for "it would be quite practical to produce a highly gifted race of men by judicious marriages during several consecutive generations." In a book published in 1883 he had proposed the term *eugenics* (from the Greek, meaning "well-born") for the applied science that would allow the prudent regulation of breeding, and he launched a eugenics movement to persuade governments to adopt these scientific policies. Nor did he rest with proposals to foster the offspring of the most gifted. He distinguished "positive eugenics," which aimed to propagate the favored class, and "negative eugenics," which was concerned to check the undesirables. Both were required for a complete policy of controlled breeding, one that would allow human beings to become successfully domesticated at last.

AFTER the pioneering efforts of Galton and Pearson, an army of psychologists developed more complicated measures of what they called "intelligence." Indeed, this project soon became central to the discipline of psychology as it established itself in Europe and the United States.

In 1904, the French ministry of education commissioned Alfred Binet to devise a test to identify children who might need special help to cope with schooling. Binet was interested in Galton's ideas, and had followed up Galton's research into the characteristics of the very gifted (including in this category not only great scientists and artists but also chess players). In 1903 he had published a study of the mental characteristics of his two daughters. Now he developed a series of measurements of mental ability based on performance in everyday tasks. Scores were related to the average performance for a child of a particular age, and children whose "mental age" lagged behind their real age were singled out for special education.

Binet denied that such tests measured uniform or innate "intelligence." They were simply a practical means to identify children who would benefit from special attention, in order to help them in their school careers. But despite Binet's reservations, his tests of "intelligence" initiated one of the growth industries of psychology, fueled in part by the demand of educational bureaucrats, and soon by the personnel requirements of the mass armies of the twentieth century.

American psychologists were entranced by the possibilities of intelligence testing, particularly after Lewis M. Terman, a psychologist on the Stanford faculty, produced a standardized test, the Stanford-Binet, which was made up of ninety tasks. Soon a whole industry developed to peddle tests to educational authorities throughout the country.

Terman was firmly persuaded that the skills measured by the tests were innate: "The children of successful and cultured parents test higher than children from wretched and ignorant homes for the simple reason that their heredity is better." He also believed that his tests could help the authorities weed out undesirables. They would identify "feeble-minded" (and hence, he argued, criminally inclined) individuals, who could be committed to preventive custodial care, thus saving the government vast amounts of trouble and cash.

The chance to demonstrate the power of the new methods came with the First World War. As the American army built up to its final wartime strength of nearly 2 million, scientists mobilized by the National Academy of Sciences were challenged to use their skills to make the army more efficient. The president of the American Psychological Association, Robert M. Yerkes, had been influenced by Galton and was eager to further the cause of intellectual testing and, if possible, eugenics. He recruited Terman, and they administered intelligence tests to 1.75 million men.

The army was doubtful about the value of these studies, but after the war this immense body of data was raked through by the psychologists. It represented the largest application of intelligence tests ever carried out, and they were determined to put it to use. Their concern was above all with the heritability of intelligence, and to sort the soldiers into groups with common descent they used vague racial criteria. But however vague the specifications, their results seemed to be decisive. Intelligence varied by "race," and so by heredity. Men of northern European ancestry had significantly higher average test scores than those of southern European or Slav origin, and all performed on average well above the norm for those they called Negroes.

In Britain the application of Binet-type tests was pioneered by Cyril Burt. As a child he had once met Galton himself. Later, borrowing Galton's *Inquiries into Human Faculty* from his school library, he experienced "a superstitious thrill when I noticed on the title-page that it first saw daylight in the same year that I was born." These remote physical connections bolstered a sense of spiritual heredity, and Burt devoted his career to the service of the Galtonian tradition.

Burt attached himself to Galton's protégé Karl Pearson (whom he was to succeed in the Galton Chair in Eugenics at University College London). Pearson had advanced the use of statistics in genetic research, and in 1909 Burt published the first of a long series of papers in which methods derived from Pearson (which he somewhat adapted) were applied to the transmission of intelligence. Burt defined intelligence, in the Galton tradition, as a package of skills that formed a unity: intelligence was "all-round innate mental efficiency," or, in a later formulation, "general, inborn intellectual ability." And, like Galton, he was persuaded that this composite ability was very largely inherited rather than acquired.

Whereas his American colleagues were interested in the inherited talents of races, Burt, as an Englishman, was more concerned with the innate worth of social classes. In an early study he compared the performance of upper-class and working-class children on his tests. The privileged children did rather better on the whole, and Burt

C YRIL BURT (1883–1971) continued the researches of Galton and Pearson into intelligence, concentrating particularly on the comparison of twins separated in early childhood. He argued strongly that intelligence was very largely determined by heredity. In 1931 he was appointed in his turn to the Galton Chair of Eugenics. After his death it was revealed that much of his data on twins was faked.

concluded that their superiority was inborn, since their educational experience did not differ enough to account for the differences in their test scores. He did not entirely discount the effects of environment, but he calculated that between 75 and 80 percent of the variation in test scores could be attributed to inherited ability.

The claims of Terman and Burt and their associates did not persuade everyone. Skeptics questioned the meaning of "general intelligence." Could all the skills that went into intellectual achievement be reduced to a single score? Respondents' scores showed considerable variation between different types of ability, for instance between verbal and abstract reasoning skills. Evidence was also accumulating that environmental differences had significant effects on test scores. Further American comparisons established that blacks in the industrialized northern states had higher average scores on IQ tests than whites in the deep South. Margaret Mead wrote her master's thesis on intelligence testing among Italian immigrants, and showed that the scores of children varied with the length of time their families had been in the United States and the amount of English spoken in their homes.

Findings of this sort should not have surprised anyone who perused the commonest IQ tests in use in America. The World War I Army Alpha test, for example, asked respondents to name the leading Brooklyn baseball team, and required the respondent to say whether revolvers were made by Swift and Co., Smith and Wesson, W. L. Douglas, or B. T. Babbitt. Whatever such questions measured, they were hardly fair to an Italian immigrant child, or a child from a poor and illiterate family in rural West Virginia.

But these scientific doubts about the value of intelligence tests made little initial impact on the eugenic cause, which soon became a major political force. Its advocates drew attention to the army tests that apparently showed that the various American "racial" groups were very differently endowed intellectually. Credence was given even to Lambroso's fanciful speculations about a primitive race of criminals that was nurtured in the bosom of civilized society. Indeed, any suggestive argument, any convenient scrap of evidence, was pounced on by people already viscerally convinced that race was destiny. And if that was true, then not all ingredients could be thrown into one melting pot. To protect the virtues of the stock it was necessary to restrict the immigration of intellectually inferior southern Europeans, Jews, and Slavs, and to prevent miscegenation between white and black.

President Coolidge was a strong supporter of eugenics, and in 1924 an Immigration Act was passed, which explicitly applied eugenicist principles to the recruitment of Americans. But merely preventing further immigration of undesirables was not enough; too many were already present. There was, according to the eugenicists, a need for more radical negative policies, particularly the sterilization of misfits.

This became an increasingly popular measure of social prophylaxis. Even the cultivated Supreme Court justice Oliver Wendell Holmes, giving judgment in 1927 in the case of *Buck v. Bell*, was prepared to countenance the involuntary sterilization of "feeble-minded" inmates of state institutions in Virginia. "It is better for all the world," he asserted, "if instead of waiting to execute degenerate offspring for crime, or let them starve for their imbecility, society can prevent those who are manifestly unfit from continuing their kind . . . Three generations of imbeciles are enough." In some parts of the south, enthusiastic sheriffs would round up "hillbillies" who seemed to them to be unfit, and have them sterilized in batches in the hospitals. In one year alone (1941), 36,000 Americans were sterilized by the authorities.

There was certainly considerable opposition to the eugenics bandwagon, and the opposition included some very distinguished scientists. The eugenics movement had initially attracted British scientists and also such radical intellectuals as George Bernard Shaw, but by the 1930s the left-leaning biologists were fiercely antagonistic. The great English biologist J. B. S. Haldane fulminated that "many of the deeds done in America in the name of eugenics are about as much justified by science as were the proceedings of the inquisition by the gospels." Haldane's colleague, Lancelot Hogben, denounced eugenics for its association with "ancestor worship, anti-Semitism, colour prejudice, anti-feminism, snobbery, and obstruction to educational progress." But the counterattacks had little political impact. A Virginia legislator, Dr. Joseph S. DeJarnette, more in tune with the times, urged in 1934 that measures of national hygiene should be prosecuted even more vigorously, pointing out that "the Germans are beating us at our own game."

That was one way of describing what was happening in Nazi Germany. Eugenics had been influential from the first in many European countries, particularly in northern Europe—the Scandinavians being especially enthusiastic—but nowhere more so than in Germany. Here too it was associated with theories of racial difference. Before Germany's colonies were lost in the First World War, German administrators had introduced strict measures to prevent miscegenation there. In the home country, after the shock of defeat in World War I, foreign elements and so-called degenerates were increasingly regarded as a threat to the racial stock.

Nevertheless, it was only with the rise of the Nazis that eugenics became the central policy of a major political movement. The Nazis gave racial science and racial hygiene pride of place in the school curriculum. Positive eugenic policies were introduced, first in the Nazi movement itself. Himmler ordered in 1931 that SS members could marry only with permission from a "Race Bureau." "Permission to marry," he announced, would "be granted or refused solely and exclusively on the basis of criteria of race and hereditary health." When they came to power, the Nazi government introduced incentives to promote the breeding of Aryans, and one of their first measures was the ban on all marriages between Jews and Germans.

Negative eugenic measures followed. In 1933 a law was passed "for the prevention of progeny with hereditary defects." This prescribed sterilization of individuals suffering from "congenital mental defects, schizophrenia, manic-depressive psychosis, hereditary epilepsy . . . and severe alcoholism." In 1939 patients in these categories began to be killed, and in the following year gas chambers were used to speed up their elimination. More than 70,000 had been killed in this way by the end of 1941. The same methods were then applied to Jews and Gypsies, and the Holocaust began. By the end of the war six million Jews had been murdered in the death camps, along with an unknown number of Gypsies, homosexuals, and so-called psychopaths and antisocial individuals, and 85 percent of the patients in German mental hospitals. Throughout the Nazi period, leading German scientists had been intimately involved in this apotheosis of the eugenics movement.

Hitler's defeat did not completely end the advocacy of eugenics, or even interrupt the careers of all the scientific accomplices of the Nazis, but there was no longer a respectable public for eugenics, and it could claim no scientific support. Racial politics had also been discredited.

Now, too, the scientific criticisms of eugenics, which had built up in the thirties, became generally accepted. Human races, so casually defined by early writers, are never pure and seldom very ancient. They are rough-and-ready classifications of populations, which rely upon superficial criteria of physical appearance. Studies of the distribution of blood groups among populations had provided early evidence that phenotypical features (especially skin color and hair type), which were the basis for traditional racial classifications, did not mirror the distribution of other inherited characters.

Population genetics drew attention to the fact that the genetic endowment of every human population was much the same. In fact, "about 85 per cent of human genetic variation (measured by any of a number of common statistics) is between individuals within a population (that is, a nation or tribe). Only about 5 per cent is between races."

Nor did racial classifications based on outward appearance fit cultural boundaries. Neighboring, genetically related communities might have very different cultures (for instance, the Bedouin of Jordan and the city people of Lebanon, the peoples of Melanesia and Polynesia, the Bantu-speaking farmers of Kenya and their Nilotic-speaking pastoral neighbors). There was no scientific foundation for racism.

T H E scientific arguments about inheritance and mental characteristics continued, however, in another politically sensitive field: intelligence testing and its application in selection for educational opportunities. Now the issue was the relative significance of inheritance and environment, nature and nurture, in shaping human abilities. Once again, political issues were implicated in the scientific debate.

By the end of the Second World War, IQ tests were firmly entrenched in educational processes. They were used to sort children into different kinds of schools in England at the age of eleven, to assess needs for compensatory education, and to select college students in the United States. The idea behind these selection methods was an odd mixture of egalitarianism and elitism. Those with the best potential should be given the most academic schooling: indeed, only they could profit from it. But ability was innate, and so selection tests should be designed to screen out the accidental advantages that accrued to privileged children through better schooling. The tests should measure intelligence, not levels of scholastic achievement.

Yet despite the fact that these tests were supposed to be both fair and efficient, and although they quickly became part of the normal bureaucratic machinery of the educational system, doubts did persist. It turned out, for instance, that coaching could improve scores on the tests to a significant extent. This suggested that the tests were not reliably measuring purely innate abilities. Moreover, although an individual's scores were stable in the short term, they varied considerably over the longer term.

But if intelligence can be measured, how can we establish whether, or to what extent, it is innate? It was true that studies showed a relationship between parental level of education and test scores. This might indicate that more intelligent parents—who had been, in consequence, more successful in educational competition—produced more intelligent children. But there was a complication: IQ scores are more closely related to the mother's level of education than to the father's. Presumably this is because the mother usually has more to do with the education of a young child than does the father.

Studies also mounted up showing the effects of cultural variables. In the United States, the first generation of immigrants tended to do rather poorly on the tests, while the performance of their children was in line with that of the general population.

The methodological question was how the effects of nature could be distinguished from those of nurture. Cultural differences were a huge complication, and so were the great discrepancies in experience between children from different social classes, or between rural and urban children. Yet within a fairly homogeneous population it might be possible to sort out the relative weight of heredity and environment. One promising route was the study of siblings; or even better, twins; or better yet, identical twins who had been reared separately.

Galton himself had thought of this, and collected extensive data on twins, but it was Cyril Burt who made the first large-scale and systematic study of separated twins. He was employed as a psychologist for the London County Council, which was responsible for education in the capital, and so he could call on help from teachers, doctors, and social workers. Soon he had built up a bank of rare material.

In his first published study, in 1943, Burt compared the IQs of identical twins (monozygotic, MZ), nonidentical twins (dizygotic, DZ), and, the rarest of rarities, fifteen pairs of identical twins who had been reared apart. Identical twins who had been brought up together tended to get very similar scores on IQ tests (with 0.86 correlation). The scores of fraternal twins who had been brought up together were less closely matched (their IQ correlation was 0.54). The crucial finding, however, was that separated identical twins had an IQ correlation of 0.77. In other words, identical twins reared apart were more likely to have similar IQ scores than fraternal twins who had been brought up together. This indicated that the effect of environment on "intelligence" could not be very significant. Genetic inheritance was decisive. The case was strengthened by Burt's further claim that in a substantial number of cases the adoptive parents of the separated identical twins had very different backgrounds from the natural parents.

Burt published additional papers on the subject in the following decades, and he also continued to build up his file of cases of MZ twins reared apart. By the late fifties Burt wrote that he and two collaborators, Miss Howard and Miss Conway, had collected over thirty such cases. By 1966 he was reporting on fifty-three pairs. The numbers are significant. It was not easy to find identical twins who had been reared separately, and Burt's fifty-three pairs of separated MZ twins constituted as large a sample as the combined cases available to all the other leading investigators in the field. And on the basis of these impressive materials, Burt claimed to have demonstrated that the effect of environment on IQ was limited. Genetic factors accounted for some 80 percent of intelligence.

In 1971 Burt died, full of years and honored as the leading British psychologist and a man who had made a central contribution to the educational policies of the nation. Three years later a Princeton-based psychologist, Leon J. Kamin, published a book entitled *The Science and Politics of IQ*. In this iconoclastic, hard-hitting, often polemical book, Kamin took an unabashedly political line, arguing that studies of IQ had political consequences and, commonly, political motives, and that they should be criticized both for their intrinsic flaws and for the purposes to which they had been put. This made his book uncomfortable reading for many scientists, who preferred to see themselves as a secular priesthood, uncorrupted by the world. But even those who frowned on his politicization of science had to concede that his scientific critique of Burt was very serious indeed.

Kamin pointed out, first, that Burt had been economical with crucial background information. He was reticent about when or how the tests had been administered. He also gave only a minimum of data about the twins themselves, not specifying, for example, the length of time of separation, or the age when it had begun. Second, there were discrepancies between the various tables in Burt's studies, and some obvious reporting errors. (Burt habitually published in journals he controlled, and editorial supervision was minimal.) But third, and most troubling to Burt's allies, Kamin showed that although the number of twins in the samples changed from one report to the next, as more cases were added, *the correlations remained constant to three decimal places.* This was statistically incredible, and Kamin concluded that "the numbers left behind by Professor Burt are simply not worthy of our current scientific attention."

A British science journalist, Oliver Gillie, picked up the trail at this point. "It seemed highly likely to me on reading Kamin's book that Burt's work must be fraudulent if Kamin's analysis was accurate," he recalled. He soon developed doubts about the existence of Burt's two collaborators, Miss Howard and Miss Conway. Officials at the British Psychological Society told him that they thought the names were fictitious. "In the context of what I already knew from Kamin this appeared to confirm the suspicions of fraud," Gillie wrote later. "Fudged statistics might make a newspaper story but non-existent people, invented in order to perpetrate a fraud, really catch the popular imagination. In newspaper terms this began to look like a big story."

In due course Gillie published the results of his detective work in the London *Sunday Times,* provoking a fierce counterattack from two of Burt's main supporters on the question of the heritability of IQ, the psychologist H. J. Eysenck and a Berkeley scientist, Arthur Jensen, who had drawn heavily on Burt's work to argue against the use of compensatory education.

In the meantime, Burt's sister had commissioned an official biography from one of the leading British psychologists, Professor L. S. Hearnshaw. Beginning as an admirer of Burt, Hearnshaw was astonished and distressed to discover that Gillie was essentially correct in his charges. "The verdict must be," he concluded, "that at any rate in three instances, beyond reasonable doubt, Burt was guilty of deception." He had indeed "produced spurious data on MZ twins." Two other old charges were also confirmed: "He falsified the early history of factor analysis . . . and he fabricated figures on declining levels of scholastic achievement." A defense can be made on Burt's behalf against some of these charges, but overall, Hearnshaw's verdict stands.

Why had Burt cheated? Fraud in science is always motivated by some combination of ambition and arrogance, the sense that one's intuitions must be right, and that slower experimentalists will one day illustrate them. There are also, however, always particular, personal factors. Hearnshaw diagnosed a susceptibility to paranoid fantasies in old age, combined perhaps with some physical illness. He suggested that as an insecure old man, Burt had been plagued by the ghosts of youthful traumas. When he was a boy his father had lost money and the family had temporarily been plunged from the middle class into the working class. Hearnshaw speculated that Cyril Burt experienced lifelong feelings of insecurity in consequence. On the defensive, as an old man, he suffered "regressive reactivation of behaviour patterns he had acquired in the London period of his boyhood, and from the 'gamin' sub-culture in which he had been immersed." This was a very British diagnosis, and perhaps a very British ailment, but it was surely ironic that Burt's downfall should be attributed to the influence of his boyhood environment.

ONE of Galton's legacies in the human sciences is the debate about the relative significance of heredity and environment in shaping intelligence. (He had been the first to counterpose that alliterative pair, nature and nurture.) He himself, and through him the eugenics tradition, always assumed that nature was dominant, and that environmental effects on intellectual development were secondary. Despite nearly a century of scientific research, some central issues remain unresolved, but in general the argument has not gone Galton's way.

Intelligence has proved much more difficult to pin down than Galton had hoped. But if its definition remains contentious, then there is little point in asking whether it can be inherited. Phillip Tobias, the distinguished South African anatomist, takes this view: "IQ tests assess such different components as memory, verbal skills, numerical skills, visualising ability, systematic thought, etc. It is inconceivable on physiological grounds that all of these faculties reflect one component . . . inherited as a genetic entity."

Even if the professionals can limit disagreement on what they mean by intelligence, and how it might be measured (and there are many out-and-out skeptics among them), the biggest problems remain. IQ tests suggest that a person's intelligence may change over a lifetime, which greatly complicates any associations that might be made between the intelligence of parents and that of children.

The concept of heritability is also a slippery one. Statements about heritability apply to a population, and individual cases may vary quite considerably. Heritability is a measure—for a population— of the relative extent of genetic and environmental influence on a particular trait. Each of these factors is extremely complex, and unstable as well. Genes interact with each other, and the gene pool is in constant flux. The environment, too, does not hold still for us; and as the environment changes, heritability will also change.

In order to simplify the problems of measurement, psychologists try as far as possible to control the variables concerned. Burt's research strategy is still used, however he abused it himself. Comparing twins who have been brought up apart is probably the best way to factor out the relationship between nature and nurture in the development of "intelligence." Such studies have become increasingly sophisticated, not least as a consequence of Kamin's critique of Burt's work. Psychologists are now acutely aware of how complex environmental factors can be. Should attention be paid primarily to the IQ of adoptive parents? Are child-rearing practices significant, or is it the internal dynamics of the adoptive family that are crucial, including the relationship between adoptive and any natural children? And are adoptive children more likely to have suffered prenatal traumas, which may affect their intellectual development?

In general, large-scale studies, which are necessary to produce statistically significant results, rely on very broad-brush measures of the environment, such as social class. One of the most sophisticated recent studies was carried out by two French psychologists, Christiane Capron and Michel Duyme, and reported in *Nature* in 1989.

Their main finding was that the average IQ score of adopted children is 12 points higher if their foster parents enjoy a high rather than a low socioeconomic status. As the American psychologist Matt McGue commented in the same issue of *Nature:* "This is a sizeable effect and approaches the difference between the mean IQ of students admitted to U.S. colleges and that of the general population." And this is clearly a purely environmental effect, though it should be emphasized that the "environment" includes diet and other factors that contribute to general health as well as the intellectual stimulation and achievement motivation that middle-class parents are supposed to transmit to their children.

But another finding was that if the biological parents were of high socioeconomic status, then their children also have an IQ advantage, even after fostering—an advantage of some 15 points on average. This may indicate a genetic effect, but the whole variance might be accounted for by prenatal environmental factors, such as the age and general health of the mother during pregnancy, her diet, prenatal traumas, delivery methods, and so forth.

In 1990 the report of a long-running Minnesota study of twins reared apart was published, and this gave more comfort to the hereditarians, even arguing that some apparently environmental factors might be shaped by genetics. The conclusion of this massive study was that "in the current environments of the broad middle-class, in industrialized societies, two-thirds of the observed variance of IQ can be traced to genetic variation."

The authors stressed that part of this variation clearly operated through an environmental filter, but the infant helps to shape its own environment, and the cues the infant gives may be genetically programmed. "Infants with different temperaments elicit different parenting responses. Toddlers who are active and adventurous undergo different experiences than their more sedentary or timid siblings. In addition, children and adolescents seek out environments that they find congenial." There are therefore, they concluded, "forms of gene-environment covariance."

These two studies do not necessarily contradict each other. The heritability of intelligence may well vary quite significantly even between societies as cognate as France and the United States. The mix between genes and environment in determining the level of intelligence may be quite different.

Studies of this sort can tell us little if anything about differences in "intelligence" between populations. Comparing test scores across cultures is a very dubious enterprise. Intelligence is defined operationally as a skill expressed in tests of verbal dexterity and the ability to solve quasi-mathematical problems. Yet even the notation of the logical tests must be learned; and vocabulary tests, which are essentially searches for synonyms, may not work in the same way in different languages. Even within a culture, the reading habits and interests of children from different social classes may be very divergent, and it is not easy to correct for such factors in devising tests.

Should a genuinely culture-free test be designed (a highly unlikely achievement), the results would still not provide a basis for comparing genetic endowment. If two populations live in very different circumstances, and value rather different skills, it will be hard to factor out environmental influences and to isolate and compare genetic potential.

The size, structure, and physiology of the human brain have been remarkably uniform among all populations of modern *Homo sapiens* for the past hundred thousand years. Within every population there is a similar range of variation. The connection between the brain itself and "intelligence" or "moral qualities" is not readily measured, not least because these qualities are extremely difficult to pin down. There is certainly no reason to believe that modern human populations differ from one another in their genetic potential for cultural success. Even within a population, it is a tricky, perhaps impossible, task to assess the relative weight of heredity and environment in promoting "intellectual" variations.

The significance of such mental or psychological variations within a population is also still a matter of debate, but there is no scientific warrant for a revival of eugenics. If a government could effectively exclude from breeding those who do badly on an IQ or personality test, it would take centuries for recessive genes to be eliminated even by the most vigilant genetic SS. Nor is it evident that the consequences would be beneficial for the future of the population. The authors of the Minnesota study believe that the variance in "cognitive and motivational" attributes within a population is itself of value. The fact that any population is a mix of different types serves to accelerate cultural change. Others have argued to the contrary that the minor variations in human psychological dispositions are part of the debris of our remote past, and without current adaptive significance.

It is ironic that the debate has focused so strongly on "intelligence," whereas Darwin himself treated intelligence as an asset largely because it served to raise the moral level of the population; and he rated the moral impulse to act for the general good as the vital human resource. "The moral faculties are generally and justly esteemed as of higher value than the intellectual powers," Darwin wrote in *The Descent of Man.* "But we should bear in mind that the activity of the mind in vividly recalling past impressions is one of the fundamental though secondary bases of conscience. This affords the strongest argument for educating and stimulating in all possible ways the intellectual faculties of every human being."

· 6 ·

THE COMMON
HERITAGE

In 1975 a book appeared with the provocative title *Sociobiology: The New Synthesis.* The provocation lay in the claim that sociobiology represented a new synthesis, for this is a loaded term in the history of biology, invoking the epochal evolutionary synthesis of the 1930s that had united Darwinian natural history and Mendelian genetics. The author of *Sociobiology,* the Harvard scientist E. O. Wilson, trumpeted an equally ambitious goal: to bring the social sciences within the ambit of modern evolutionary theory. Sociobiology would demonstrate that a single neo-Darwinian theory could explain the behavior of human beings in the same terms as the behavior of other animals (and, indeed, of birds and insects too).

This was heady stuff. Yet sociobiology was neither as new nor as all-embracing as it appeared at first sight, and the fuss that was provoked by Wilson's paean to genetics obscured the most promising aspect of the theory. A little history is needed to put human sociobiology in a proper perspective.

In the 1930s a small group of scientists interested in the comparative study of animal behavior established a new discipline, which they called ethology, from a Latin term meaning the art of depicting character. The aim of these scientists was to develop a Darwinian science of behavior, and perhaps their favorite text was the book that Darwin published immediately after *The Descent of Man,* his *Expression of the Emotions in Man and Animals* (1872), in which he attempted to show that humans and animals experienced common emotions, displaying them with the same repertoire of gestures and facial expressions.

The founding fathers of ethology were Konrad Lorenz, Nico Tinbergen, and Karl von Frisch. Their main interest was the study of animal behavior, under laboratory conditions and in nature, but Konrad Lorenz in particular was convinced that ethology must implicate human behavior in its comparisons.

The son of a physician, Lorenz was born in Vienna in 1903. He studied medicine but at an early stage became fascinated by the experiments of a German zoologist, Oskar Heinroth, who showed that grayleg geese, reared from the egg by humans, would follow their keeper as though he were a mother goose. This finding led Lorenz on to a series of ingenious experiments that established what he termed "imprinting," the process by which an animal becomes fixated at a very early stage on a particular individual. If this individual is of another species, the adult goose (to take the most famous example) may be incapable of appropriate sexual interest in birds of its own species. Imprinting became an instance of what Lorenz called a "fixed action pattern," an instinctive series of responses that were triggered and guided by environmental circumstances.

The basic premise of ethology was that instincts, like organs, were inherited and had been formed by natural selection. Instincts or drives—in later formulations, programs of the central nervous system, and later still, genetic programs—were often shared by different species, which inherited them from common ancestors. The innate programs expressed themselves in particular sequences of behavior. These were adaptive, which was why the programs persisted. Human beings shared many instinctive drives and responses with other species, even with birds and insects. Lorenz himself drew particular attention to aggression and territoriality, and celebrated the evolutionary advantages of kinds of behavior that civilized people were supposed to deprecate.

The argument from animals to humans could work only if culture did not greatly modify innate patterns of behavior, and Lorenz took the view that culture was a superstructure built upon the instincts. It refined instinctive action patterns but did not discard them. The model here was what the ethologists termed "ritualization." An innate pattern of behavior could be modified by natural selection to serve as a form of communication. An instinctive response of aggression, for instance, could become a warning display: less risky, but almost equally effective. This, Lorenz argued, was the direction in which culture tended to modify innate behavior.

There was nevertheless a danger that culture might get out of hand, that artificial selection could pervert the instinctive programs. Lorenz was convinced that if domestication did thwart instinctive action patterns, this could only lead to trouble. "There is no doubt," he wrote in a popular book, *Civilized Man's Eight Deadly Sins,* "that through the decay of genetically anchored social behavior we are threatened by the apocalypse in a particularly horrible form."

Lorenz believed that ethology had a moral and even a political dimension. He flourished under the Nazis, who likewise celebrated the instincts, and who had a proper appreciation of the advantages of aggression. After the war Lorenz half-apologized for his record. "I hoped that National Socialism would have some good effects, since, for instance, it held the biological perfection of Man in such high esteem and had a poor opinion of attempts at domestication, and so on. At the same time, I really didn't believe that these people meant murder when they spoke of 'eradication' or 'selection.'"

Be that as it may, in 1940, in a paper entitled "Disturbances of Species-specific Behavior Caused by Domestication," Lorenz compared individuals "who have become asocial because of their defective constitution" with cancerous tumors. His conclusion was fully in keeping with the *Zeitgeist.* "Fortunately, the elimination of such elements is easier for the public health physician and less dangerous for the supra-individual organism, than such an operation by a surgeon would be for the individual organism." In the same year he proclaimed in a published paper that it was "one of the greatest joys of my life" to have converted a student to National Socialism.

In 1973 Lorenz shared the Nobel Prize for Physiology or Medicine with the co-founders of ethology, Nico Tinbergen (who worked at Oxford University from 1949) and Karl von Frisch. Neither the Dutchman Tinbergen nor von Frisch, who was best known for his study of communication among bees, was tarnished by association with the Nazis. Their reputation helped to save ethology from a too-easy equation of instinct theory with the politics of the blood that the Nazis espoused. The dangerous extrapolations in which Lorenz engaged did, however, deter more cautious scientists from pushing too far the analogies between animal and human behavior. There was also a revulsion against the view—which had seduced D. H. Lawrence and other writers in the interwar years—that human fulfillment would come only if we gave the instincts full reign.

The books and articles of Lorenz and of Tinbergen (who was also interested in aggression in humans) inspired a number of anthropologists to develop ethological ideas. One of them was Robin Fox, a British scholar who moved to the United States in 1970 and made his career at Rutgers University.

Fox has a rare command of the evidence from cultural anthropology. He also has a cultivated awareness of the philosophical roots of the debates between the proponents of an innate human nature and their opponents. He deploys a fund of citations from their most literate exponents over the centuries, and he knows more than enough history to turn away the accusation that the innatists are bound to be conservatives, if not, indeed, fascists. Rousseau, after all, believed in innate, natural human qualities, while his English critic, the conservative Edmund Burke, would be called a cultural relativist today. Nonetheless, Robin Fox's own political sympathies are with the pessimistic conservatives, and his fiercest scorn is reserved for "all sanctimonious manipulators from Mill through Stalin." For he is not just a scientist who wishes to understand the world: he is a moralist who wants to change us.

Fox's central thesis is that human beings do have a common nature, which is the consequence of natural selection. It is not a bundle of instincts but rather a set of genetic programs which require environmental triggers, and which can be frustrated or perverted. A woman will probably not be a good mother unless she herself experienced good mothering, but the basic responses are there, if properly fostered.

This human nature matched the human condition as it was for 99 percent of our existence as a species. Traditional cultures were particular expressions of universal and necessary habits and guidelines that have been bred into us. As long as cultures respected these natural parameters, we flourished. The highest point in our history was the Upper Paleolithic, which Fox celebrates as the "Paleoterrific." Then came the Fall.

The flaw in our nature was imagination, necessary to predict the behavior of others, fatal once we began to reflect on ourselves and to moralize. Once we invented the bow and arrow we were on a slippery path, and "all 'history' is a series of wilder and wilder divergences from a Paleolithic norm." In Fox's view, the cultural evolution of an increasingly self-conscious human species will ultimately prove to have been self-destructive. There is more than a hint here of Lorenz's fear that cultures might pervert human instincts.

There is some hope, perhaps, but only if we recognize our true nature and reconstruct some of the conditions of Paleolithic life. Evelyn Waugh once complained that a British Conservative government had not turned the clock back even by one minute. Robin Fox wants to turn it back by 10,000 years.

Leaving aside the admittedly considerable practical difficulties with Fox's prescription, the argument itself is seriously flawed. A naturalistic ethic, he tells us, "would state that all human action, that all social policy, should operate within human parameters and hence avoid the inhuman." But what are these human parameters? What is inhuman?

One of Fox's propositions is that the sin of Cain, aggression and violence, is the mark of humanity. It is human, and therefore humane. "Since man evolved as a hunting, omnivorous species, it follows that he will destroy animals, plants, and even other members of his species who threaten him. He is right to do so. All these things are totally natural, totally within a comprehensible scheme of evolution. They are not problems." The danger does exist that this violence will get out of hand and result in our own destruction as a species, but this is the consequence of historical perversions that followed from technical development and population pressures. Human nature is good, but culture has betrayed it. He insists that "the problem is not violence, but war; the problem is not aggression, but genocide."

Yet we can only observe modern human beings, and since their spoiled nature is apparently no guide to their true nature, we have no scientific basis for deciding what human nature was really like before the Fall. Fox writes of "the violence in man that drove herds of horses and ungulates over cliffs by the hundreds, or fought for diminishing hunting ground during the glacial periods"; but he is just guessing. An equally good guess might be that Paleolithic man relied more on his cunning than on violence, scavenging carcasses or trapping game in carefully disguised falls, and retreating in the face of stronger rivals. In truth, we do not know, and so we cannot say if there was once a common human culture that was more in tune with our nature.

Ethology was never a major force in American biology or anthropology, and it is perhaps worth remarking that Robin Fox and his close associate, the Canadian Lionel Tiger, are both foreigners who live and work in the United States. In any case, American scientists embraced sociobiology in the mid-seventies as a revelation, or repudiated it as a dangerous new heresy, whereas European ethologists welcomed it as a modernized version of ethology rather than a wholly fresh project. Neither appreciation was altogether accurate.

It is certainly true that sociobiology covers much the same ground as ethology, and reaches parallel conclusions; but it did introduce a quite different logic into its evolutionary arguments. Yet the precise character of this novel element is not easy to determine, for sociobiology got off to something of a false start. This was because it could not resist the temptation to hitch its star to the glamorous project of molecular biology.

In 1953 Francis Crick and James Watson discovered the structure of DNA. Once the structure was known it suggested the mechanism by which replication occurs, and led to an understanding of how the gene passes on its messages, programming the development of the organism. These discoveries marked the coming of age of molecular biology and inaugurated a scintillating phase in the history of modern science. "It could only be remarkably poor judgment or envious resentment," a great biologist has remarked, "that would deny molecular biology's claim to be the source of the most brilliant discoveries in Biology since the days of Darwin and the great post-Darwinian generation of comparative anatomists."

In the decades following the discovery of the structure of DNA, rapid progress was made in the physical specification of genetic processes, and genes were identified that transmit high probabilities of contracting particular diseases. The human genome project promises at last a reliable cartography of the human animal.

It is obviously tempting to suppose that molecular biology will eventually deliver new certainties about the roots of human behavior. We know now that our common heritage has a physical existence: it runs through the DNA that is passed from one generation to the next. Our DNA is remarkably similar to the DNA of chimpanzees, and clearly cognate with the DNA of all living things. It codes the makeup of our bodies, and carries instructions for behavioral responses to stimuli.

Even the agencies and processes of cultural evolution may prove to be genetically encoded. Perhaps genetics will replace psychiatry, sociology, psychology, even history. This was the imperialistic claim of Wilson's manifesto, *Sociobiology: The New Synthesis.*

D ISAPPOINTMENT awaited those who took the promise too literally, who may even have expected soon to be able to study political science or economics by observing segments of DNA under a microscope. To date, nobody has identified specific genes that determine psychological dispositions or strategies of social action. Some now deny that this was ever the point of sociobiology, but in the initial flush of enthusiasm Wilson did talk as though such genes would indeed soon be discovered. Extravagant early claims laid sociobiology open to the charge that it could not deliver what it promised.

"What is the direct evidence for genetic control of specific human social behavior?" demanded Stephen Jay Gould soon after the publication of Wilson's book. "At the moment, the answer is none whatever." Fifteen years later, the same answer must be returned, but nobody is surprised any longer.

The quest for a genetic grail was probably always doomed. "A single gene is often involved in the expression of many characteristics," writes the French Nobel laureate François Jacob, "and one characteristic may be controlled by many genes which we are not able to identify." There may well often be a genetic factor which makes a particular type of complex human action more likely (though geneticists speculate that the heritability of such a gene in humans might be quite low), but its location and impact must remain a matter of speculation.

In practice, the human sociobiologist is usually content to argue that there are predispositions to act in certain ways. Although the modern idiom of genetics is preferred to the old-fashioned talk of instincts, this premise is not very different from that of classical ethology. Indeed, they may merge seamlessly, as in Wilson's remark that in the avoidance of incest "human beings are guided by an instinct based on genes."

The real promise of sociobiology lies rather in its ideas about selection, and here the argument derives from another tradition in genetics, population genetics, which studies genetic variation in populations and tries to account for this variation. Given to mathematical models, population genetics began in England, growing out of the deductive models that Galton's associate Pearson began to develop at the beginning of the twentieth century. Its great theorist was Sir Ronald Fisher, who succeeded to the Galton Chair of Eugenics at University College London in 1933. Here and later at Cambridge University he inspired a brilliant generation of geneticists, including some who took the new ideas abroad with them, like the aristocratic Italian Luigi Luca Cavalli-Sforza, who went to Stanford.

One of the puzzles thrown up by Darwinian theory was the problem of altruistic behavior, particularly among social insects and birds. Worker bees and soldier ants are sterile, slaving away to serve the few fecund females in the population. A sentinel bird will call to warn others that a predator threatens, although it thereby puts itself at greater risk. What could explain such behavior? And how was it transmitted to the next generation?

A persistent heresy in biology is that altruistic behavior makes evolutionary sense because it serves the group or even the species. That was the rough-and-ready solution that was initially accepted by Lorenz and his colleagues. It was, however, diametrically opposed to the Darwinian premise that natural selection operated on the individual, selecting modifications "profitable to the individual under its conditions of life."

As so often, the solution harked back to a suggestion made by Darwin. He too had worried about how unselfish behavior might be transmitted. How does the sterile soldier ant pass on its traits, or the rash sentinel bird, which sacrifices its life? The puzzle appeared, at first sight, to be insuperable, but Darwin suggested that the difficulty "is lessened, or, as I believe, disappears, when it is remembered that selection may be applied to the family, as well as to the individual, and may thus gain the desired end." He cited his breeders in confirmation. The farmer might pick out a particularly flavorsome vegetable for his table, but will take care to sow seeds from the same stock. So too, the sterile ant dies without issue, but it has helped its relatives to flourish, and they share a common heredity.

As it proved, Darwin was moving in the right direction. It would have been easier had he known, as we do, that worker ants and bees are not only closely related, as sisters, but actually—because of the sex-determining mechanism of these species—share three-quarters of their genes, rather than the half that sisters share among most animals.

Those in the group around Fisher were particularly interested in the genetic makeup of populations, rather than in individual genomes, and so they were primed to develop this Darwinian hint. The theatrical polymath J. B. S. Haldane, in a popular lecture in 1955, asked the members of his audience to imagine that they were standing together on the bank of a river. We see a drowning child. You have a rare gene that will affect your judgment in such a way that you will jump in and save the child, although you have a one in ten chance of being drowned yourself. I, Haldane offered, do not possess the gene, and remain safely on the bank. If the child also happens to be your own, then it will have an even chance of carrying that gene. If you make a habit of risking your life to save your close kin, then the chances are that the gene will be perpetuated in your family. In a small community of close relatives—say among a flock of birds—this would lead to the transmission of some unselfish forms of behavior.

Haldane was, of course, teasing, shocking his audience with the suggestion that apparently altruistic conduct had a selfish evolutionary basis. The serious theory behind this coat-trailing was set out by W. D. Hamilton in two papers in the *Journal of Theoretical Biology* in 1964. Hamilton proposed a mathematical model that suggested an evolutionary basis for behavior that favored kin. In classical Darwinian theory, a modification is selected because it promotes fitness, the survival of an individual and its progeny. Help given to offspring and to other relatives must also pay off, but the advantage it offers might be bought at some cost to the individual: at the extreme, it might cost its life, or the sacrifice of its chances of propagation. The yield is the added chance that its genes will be perpetuated, if only by way of the replicas of those genes that are carried by siblings or other close relatives. Hamilton coined the term "inclusive fitness" to cover this broader conception. (Inclusive fitness is a measure of the reproductive success of an individual plus the contribution of the individual to the reproductive success of relatives, this being weighted for the degree of relatedness.)

Here was a fresh approach in evolutionary theory, and it inspired an explosion of models of strategic behavior that might promote inclusive fitness. R. L. Trivers, an American theorist of kin selection (who has been called the Bobby Fischer of sociobiology), began to explore strategies that involved give-and-take between unrelated partners, like the cuckoo and its host. He also modeled competitive games, which might, for instance, pit against one another parents and children, each following their own strategies to further their selfish interests.

The population geneticists had come up with mathematical models that accounted for stable distributions of different genes in a population. Sociobiologists suggested that competing social strategies might also become conventionalized in a particular community. Individuals adopt cynical, calculating policies to maximize reproductive success, but they have to take account of the tactics that others are trying out. In the end, a set of games and strategies becomes established in a population. The individuals act unreflectingly, for they are geared to sequences of action and reaction; and that is just as well because they are serving not themselves but their genes.

Readers of this new genre became familiar with an amoral world of sexual deceit, childish ingratitude, and manipulative parents. As one commentator remarks, it "has resulted in the introduction into the literature of an emotionally loaded vocabulary containing such words as 'desertion' and 'cuckoldry' and a general aura reminiscent of Restoration comedy." Others, perhaps less cultured, think of the soap opera *Dallas*.

THIS was the main theoretical tradition on which E. O. Wilson drew in his *Sociobiology.* Wilson is an entomologist, and the power of these new theories was most evident in accounting for the behavior of the social insects and birds, but like Lorenz before him he was tempted to extend the theory to incorporate human beings. It was the final chapter of Wilson's book, in which he explained the application of sociobiology to humans, that caused the extraordinary explosion of interest in the theory. Wilson followed up in 1978 with a more popular book that was concerned only with humans, *On Human Nature,* and human sociobiology took off.

Wilson begins his exposition in *Sociobiology* by recalling Samuel Butler's quip that a chicken is only an egg's way of making another egg. Updated, he remarks, this should read: "the organism is only DNA's way of making more DNA." Genes are the lead actors in evolution. Their carriers humbly serve their interests. Social arrangements are to be understood as ways of improving an organism's chances of passing on DNA. In the now famous phrase of the Oxford biologist Richard Dawkins, the mover and shaker in evolution is "the selfish gene." (Dawkins is the great phrasemaker of the new sociobiology. "The genes march on . . . That is their business. They are the replicators and we are their survival machines. When we have served our purpose, we are cast aside. But genes are denizens of geological time: genes are forever." He is also the best writer in this tradition, and one of the most original.)

An individual will favor biological relatives in all sorts of ways, because such behavior will increase the reproductive chances of their shared genes. Nepotism, on this view, is nothing if not natural; and certainly it is common enough. Other practices that appear to be counterproductive on a test of "fitness"—for instance, sexual abstinence, homosexuality, or infanticide—may also make good evolutionary sense if they favor the collateral carriers of an individual's genes.

In Wilson's own work there is the clear implication that practices likely to promote the interest of kin, which sociobiologists gloss as "altruistic," are themselves programmed genetically. Altruistic behavior fosters the chances of survival of related organisms; and these will very probably carry the same genes for similar altruistic behavior.

This argument requires that some quite complex forms of human social behavior must be under genetic control, and must promote inclusive fitness. That may seem a plausible assumption to make, but it is not easy to pin down which patterns of behavior are genetically programmed. There is nothing comparable to the evidence that neurologists have built up to show that specific parts of the brain control certain functions, such as speech. The strategy of the sociobiologists is therefore to assemble indirect evidence, as indeed Darwin did for his theory of natural selection.

Their characteristic procedure is to identify general human—or better still, primate, or best of all (and recall that Wilson is an entomologist by trade) virtually universal—forms of behavior. These must have been inherited, since they are shared by other species; and they are so widespread because they promote inclusive fitness. Candidates are Hamilton's nepotism, and Lorenz's duo, aggression and territoriality.

One great difficulty with this procedure is that modes of behavior are less easily specified than the physical features that are the traditional concern of evolutionary biology. Anatomists can identify vestigial tails in humans, or establish morphological similarities between the limbs, fins, and wings of different genera. Patterns of behavior are unfortunately more elusive.

For example, Wilson takes up Lorenz's notion that human beings, and all primates, are territorial in their behavior; but although this view is now widely held, it is not easy to specify what constitutes territorial behavior. The difficulty is compounded when more imaginative authors (including both Lorenz and Wilson) extrapolate from birds defending their nests to primate conflicts and on to colonial wars.

The evidence for territorial behavior among humans is by no means unambiguous, and on any definition the degree of territoriality is very variable. One Bushman group in the Kalahari desert, the !Xo, have been described by their ethnographer, H.-J. Heinz, as being extremely territorial. But as another Bushman specialist, Alan Barnard, has pointed out, the !Xo are exceptional among Bushmen, who generally take a flexible view of group membership and access to resources. Barnard argues that even the !Xo do not exhibit a high level of concern for the defense of boundaries or resources. What marks them out is rather their high regard for group solidarity, and this, he suggests, is a result of their vulnerability to incursions from outsiders in the central Kalahari, where they live.

Furthermore, notions of ownership are culturally coded. Ideas current in other cultures about rights in people and in things are often hard to translate into our own capitalist terms. Modern governments which try to accommodate the claims of culturally remote hunter-gatherers sometimes find it virtually impossible to understand what territories meant to (for example) the native peoples of Alaska or Australia. It may therefore be difficult to specify what some people have to be territorial about.

The argument on human aggression is also difficult to establish. The thrust of the sociobiology argument is that institutionalized patterns of violence must serve the realpolitik of the genes. Directly or indirectly, violence should therefore promote the chances of one's close kin. Accordingly, violence between individuals, and especially homicidal violence, should occur more commonly between unrelated individuals, and least often between closely related individuals. The theory predicts that occasions of violence should also be related to genetic success. Men will risk violence in competition for women, or to control vital resources; and successful aggression will be rewarded in the genetic stakes.

Bruce Knauft, an anthropologist at Emory University, tested the first prediction on data he collected between 1980 and 1982 while studying the Gebusi, a small tribe in lowland New Guinea. The Gebusi number only some 450 individuals. They make a living from hunting, foraging, growing bananas in unfenced gardens, and their few semi-domesticated pigs. There is no land shortage, and little competition for natural resources. Interpersonal relationships are uncompetitive; people try to be self-effacing and display mutual deference.

Nevertheless, the Gebusi have one of the highest ever recorded homicide rates. In the immediate pre-contact period, their homicide rate was nearly 700 per 100,000 of population per year, and even in the period 1963–1982, the rate was 419 per 100,000. This compares to a rate of 4.8 per 100,000 in the United States, and 0.5 per 100,000 in Britain. Given the fact that this is a tiny community, and largely endogamous, it is obvious that most violence will be between relatives. Yet contrary to what a sociobiologist would predict, the closer the relationship between Gebusi individuals, the greater are the chances of homicidal violence.

The second prediction, that violence will be directed mainly to the control of women and of resources, has some cross-cultural support. Bruce Knauft found that among the Gebusi and many other small-scale, egalitarian societies, conflicts between men over wives and mistresses were the most common cause of violence. Cross-cultural comparisons provided less support, however, for the proposition that aggressive men are particularly successful in propagating themselves.

The Gebusi—a tiny community of relatives—do not, perhaps, represent a good test case. It may be that their violence has something to do with the intimate, claustrophobic scale of their social relations. A more complex set of societies that feature prominently in discussions of violent behavior are the Yanomami, slash-and-burn farmers and hunters in the Amazon dubbed by an ethnographer "the fierce people."

The 22,500 Yanomami are distributed throughout a territory of some 192,000 square kilometers in Venezuela and Brazil. They are divided into communities that differ from each other in size, economy, and degree of contact with outsiders, but everywhere they seem to rejoice in violent encounters. They conduct fierce raids on neighbors and capture women and children. In consequence, they have a homicide rate that is far in excess of those to be found among most sedentary populations in the world today (though well below that of the Gebusi).

Napoleon Chagnon of the University of California, Santa Barbara, has become famous as an ethnographer of the Yanomami, and over the past twenty-five years he has made fourteen field trips to study them. His popular ethnography, *Yanomamo: The Fierce People,* is one of the anthropological best-sellers of the past twenty years, and he has written many articles on their culture. His best-known thesis, however, is that most homicidal violence among the Yanomami has to do with the control and even capture of women, and that men who have the worst record as killers also father the most children. He leans toward a sociobiological explanation of these findings.

Two French anthropologists based in Brazil, Bruce Albert and Jacques Lizot, have criticized Chagnon's ethnography. First of all, they point out that there is wide variation among the dispersed Yanomami communities, and this applies also to the homicide rate. Male mortality in warfare may be very high indeed for the group among which Chagnon mainly worked, but elsewhere it is substantially lower. Similarly, they report that the abduction of women in war, which Chagnon emphasizes, is quite exceptional. Lizot, who has spent two decades almost continuously with one large community, claims that here fewer than 1 percent of the wives had been captured.

Second, they argue that the image the Yanomami give of themselves must be decoded. For instance, it is not always clear what the Yanomami mean by a "killer," for they elide homicidal violence and supposed killing by sorcery. In warfare, a corpse is often pierced by the weapons of several men, each of whom then qualifies as a "killer," at least in the sense that he has to go through the appropriate ritual, and takes the fearsome title of *unokai.*

There is a political dimension to the argument as well, which has embittered it. Chagnon's findings were convenient for the miners who wanted to move into the Amazon territory of the Yanomami. They were opposed by advocates of native rights and by preservationists, and the miners countered their objections by arguing that the Yanomami were violent savages—hadn't Chagnon proved that?— and that humanity would be best served if they were brought under civilized control.

As so often in ethnography, there is also a personal dimension. Napoleon Chagnon is an assertive, even aggressive man, and close colleagues think that he sees something of himself in the Yanomami. Chagnon is no reflexive postmodernist, however, and he insists that his overriding allegiance is to science, and that the data are unambiguous. He has angrily distanced himself from opportunistic abuse of his research for political purposes, and he has vigorously countered the criticisms from other ethnographers; but while he may well be right about the particular Yanomami whom he studied, it does seem that among these people—as among the Bushmen—there is considerable local variation, some of it probably due to differential contact with outsiders.

There are also societies in which violent behavior is channeled into conventional forms that seem to have little to do with the individual's reproductive fortunes. Among the pre-conquest Cheyenne of North America, a highly militarized society, warrior chiefs favored celibacy and usually died young, either in battle or as a consequence of ritual suicide. In contrast, the so-called peace chiefs, who eschewed warfare, were typically polygynous, long-lived, and fertile.

Opportunities for sexual entrepreneurs may also be culturally restricted. Polygamy is rare in hunter-gatherer societies, and in many complex societies—all Christian societies, for example—it is banned, and extramarital pregnancies (until recently) were strongly sanctioned.

Chagnon denies that his observations necessarily imply that all men are aggressive. His conclusion is rather more in line with Lorenz's own: we all have an innate potential for aggression, which will be triggered if competition reaches a certain point. But one could just as well argue that the most competitive and aggressive Yanomami men may have an innate potential for cooperative, unselfish behavior, which needs only the appropriate environmental signal to be released. This would suggest that we are not very strictly programmed after all. If each of us is potentially either Jekyll or Hyde, we may be able to manipulate the environment in order to foster less aggressive or territorial citizens. One culture may reward the strategies of doves and punish hawks, while another will do precisely the contrary.

UNIVERSAL human strategies are evidently elusive, but by its very nature human sociobiology has little to say about change and cultural variability. This is no minor drawback. Cultural practices change quickly, and are readily borrowed and adapted. Field research by social anthropologists among supposedly traditional communities has documented vertiginous processes of cultural change, and it is striking that people are not necessarily helpless victims when faced with overwhelming technological superiority. Arc-tic peoples adapted to the incursions of Europeans (beginning in the seventeenth century), resisting, organizing, selectively adopting techniques and institutions, and many of them have managed to retain the option of living a nomadic, hunting way of life in the late twentieth century, though comfortably provided with snowmobiles, rifles, and radios, and participating shrewdly in the market.

If anything, human beings are specialists in learning new tricks. This might be the most obvious generalization about human social behavior: that it is extremely plastic and variable. Ernst Mayr, one of the architects of the evolutionary synthesis, has defended Wilson against charges of all-or-nothing genetic determinism, but he re-marks that "the profound differences in social behavior among hu-man groups, some of them closely related, show how much of this behavior is cultural rather than genetic."

Or could it be that cultural variation is bound up with genetic variation? Wilson's first impulse is to look for universals, but he concedes that some practices are restricted to a particular commu-nity, and he is prepared to argue that this may be because the mem-bers of the community share a specific genetic tendency which favors that practice. After all, he points out, the distribution of some inher-ited traits does vary between populations:

> Moderately high heritability has been documented in introversion-extroversion measures, personal tempo, psychomotor and sports activi-ties, neuroticism, dominance, depression, and the tendency toward cer-tain forms of mental illness such as schizophrenia. Even a small portion of this variance invested in population differences might predispose societies toward cultural differences.

This is a tricky case to argue. Most of the traits that Wilson lists are hard to define and to measure, and they are all susceptible to considerable environmental influence. "Sports activities," to take one of his examples, are culturally specific, and even within a culture they may be more important to some categories of people than to others. Baseball skills are likely to be fostered among American boys but not American girls. Black American men dominate the world of heavyweight boxing. This may be because they have some genetic advantage, but it is also the case that professional sports provide rare opportunities for ambitious young men in the United States who suffer from racial discrimination and educational deprivation. For the same reasons, young Jewish men from London's East End were a considerable presence in British boxing at the turn of the century.

Retreating from their initial uncompromising program, the sociobiologists are latterly inclined to make a rather more subtle argument. Genes may code potentialities rather than program fixed sequences of action. This is, of course, well recognized. "While in lower organisms, behavior is strictly determined by the genetic program," François Jacob wrote, where more complex organisms are in question, "the genetic program becomes less constraining . . . Instead of imposing rigid prescriptions, it provides the organism with potentialities and capacities." Among human beings there may even be positive selection for genes that promote flexibility and foster innovative strategies. If so, one might conclude that the genetic constraints on culture are rather permissive, loose enough to allow for a great deal of cultural variation that must be explained in quite different terms.

Even the very general forms of behavior that the sociobiologists take as their special object, and ascribe to instincts or genetic programs, could well have developed by trial and error, and been transmitted by learning. Parental investment and nepotism may be taught because they have proved to pay off. People may invest in their children in the hope that their children will return the favor in the parents' old age. Experience may have taught that infants and their mothers stand a better chance if they are protected by attached males. Perhaps we have learned by trial and error that incest increases the risk of genetic damage.

A contemporary sociobiologist might concede these arguments, but go on to suggest that even if a form of behavior is not genetically controlled, it could still serve to increase the number of surviving offspring of those who practice it. For example, a rule against incest may not be genetically implanted, but incest avoidance will nevertheless improve the fitness of one's descendants. Since parents teach their children how to behave, they will also pass on the adaptive

customs. Children who follow these parental teachings will be relatively more successful than those who do not, and in consequence
the customs will become increasingly general.

This is plausible enough, although it does not follow that the bottom
line for all social practices is the genetic payoff. Moreover, the nagging
criticism of the cultural anthropologists cannot be evaded: sociobiology leaves aside the problem of variation. There are well-documented
cases of institutionalized brother-sister marriage in Iran and Egypt
early in the first century A.D. Some societies ban sexual relations not
only with siblings but with all cousins, while others permit sexual
relations with some first cousins but not others, and many modern
industrial societies have no formal sanction against sexual relations
between any cousins. Some degree of incest restriction may be genetically required, but this will not explain the variable incidence of
incest regulations in human societies.

The potential of human sociobiology is obviously not as great as
it may have seemed twenty years ago. It will not replace the other
human sciences. There are good judges who think little of its prospects altogether. *"Human ethology,"* Sherwood Washburn wrote in
thunderous italics, *"might be defined as the science that pretends
humans cannot speak."* And the same, he said, goes for its successor,
sociobiology. Peter Medawar, a Nobel Prize winner, spoke for many
when he mocked the "simplistic notions of geneticism [that] make
themselves apparent in sociobiology," and would only concede that
the theory might yet "prove itself in the interpretation of the social
behavior of lower animals."

THE bold claim that genes physically determine culture is now
muted, the central importance of learning in human life acknowledged. Alongside sociobiology, another series of research programs
has developed that explore other ways in which the tantalizing successes of population genetics may be tapped to explain human behavior and cultural history.

One was conceived in Fisher's Cambridge laboratory by Luigi Luca
Cavalli-Sforza—"a project," he wrote forty years later, "so ambitious
it seemed almost crazy: the reconstruction of where human popula-

tions originated and the paths by which they spread throughout the world. I reasoned that the task could be accomplished by measuring how closely living populations are related to one another and by deducing from this information a comprehensive family tree." At first, adequate data were available only on blood groups, but in the 1980s it became possible to study molecular data coded in DNA.

One spectacular finding was that the genetic distance between Africans and non-Africans is twice that between Asians and Australians, which in turn is twice that between Asians and Europeans. This is precisely what would be expected if modern humans originated in Africa, as some archaeologists and paleontologists were suggesting. Asians and Europeans had separated from one another comparatively recently, and had probably maintained more contact. Australians had separated from Asians at much the same time, but had lived in isolation since then. There have been serious criticisms of the methods used by Cavalli-Sforza and his associates, and the results are questioned by some specialists; but this line of research will certainly be pursued.

Cavalli-Sforza's next project was even more daring, and yet more controversial. A colleague at Stanford was the historical linguist Joseph Greenberg, who had published in the early 1960s a radically simplified classification of African languages. After much debate, his ideas had been generally accepted, and in the meantime Greenberg had moved on to reclassify the native languages of the Americas, which he eventually arranged into just three families. Cavalli-Sforza matched Greenberg's language families in Africa and the Americas with genetically defined populations, and was able to show that the two separate mappings fitted very well together. Even more global comparisons of genetic groupings and language phyla pointed to a high degree of overlap.

Cavalli-Sforza insisted that genes do not determine language. Nor, on the contrary, do language differences suffice to establish impermeable barriers between populations, which prevent intermarriage. Rather, he maintained, both linguistic and genetic divergence resulted from population movements. The distribution maps of languages and genetic traits could therefore be used to reconstruct the great population shifts in prehistory. Cavalli-Sforza emphasized that his genetic maps were most reliable where populations were isolated and conservative. He had in mind traditional societies in which people transmit their culture, like their genes, from one generation to another, rather than borrowing innovations—or welcoming marriage partners—from foreign peoples.

Reflecting on the relationship between the ways in which genes and culture are transmitted, he began another project, with his Stanford colleague Marcus Feldman, on cultural evolution. Feldman is a brilliant mathematical population geneticist, and together they developed models, drawn from population genetics, for the study of the transmission of cultural traits. In 1981 they published an influential book, *Cultural Transmission and Evolution: A Quantitative Approach.*

Their initiative inspired others, notably an anthropologist, Robert Boyd, and an ecologist, Peter J. Richerson, who collaborated on another widely read book, *Culture and the Evolutionary Process* (1985). Boyd and Richerson draw on modern psychology to specify the very distinctive ways in which people learn (as Darwin had it, by way of "habit, example, instruction, and reflection"). They then argue that learning combines with the very different process of genetic transmission to constitute a "dual inheritance" system which is uniquely human.

The bold models drawn from population genetics are richly suggestive, but full of problems too. To begin with, they require the isolation of cultural units, rather like genes. Yet there are obvious differences between genes and cultural traits. For one thing, genes really are discrete entities, while a culture is not self-evidently constituted by a series of distinct items. Anthropologists are accustomed to insist that cultural traits do not come in discrete packages.

One example of a gene-like cultural trait proposed by Cavalli-Sforza and Feldman is a belief in the afterlife. But this belief entails a whole system of ideas, including most obviously a belief in the existence of the soul and a belief in God. Neither of these beliefs can be sustained in isolation. They require adherence to a whole religious system, such as Christianity; and the Christian religion itself could not exist without churches and clergy and missals and bibles. The Stanford men are perhaps on firmer ground when tracking the spread of individual technical innovations, but even these usually require

for their adoption further changes in work habits and social organization, which greatly complicates the application of genetic models.

A second problem is that the carriers of culture are treated as
independent and equivalent individuals, like the carriers of genes.
But culture is not passed on in a single, biological act; it is acquired
within a matrix of social relations. This Boyd and Richerson acknowledge in principle, but they do not allow sufficient weight to the social context.

Consider their treatment of the problem of "altruism" (which they
understand in a rather more conventional sense than the sociobiologists would like). Individuals, they argue, will tend to be rather selfish.
Communities may nevertheless benefit if individual demands are
moderated in the common interest. They then identify situations in
which individuals might learn that it is advantageous to cooperate,
concluding that where groups are in competition, individuals will
discover that they are well advised to restrain their selfishness.

This argument obliges them to move uneasily between appeals
to individual rewards and community benefits. Biological evolution
deals with individual advantage, but human beings often operate as
collectivities. Like many before them, Boyd and Richerson cut this
knot by assuming that group gains redound to the benefit of the
individual, and vice versa.

There are certainly circumstances in which what is good for General Motors is good for America, and also for all the employees of
General Motors and even perhaps for all Americans. Yet quite often
corporate interests conflict with other corporate interests, and with
some individual interests. Boyd and Richerson consider this unap-
pealing prospect, but they shy away from it. "It might be argued
that individuals co-operate in order to avoid punishment by other
members of their own group," they write. They admit that this con-
forms to common experience. But, they go on, this "does not solve the
theoretical problem; it only raises the new problem of why individuals
should cooperate to punish other individuals." One could surely
imagine a dozen reasons, the most likely being that they are rewarded
for so doing by more powerfully placed individuals.

Boyd and Richerson create these problems for themselves because
they fail to acknowledge that a social system is something more than

a collection of self-propelled individualists. Some people find either pleasure or profit in coercing others, and a few succeed in institution- alizing their advantage. Every known society has its techniques of coercion and repression. The forces that determine the selection of cultural norms cannot therefore be discovered by assessing individ- ual advantage, without regard for the power of the individual in question.

A third problem has to do with the analogies between biological and cultural selection. Cultural preferences may actually be detri- mental to biological fitness. For example, many peoples practice male circumcision. In the absence of modern hygienic procedures, this carries a high risk of infection. A significant proportion of initiates die as a result of their wounds; others become impotent. There is no evidence to suggest that those who suffer infection are less brave, generally less healthy, or otherwise less desirable sources of genes than those who recover from the operation unscathed.

Cavalli-Sforza and Feldman accept this. They explicitly contrast "cultural selection" with "natural selection," and they concede that the two modes of selection may be in tension with each other. They admit that cultural selection does not necessarily promote Darwinian fitness and recognize that it may actually inhibit fitness. But they will not concede that it is therefore a very misleading way of talking. In fact, they are confusing two completely distinct senses of the term "selection." The one sense has to do with the elimination of unfavorable adaptations by natural processes; in the other sense the term connotes the expression of individual preferences and choices. It is because these mechanisms are so distinct that one can ask what consequences, if any, cultural selection may have for natural se- lection.

All these criticisms boil down to the simple objection that one should not be carried away by analogies between genes and cultural traits, genetic mutation and cultural change, natural selection and cultural selection. Metaphors may be seductive, but they should not be taken too far.

Richard Dawkins was a pioneer of the metaphorical school of cul- tural genetics. "Cultural transmission is analogous to genetic trans- mission," he wrote in *The Selfish Gene*, "in that, although basically conservative, it can give rise to a form of evolution." He later coined the term "memes" to stand for cultural analogues of genes. Cavalli-Sforza and Feldman argued from the more specific premise that "we have in cultural transmission the analogs to reproduction and mutation in biological entities." Boyd and Richerson were perhaps more utilitarian, but no less imaginative. "The main reason we are interested in using the inheritance system analogy is practical," they explained. "To the extent that the transmission of culture and the transmission of genes are similar processes, we can borrow the well-developed conceptual categories and formal machinery of Darwinian biology to analyse problems."

This sort of language may have a fine scientific ring to it, but genetic analogies bring in their wake, often unremarked, very problematic assumptions. The genes are anarchists. They are no respecters of status; they make no alliances, take no hostages. People, on the contrary, are constrained by social rules and social relationships. A history written on the analogy of genetics is a history made by equivalent individuals, who are operating without principles in an efficient market. This view of human motivation and behavior may have something to do with the appeal of all genetic analogies in the human sciences. They make nature seem like a perfect market economy; and perhaps, in consequence, they suggest that market economies are perfectly natural.

FIRST
FAMILY

Evolutionary theory directs attention to breeding, and so to mating; and so, where human societies are in question, to marriage. The early Darwinian anthropologists displayed great ingenuity—and a certain prurient delight—in their speculations about early human mating practices. Savages, they believed, abandoned themselves to lust. They respected no incest taboos or marriage vows. They were not constrained by feelings of modesty, or by jealousy. There were no families among them. In that dissolute world of savagery, no man could even be sure who his children were. Then at some stage instinct began to be checked by morality. Ultimately, sex was restricted to the marriage relationship, and the family evolved. The Victorian nuclear family, with its stern father, chaste mother, and modest and obedient children, represented the civilized solution to the vulgar necessity of propagation.

Perhaps the most influential example of this anthropological genre was a book entitled *Primitive Marriage,* published in 1865 by a radical Scottish lawyer and journalist, John Ferguson McLennan. McLennan conjured up a band of warrior braves engaged in constant battles with rivals. He suggested that a winning tactic in this fierce competition was to kill off female children, who would otherwise be a burden to warrior bands. "As braves and hunters were required and valued," he argued, "it would be in the interest of every horde to rear, when possible, its healthy male children. It would be less in its interest to rear females, as they would be less capable of self-support, and of contributing, by their exertions to the common good."

When they needed wives, the warriors captured women from other groups. Mating was therefore "exogamous," to use the term coined by McLennan himself. Wives were outsiders. They were held in common by the warriors, and in consequence the only blood relationship that was recognized was that with the mother. Children regarded all the men of the group in the same way, as common fathers.

In societies at a more sophisticated level of development, a set of brothers would share their wives. Gradually the idea of descent through a line of males—patrilineal descent—would take root. As moral standards improved, each child would know it had a single father, just as it had its own mother.

There was no direct evidence for the mating arrangements of early human populations. However, the anthropologists assumed that contemporary foraging populations in Australia and the Americas preserved some primeval customs, if only in symbolic form, and they scoured the literature for indications that would support their reconstructions.

McLennan cited a report that female infanticide was not uncommon in North India. He pointed to some marriage ceremonies in which the bride was dragged, with every appearance of reluctance, to her husband, and argued that these wedding rites recalled the earlier practice of marriage by capture. There were hunter-gatherers who did indeed trace descent through a line of women. Some—like the aboriginal peoples of Australia—even denied the role of the father in propagation, believing that women were made pregnant by spirits.

Darwin was intrigued by the writings of the anthropologists, but he was skeptical about the stories they told regarding primitive mating customs. He also pointed to evidence that tended to subvert their imaginative reconstructions. "The licentiousness of many savages is no doubt astonishing," Darwin observed, "but it seems to me that more evidence is requisite, before we fully admit that their intercourse is in any case promiscuous." Andrew Smith, a scientist who had studied primates, and who had firsthand knowledge of the South African Bushmen and Hottentots, had "expressed to me the strongest opinion that no race exists in which woman is considered as the property of the community."

Darwin also noted that no other primates were known to be sexually promiscuous. Some primate species were monogamous, others polygamous; but in none, he thought, was copulation random. On the contrary, all male quadrupeds were typically jealous and armed by nature to fight off rivals. He found it hard to believe that early men were in the habit of sharing their women.

Darwin suggested it was more probable that early human groups were like gorilla bands, in which the male leader monopolized sexual access to females. He would not tolerate competition from young males, expelling them from the group as they reached maturity. As soon as the silverback faltered, the younger males would fight to displace him. "Therefore," Darwin concluded, "looking far enough back in the stream of time, and judging from the social habits of man as he now exists, the most probable view is that he aboriginally lived in small communities, each with a single wife, or if powerful with several, whom he jealously guarded against all other men."

Darwin also suggested that he and the anthropologists were addressing quite different questions. As a biologist, his interest was in mating. If powerful males controlled females, jealously guarding them against other males, then the mating practices that resulted were not genuinely promiscuous from a biological point of view. The anthropologists, he pointed out, were concerned not with the biology of mating but rather with the sociology of marriage. When they wrote about promiscuity among savages, they were commenting on the absence of rules and institutions governing sexual conduct.

The question facing the anthropologists could therefore be rephrased: What marked the transition from mating behavior regulated only by force? What was the first rule that humans invented to check the free play of instinct? The answer, it was generally agreed, must have been the incest taboo.

THE three classic theories of human incest avoidance were advanced by Edward Westermarck and Sigmund Freud at the turn of the century, and a generation later by Claude Lévi-Strauss. Their theories all assumed that incest avoidance was a specifically human trait, and indeed that the ban on incest was the first taboo. The prohibition of incest marked the beginning of a truly human culture, a way of life that inhibited the acting out of instinctive desires.

Edward Westermarck, a young Finnish scholar, had been drawn

to this problem by reading *The Descent of Man,* and in particular Darwin's review of contemporary anthropological theories. Notwithstanding Darwin's criticisms, Westermarck was at first prepared to credit the accounts of primitive promiscuity, but as he followed up the works of the anthropologists cited by Darwin he began to have serious doubts. He read voluminously in the ethnographic literature, and sent out questionnaires to Europeans living in the tropics who were studying exotic customs. His doubts grew as he accumulated information. He also questioned the methodology of the anthropologists, who assumed that customs of contemporary peoples could be interpreted as survivals from early forms of organization. When he finally published his findings in 1891, at the age of thirty, he was a master of the field, and he had reached the conclusion that with respect to human marriage practices, Darwin's critique of the anthropologists was essentially correct.

Darwin had cited evidence which suggested that the apes were not given to promiscuity. Westermarck pointed out that among the primates closest to human beings, the male partner of a pregnant female looked after her, and later her young, and acted very like a true father. Apparently paternity was socially significant among primates in general.

After an exhaustive and critical review of the available information, Westermarck concluded that even among the Australian aborigines and other peoples who do not recognize the biological necessity of fathers at all, social fathers are still very much in evidence. The Polish social anthropologist Bronislaw Malinowski, who joined Westermarck at the London School of Economics in 1910, scoured the Australian sources and established that even though the aborigines denied the physiological role of the father, children and mothers were indeed closely associated in family units with husband/fathers. The husband of the child's mother had special rights over the child, and accepted responsibilities toward it. The child inherited certain rights through the father, including the right to membership in a local band, although other significant rights were inherited from the mother's side of the family.

There was certainly considerable play in the ideas that people had about the biology of procreation, and the male role in impregnating the female might be denied. Nevertheless, Westermarck concluded that in most if not all societies a child recognizes a particular man as his or her social father. There were good evolutionary reasons why this should be so. A woman carries a baby for nine months, and in that time she is increasingly physically restricted. After she gives birth, she and the baby are helpless for a time. Then she must feed the child and keep it close to her, and so for months or even years she is unable to range widely and cannot easily defend herself or her child. Those women and small children who are associated closely with a man, a man who is devoted to their care and protection, will be more likely to survive. Fatherhood—in this social sense—favors reproduction.

Freud argued that fathers are also psychologically necessary, instilling discipline and providing children with a model of adult manhood. Part of growing up involves making the father's rules one's own, internalizing them, and, for a boy, matching oneself against this male authority.

The argument could be broadened, to take account of intellectual development as well as physical and emotional growth. The human infant remains immature and vulnerable for longer than the young of other species, and so requires extended nurturing. This uniquely extended period of immaturity is perhaps a necessary condition for the transmission of cultural knowledge. The price of cultural learning is prolonged dependence on the parents. (Malinowski added a rider to this: the educational role of the family could be fulfilled only if the authority of the parents was not confused by sexual passions, so that the incest taboo was necessary to protect the educational mission of parents.)

Westermarck therefore concluded that marriage and the family were universal among primates. "Human marriage," he remarked, "appears, then, to be an inheritance from some ape-like progenitor." Yet the human family did differ in a very important way from the primate family, if only because it persisted for longer than among other primates. Among the apes, the dominant male forced out other males as they matured, including its sons. "The younger males," Darwin had written, "being thus expelled and wandering about, would, when at last successful in finding a partner, prevent too close interbreeding within the limits of the same family." Among humans, in contrast, the family stayed together while the young matured, and so brothers and sisters were raised together. There had to be some special mechanism that would prevent incest between siblings, for incestuous breeding had deleterious effects. A population that tolerated widespread incest might not easily survive the long-term consequences. Westermarck suggested that this mechanism was part and parcel of the very process of family life. Growing up in intimacy reduced sexual attraction. Children who were raised together tended to feel a positive aversion to the idea of sexual contact with one another.

Two modern studies provide support for Westermarck's central thesis. The first one focused on the kibbutz, a utopian socialist invention of the first Zionist settlers in Israel in the 1920s. Their aim was to foster social pioneers who would work on the frontiers of Israeli society, forging a model of the ideal, socialist society that others could follow. Like many utopian theorists, the founders of the kibbutz movement believed it was necessary to marginalize the family, the most potent source of traditional social attitudes. Children were therefore raised communally. Age-mates lived together, in collective nurseries and boarding houses. Here children would be molded from birth to form a social avant-garde.

Children of both sexes lived, played, and bathed together, and young boys and girls formed close partnerships. Nevertheless, children brought up together from infancy under these conditions were extremely unlikely to form sexual relationships at adolescence. An Israeli sociologist, Yonina Talmon, pointed out that the members of the kibbutz favored in-marriage, since they wanted to keep their carefully fostered members; but when they grew up, kibbutz children were reluctant to oblige. Talmon collected statistics to illustrate this conclusion, and later studies confirmed it. Another Israeli researcher, Joseph Shepher, analyzed material on 2,769 marriages from 211 kibbutzim. Only 14 of these marriages involved a couple who had been brought up in the same peer group, and only a handful of these couples had been in the same peer group from under the age of five. Shepher argued that his findings provided "a strong case for Westermarck's instinctive avoidance theory."

The second study was carried out by Arthur Wolf, an American anthropologist working in Taiwan in partnership with a Chinese anthropologist, Chieh-Shan Huang. The two researchers studied a traditional Chinese form of arranged marriage, *sim pua* or "minor" marriage, in which a family adopts a young girl as an infant and raises her to be a wife for their infant son. Here was an ideal opportunity to test Westermarck's aversion thesis, and they proceeded to collect all the relevant data, which they presented in a massive book, *Marriage and Adoption in China, 1845–1945*. They found that couples who were raised together were generally reluctant to go through with marriage when they grew up. Quite often the young man would run away to avoid his fate. Further, these marriages were on average less fertile than marriages contracted by adults, and rates of both adultery and divorce were higher. The earlier the children were brought together, the greater was the likelihood that the marriage would end in divorce.

FREUD began to develop his very different theory of incest at the turn of the century, and he published his fullest account of his thinking on the subject, *Totem and Taboo*, in 1913. He began by restating an obvious objection that had already been raised against Westermarck's thesis. Why make something taboo if people won't do it anyway? If people feel a natural aversion to incest, it should not be necessary to prohibit it. Yet rules against incest are universal, and infringements cause horror.

The truth, according to Freud, is the very opposite of Westermarck's proposition. Children experience a powerful sexual attraction toward members of their family. A young boy desires his mother, and resents his father as a rival for her love. In fantasies he is married to his mother and kills off his father (as the unfortunate Oedipus did, following a series of ghastly accidents). But a boy fears that his father can read his erotic longings and will punish him violently—indeed, by castrating him. This fear is transformed, as the child's conscience develops, into feelings of guilt and shame. With maturity, he transcends this initial complex of emotions and fantasies, and redirects his sexual interest to persons of the opposite sex outside the family.

Healthy children overcome their Oedipal desires: only neurotics fail to resolve them.

Freud used Darwin's description of the sexual behavior of the higher apes as the point of departure for the story he had to tell. The gorillas lived in small communities dominated by a single mature male, who monopolized sexual access to one or more females. According to Darwin, "when the young male grows up a contest takes place for mastery, and the strongest, by killing and driving out the others, establishes himself as the head of the community." Freud assumed that this was also true of early human bands.

Freud was writing at a time when Vienna was at the epicenter of revolutionary movements, and he proposed that at some stage the young men who had been driven away would have formed a conspiracy, ganging together to kill the father-overlord and to take his wives for themselves. This primal crime enacted the secret wish of every young man to displace his father and possess his mother.

But the revolutionary overthrow of the father threatened the foundations of social life. No society could permit men to mate with their mothers. Accordingly, taboos and magical beliefs grew up that equated the father with a god and imposed supernatural penalties upon the sexual possession of a mother. Culture repressed natural sexual desires, imposing a painful growing away from first love and the denial of the most basic jealousies and fears. Freud made the Oedipus complex and its resolution the motor of moral evolution.

Freud now had a theory about individual sexual development and a thesis about the history of the human family. To link the two, he invoked an evolutionary theory that was particularly fashionable in Germany. It had been developed by Haeckel, the leading German Darwinian, and was summed up in the phrase "ontogeny recapitulates phylogeny." In other words, in the course of its development the organism passes through the same stages as those that had marked the evolution of the species. Each growing person relives the whole history of humanity. The child is a primitive; the adolescent reenacts the Oedipal struggle and the birth of culture; and only the adult is a modern and civilized person. The adolescent boy wrestling with his Oedipal fantasies relives the guilt of the ancient revolutionaries who killed their father.

Freud drew his evidence for the persistence of Oedipal desires in civilized society from his clinical experience. Yet Freud's patients were in fact mostly young women. In his day-to-day practice he was dealing with the fixation of daughters upon their fathers, a relationship that had not been emphasized in his great myth of origin of the incest taboo.

Time and again, Freud's female patients reported under analysis that they had experienced sexual encounters with their fathers. Initially, in the 1890s, Freud had concluded that these incestuous experiences caused their adult neuroses. Later he altered his diagnosis and insisted that these reports were fantasies. The cause of the neurosis was an unresolved infantile fixation on the father. The women dreamed that their desire for a sexual relationship with their fathers had been consummated, and they were then tormented by feelings of guilt.

We now know that some of Freud's women patients were indeed victims of sexual abuse as children, as are many children in modern societies. Children may or may not harbor secret lusts for their parents, but a significant number of parents quite evidently do force sexual relations upon their children. A Freudian, inclined to assert the effect of childhood experience on the adult personality, might suggest that the incestuous parents are reenacting the confused, unresolved fantasies of their own childhood. Healthy adults do not behave in this way.

In Freud's theory, culture normally triumphs over nature. The incest taboo checks natural drives and incidentally diverts a growing boy's sexual energy away from his mother, liberating energies that can be turned to cultural creativity. Civilization, according to Freud, was built upon the repression of instinct.

In Westermarck's theory, culture follows nature. The cultural rule echoes a biologically necessary and naturally produced aversion to incest. Westermarck countered Freud's objection that a natural aversion would not require reinforcement by a rule. Why then, he demanded, did human beings universally prohibit bestiality? Did Freud suppose that there was a general temptation to engage in unnatural connections with animals? Rules could go with the grain of natural inclination; culture could underwrite nature.

Westermarck's theory won support from ethologists and sociobiologists, who were also inclined to the view that culture articulates natural patterns of behavior. Where the natural pattern has been disrupted, culture may compensate. Robin Fox argued that incestuous desires arose only in societies where brothers and sisters were raised apart. There was also evidence suggesting that children were more exposed to the danger of sexual abuse if they lived with a stepfather rather than a biological father. It was in such circumstances that an incest taboo was required.

The evidence for Westermarck's hypothesis is rather better than that for Freud's. There are also powerful objections to Freud's account. Freud represented the authority of the father as the main check on incest, but it could be argued that the power structure of the family actually fosters the abuse of young people by parents and older siblings. Considered as an evolutionary hypothesis, Freud's scenario also suffers from the fact that mother-son incest is extremely unusual among all primates: its prohibition is therefore unlikely to have represented a revolutionary event in the cultural development of humans.

Yet the theories of Westermarck and Freud are not necessarily in competition with each other. They identified different mechanisms that inhibit incest, but then each was primarily concerned with only one form of incest. Westermarck dealt mainly with sibling incest, arguing that sexual attraction is rare between brother and sister, and that this indifference is a consequence of their being raised together. Freud highlighted the issue of mother-son incest. A growing boy, he believed, will naturally be sexually attracted to his mother, and this attraction must be checked by cultural mechanisms as he matures. Both identified the inhibiting factors within the structure of the family.

Either theory may be reconciled with explanations that invoke the biological benefits of outbreeding. Marrying out avoids the genetic penalties of sustained inbreeding, which arise from the greater chance that deleterious traits carried by recessive genes will be transmitted to offspring. Whatever mechanisms achieve this end will tend to increase fitness and thus would be preserved and would spread.

THE third theory proposed a quite different origin for the rules of the incest taboo and the regulation of marriage. The father of English anthropology, E. B. Tylor, an associate of Darwin, was a Quaker. He recoiled from McLennan's fierce view of primitive hordes living by warfare, infanticide, and the kidnapping of wives. Instead he suggested that early humans would have been peace-lovers, diplomats, coalition-builders. Their subtle strategies would have been pursued with the only resources to hand: their women. In 1889, Tylor put forward his famous hypothesis: "Among tribes of low culture there is but one means known of keeping up permanent alliance, and that means is intermarriage." Intermarriage allowed a growing tribe to maintain contact with outlying segments, sustaining a broadly based military force that was more than sufficient to match the inbred, isolated populations of their enemies. "Again and again in the world's history," he concluded, "savage tribes must have had plainly before their minds the simple practical alternative between marrying-out and being killed out."

This hypothesis is the basis of a modern anthropological classic, *The Elementary Structures of Kinship,* originally published in 1949 by Claude Lévi-Strauss. Tylor's insight, according to Lévi-Strauss, could be used to solve the problem of the incest taboo: it was the necessary precondition for a system of marriage alliances. When a man gave up his sexual rights to his daughter and his sister, he was obliged to marry them off to men outside the family. That act of renunciation gave him a claim to marry their sisters and daughters in exchange. The payoff for the regulation of incest was the institution of marriage exchanges, and marriage alliances provided the foundation for a broader sociality.

The incest taboo marked the boundary between nature and culture, for it was the first rule. Precipitating the primal exchange—of the super-gift, women and children—the ban on incest also made human society possible. Lévi-Strauss accepted the universality of the nuclear family, but he insisted that the basic unit of human society was the nuclear family plus the wife's brother, the man who gave his sister to a husband, so constituting the family. The tie between brothers-in-law was the foundation of society.

Lévi-Strauss argued further that there are only a limited number of ways in which a systematic exchange of women can be organized. He identified three widespread formulas that drive the repetitive exchange of women between the same family groups, from generation to generation. The first was the immediate and direct exchange of sisters between two men. Their sons would repeat the exchange, marrying each other's sisters. The second formula was a delayed exchange: a man married his sister to another man and received a return in the next generation, when his son married that sister's daughter. The third, most widespread formula Lévi-Strauss termed "generalized exchange." This was based on the repudiation of a direct return. A man gave a sister to a second party, who gave a sister to a third, forming a chain of indefinite extent, at the end of which was a man who gave a sister in marriage to the initiator of the cycle.

These elementary systems of exchange cropped up again and again all over the world, and probably corresponded to the arrangements developed by early human communities. Only in complex modern societies, with political structures no longer based on kinship alone, has something approaching a free market for marriage come into being.

This is a powerful, elegant model, but it has serious deficiencies. One concerns its range. Like the anthropologists of the nineteenth century, Lévi-Strauss paid especial attention to the Australian aborigines, and they operated perhaps the most complicated "alliance" system that has ever been discovered. But we no longer regard the Australian aborigines as prototypes of primitive humanity, and their wonderfully elaborate marriage systems are not typical of foraging societies. Among such well-documented societies of hunter-gatherers as the Inuit of Alaska, the Andaman Islanders, the Pygmies of the Zairean rain forest, or the Hadza of Tanzania, there is no regular pattern of marriage alliance. Lévi-Strauss's elementary systems of marriage alliance are probably more typical of complex Far Eastern societies, including, for instance, South Indians and Chinese populations, than they are of hunter-gatherers. In the Arab world there are also apparently contradictory rules that favor in-marriage with close kin on the father's side, within the extended patriarchal family. Probably the majority of known societies do not circulate women along fixed paths between the same family groups.

It is therefore not easy to believe that the early human societies were all based on Lévi-Straussian systems of repetitive marriage alliance. Nevertheless, it is certainly plausible that marriage alliances are among the fundamental social bonds, and that they may provide the basis for the structure of a simple society. Lévi-Strauss insisted that it was this social imperative that required the institution of the incest taboo. Human society could come into being only after men were obliged to seek wives outside the family.

One thing all these theories of incest regulation had in common was the premise that the taboo on incest distinguished human beings from all other animals. This assumption was based on observations of domestic animals and of the denizens of zoos. Solly Zuckerman, studying primates in the London Zoo in the 1920s and 1930s, even found an incestuous mother-son pair. Apparently, therefore, incest avoidance was a uniquely human trait.

As it turns out, this conclusion was false. Incestuous sexual contact is uncommon among most animals in nature. Generally, maturing males are expelled from the home group and are obliged to seek partners elsewhere. In some species, males and females scatter, thus reducing the probability of incestuous sexual relationships. Even where opportunities for incestuous mating exist, it may not occur. George Schaller found that in a gorilla band, a young female will not mate with its father or brother. Ironically, theories about incest and human culture were based on a contrast between humans and incestuous domesticated animals. This distinction vanished if humans were compared with animals in the wild.

But if most animal populations prove to have a low incidence of incest in practice, it has also become evident that incestuous sexual relationships are by no means unknown among human beings. Incest is not even universally prohibited by human laws. Various god-kings, including the Pharaohs, married their sisters, and widespread brother-sister marriage is well attested in Persia and Egypt during some historical periods. While it is nevertheless true that marriages between brothers and sisters have only rarely been permitted, rules regulating marriage between cousins, nieces, nephews, uncles, and aunts are quite variable.

WHAT of Westermarck's thesis that marriage and the family are universal human institutions? One of the first modern ethnographic studies was carried out by Bronislaw Malinowski, who had worked closely with Westermarck at the London School of Economics, documenting the existence of families among the Australian aborigines. During the First World War Malinowski made a pioneering intensive field study in the Trobriand Islands, off New Guinea, spending two years living in the community on intimate terms with the people, and learning the language fluently.

Here was another society in which the biological facts of paternity were disputed. A woman, it was believed, could only be made pregnant by the intervention of a spirit, a dead person pressing to be reborn. Moreover, the Trobrianders traced politically crucial relationships through the mother's line rather than through that of the father. A man inherited not from his father but from his mother's brother, and at adolescence he moved away from his parents to live with his maternal uncle. (The anthropological term for this package of arrangements is matriliny, and societies that go in for it are called matrilineal societies.)

As a consequence of these matrilineal dispositions, the mother's husband was not a disciplinarian or a figure of authority for the children; rather, he was an attentive, loving friend. It was the mother's brother, as head of the extended family, who disciplined children and taught them to observe the rules of the wider society. Yet while a Trobriander inherited from his mother's brother, his father's connections were useful to him, and fathers taught their sons esoteric skills and secret magical formulas.

Malinowski used this Trobriand family variant to probe Freud's claim that the Oedipus complex was universal. According to Malinowski, the Trobriand boy did not secretly lust after his mother and dream about disposing of his father and replacing him. Instead he had an emotionally fraught and ambivalent relationship with his sister, whose sons would eventually succeed him; and he hated and resented his mother's brother, who disciplined him, and whose death would eventually deliver his inheritance.

Notwithstanding these matrilineal complications, the nuclear family of father, mother, and children could be found in a recognizable form in the Trobriand Islands. Husbands and fathers are very much in evidence in most matrilineal societies, and the nuclear family is commonly a living unit, at least while the children are young.

Yet a man in such a society cannot freely exercise authority over his children, since their uncle is their legal guardian. He may also have to defer to his wife's father or brother when it comes to controlling his wife. Women may be inclined to move with their children to live with their brothers. Divorce rates in matrilineal societies tend to be high, and domestic life is characterized by power struggles over women between their husbands and their brothers. At the extreme, there are some cases where fathers and husbands may become marginal figures in the society. There is one famous ethnographic case, that of the Nayar, in which they seem to have been vestigial.

The Nayar live on the Malabar Coast at the extreme southwestern tip of India. This is a region where caste distinctions have traditionally been very strong, and the Nayars, a military people, were sharply distinguished from their Brahman neighbors, and from the majority of the local people, who were regarded as untouchables. Their strange kinship and marriage practices were reported in some detail by a Portuguese traveler, Duarte Barbosa, who spent several years in the region in the early sixteenth century and learned the local language.

Barbosa reported that among the Brahmans, only the eldest son married. Brahman women had to be pure, and most never married or formed sexual alliances. The younger sons of Brahman families formed alliances with Nayar women, and these women, Barbosa reported, "hold it to be a great honour, and as they are Brahmans no woman refuses herself to them, yet they may not sleep with any woman older than themselves."

There are many societies in which aristocratic men can have their way with lower-status women. The real oddity was the behavior of the Nayar themselves. The Nayar men, Barbosa reported, "are not married, their nephews (sisters' sons) are their heirs. The Nayar women of good birth are very independent, and dispose of themselves as they please with Brahmans, and Nayars, but they do not sleep with men of caste lower than their own under pain of death."

The Nayar lived in long-houses where a woman, her daughters, and her daughters' daughters would bring up their children, attended by their brothers and mother's brothers. Lovers would visit them, but there was only the faintest trace of wedding rites (which were merged into the puberty ritual). An appropriate man had to acknowledge paternity of a child in order to establish that no caste or incest rules had been broken, but there was virtually no social relationship between this nominal father and his children.

According to most authorities, the explanation for the Nayar system lay in their unusual economic specialization. The men were employed largely as mercenary soldiers, and were therefore absent for long periods. The female-based family arrangements they had developed made this way of life possible. This was indeed the deduction of the French philosopher Montesquieu, writing in 1748. The Nayar are soldiers, he noted. "In Europe, soldiers are forbidden to marry; in Malabar, where the climate requires greater indulgence, they are satisfied with rendering marriage as little burdensome to them as possible: they give one wife amongst many men, which consequently diminishes the attachment to a family, and the cares of housekeeping, and leaves them in the free possession of a military spirit." In North India, where there were also communities that specialized in the provision of mercenary soldiers, some had developed an alternative system to deal with the problem of marriage: they had a system of polyandry, with a group of brothers marrying one woman and rotating the privilege of living at home with her.

The British annexed Malabar in 1792, and the military system that had sustained the Nayar was suppressed. Early in the nineteenth century the polyandrous system died out, and increasingly the Nayar began to favor permanent relationships between a single man and woman. The prestige of the higher-caste practices of marriage and family life also probably had an influence on the behavior of the Nayar, once the economic rationale behind their traditional arrangements disappeared. Economic changes in the nineteenth century also gradually undermined the matrilineal system. Today the family life of the Nayar is very much like that of their neighbors.

Other communities in which fathers are marginal are also typically minorities living as part of a larger social system, often in poverty-stricken enclaves in richer societies. Where men can contribute little to their women and children, the family is weak. However, the poor aspire to the values held by the broader society, and they typically try to establish viable families.

It has sometimes been argued that black American family arrangements differ from the white American norm because of the effects of slavery on family life, or because the slaves brought with them matrilineal customs from West Africa. However, Herbert G. Gutman has shown that between 1855 and 1880, 90 percent of black households contained a married couple with children, or a father with children. The rise in the number of female-headed households among black Americans coincided with the move to lives of poverty in the ghettos of northern industrial cities. On the other hand, the economic and social pressures they experienced made people more dependent on other kin: black American adults are nearly twice as likely as American whites to share households with relatives other than a husband or wife.

There are, then, few significant exceptions to the general rule, and these can be accounted for as temporary or local deviations from the normal pattern of family life, established under peculiar and usually transient circumstances. There is little reason to suppose that our distant ancestors arranged their domestic affairs very differently. In most band societies where people live by foraging, fathers feature prominently, and nuclear families are central to social arrangements. The Algonquin Indians, Congo Pygmies, Kalahari Bushmen, the native peoples of Australia, the Amazon, the Arctic, all organize themselves in nuclear family units.

Westermarck apparently read the evidence correctly a century ago. Authoritative comparative studies by later anthropologists confirmed his conclusions. The American anthropologist Robert Lowie reviewed the theories of the family and the ethnographic record in his *Primitive Society* in 1920 and concluded that the family could be found everywhere, with the same fundamental structure, linking children with both mother and father. "A man may spend the major part of his working and sleeping hours away from his wife, but for all that he is linked to her by the common interest in the children of the household, really or putatively his own, and by their economic industrial partnership." The economic and political arrangements of the society will "often strangely affect the dynamics of family life," but "the bilateral family is none the less an absolutely universal unit of human society."

THE nuclear family, complete with a father figure, hedged around with incest taboos, may be very ancient; but until recently historians and anthropologists were still inclined to believe that it was once much less important than it has since become. They believed that it was traditionally only a segment of a larger kinship institution.

The anthropological orthodoxy held that most human communities, for much of their history, were organized into large aggregates of kin, which they called clans or lineages. The Victorian scholars, who went in for elaborate speculative reconstructions, took the view that early societies developed a system of matrilineal descent groups, since the father was marginal and paternity uncertain. Only after a lengthy period of social development did matrilineal societies become obsolete. Descent traced in the male line then became the basis for organizing political groups.

This thesis was soon discredited. It turned out that a majority of matrilineal societies were rather complex and sophisticated, and that few extant hunter-gatherers were matrilineal. Yet the fundamental element of the Victorian model continued to command assent. Anthropologists in general believed that in so-called primitive societies, large descent groups provided the basis for social organization. Nuclear families formed distinct but subordinate parts of such larger corporations. Where polygamy was practiced, the nuclear family was in any case only found among the poor.

Historians of Europe, India, and China delineated what was taken to be a more advanced form of community life, in which the clan had declined and been replaced by the extended family. An older couple and their married children formed a single extended family. The several nuclear families that made up an extended family shared a household and held property in common. Such extended families united three generations in a complex and harmonious enterprise: the family joint stock company.

In modern times, the extended family had withered away. The state assumed its traditional welfare functions, educating children and caring for the aged and infirm. Industrialization had removed the workplace from the cottage or the family farm, and imposed a high degree of mobility of labor. The nuclear family, the small unit of parents and children, continued, but it was now vulnerable, isolated, striving to fulfill a new and difficult role: to provide a haven in a heartless world.

In the mid-twentieth century, mainstream sociologists and psychoanalysts tended to represent the family as a crucial source of social stability, but critics, less content with the outcome, were less respectful of the family itself. The modern nuclear family was quite commonly represented as the source of grave, perhaps terminal social problems. It was too authoritarian, too claustrophobic, riven by irresoluble emotional strains. The family restricted the opportunities of women, fomented emotional crises that it could not resolve, protected perpetrators of violence and child abuse. The anthropologist Edmund Leach shocked the British public in his BBC Reith lectures in 1967 with the claim that "far from being the basis of the good society, the family, with its narrow privacy and tawdry secrets, is the source of all our discontents." The family was even blamed for the political ills of the society. The dissident psychoanalyst Wilhelm Reich described the "authoritarian family" as "the factory in which the state's structure and ideology are moulded."

But if the isolated nuclear family was itself a modern institution, then one might expect it also to be transient. This was a familiar radical theme. In 1884 Friedrich Engels wrote that the family would eventually wither away, along with the state and with the institution of private property which sustained both. A decade later, Emile Durkheim predicted that in modern industrial societies associations of workers would take over many of the present functions of the family. And feminists argued that the father is an unnecessary addition to the natural domestic unit of mother and children. Why not use artificial insemination and eliminate the middleman?

These predictions of dissolution are not on the face of it implausible. The nuclear family is clearly less stable today than it was half a century ago in the major Western industrial countries. Peter Laslett, the pioneer of family history in Britain, described the 1950s and 1960s as "the time of the Grand Climacteric in the family life of

Western societies. It was then that consensual unions began to be widespread, abortions to be exceedingly common, contraception to be universal and the numbers of births to fall so far that it is now doubtful if many Western populations can maintain their numbers in the long run."

The divorce rate, which shot up briefly at the end of both world wars, began a rapid and apparently relentless climb in the sixties and then accelerated dizzyingly as industrialized Western societies instituted "no fault" divorce laws. By the 1990s, about half the marriages contracted in the United States and a third of those in the richest European countries were evidently destined for legal termination.

Not only are more marriages breaking up. An increasing proportion of people saw no point in marrying, opting for "living together." In the United States, half a million people were cohabiting unmarried in 1970. By 1980 the number had increased fourfold. Western Europe is moving in the same direction.

What is perhaps most striking, the Grand Climacteric in family life marked a transformation in the position of women. They were no longer restricted to hearth and home; indeed, the home itself could be represented as a prison for women, the last stronghold of male domination. By the 1980s, over half the married women in advanced industrial societies were employed outside the home, and the numbers were rising. In more and more countries, discrimination against women in public life and in employment was made illegal. Increasingly, women did not require men to support them. Marriage became something of an optional preliminary to motherhood. In Sweden, half of all births are outside marriage, and even in England and Wales one in five children is born to an unmarried mother.

All in all, a number of sober and well-informed observers have concluded that the nuclear family is a rather recent innovation, perhaps adapted to one phase of industrial society, but plagued by growing psychological and moral problems. It will soon, perhaps thankfully, be rendered obsolete. Accordingly, any theory of human social life that takes for granted the centrality of the family is fatally limited.

These arguments combined to suggest a clear progression. Primitive societies were organized into clans and lineages. The sprawling extended family served traditional societies in Europe, India, and China. In modern society we have the naked nuclear family. In the near future this will be superseded by something else, perhaps by free partnerships of liberated individuals, perhaps by a system of female-headed households that will marginalize men.

This neat historical sequence is no longer accepted by scholars. Contemporary social anthropologists are skeptical about the models, current until recently, which represented African, American, and Pacific societies as associations of large corporations of kin that swallow up the family and the individual in a great collective of blood-kin. On the contrary, nuclear families crop up everywhere, and they are usually the most important domestic institutions, their heads making pragmatic choices of political alignment. Nor does polygamy greatly affect the matter. Even in polygamous societies, most men have only one wife; and polygamous families tend to operate as a cluster of nuclear families with a common patriarch.

Historians have discredited the established view that in pre-modern Europe most people lived in extended families, intergenerational corporations, which were eventually dissolved by the acid of industrial society. The French *Annales* historians, followed by Peter Laslett in Britain, showed that from the sixteenth century the nuclear family was the predominant domestic institution. The households of richer families included servants or apprentices, but seldom grandparents, or adult brothers and sisters. In Britain, Laslett found, the mean household size remained constant at 4.5 to 5 people per household from the sixteenth century into the early twentieth century. Remarkably similar findings were reported for other parts of pre-industrial Europe and America. The nuclear family turns out to be the traditional family form in the West.

Finally, the prediction that the family in modern societies is on the point of obsolescence has been radically qualified. In the United States, more people are getting married than ever before. There are fewer of the confirmed bachelors and spinsters so common in the nineteenth and early twentieth centuries. This rise in the incidence of marriage is, indeed, one of the reasons for the increase in the incidence of divorces. Moreover, one great risk to the security of the child has been lessened. In the early period of industrial society there was a constant fear that a child would be orphaned, for adult mortality was far higher than it is in advanced industrial societies, and women risked their lives in childbearing.

Today, despite the rise in illegitimacy and divorce the great majority of children in the rich industrial societies are still raised by their own two parents. Only a small minority are raised outside a nuclear family unit, although in an increasing proportion of cases the parental couple may not be legally married to each other. In Great Britain in 1985, for example, 78 percent of children under fifteen were living with both natural parents, who were married to each other. A further 7 percent lived with their natural mother and a stepfather, to whom their mother was married. Two percent lived with both natural parents who were not married, and a further 2 percent lived with a natural mother and an informal stepfather. In all, then, almost 90 percent of British children still grow up in a nuclear family.

In America too illegitimacy figures have risen, but many couples raise children in a stable relationship without the benefit of marriage, and such arrangements are more acceptable to the broader society. Divorce rates have escalated, but the remarriage of divorced persons is common. Eighty percent of American children live with both parents, and many of the remainder live with one parent and his or her partner. Nuclear families without young children are unstable; many women postpone childbearing for longer than their mothers did; a significant proportion avoid having children altogether; and couples without children see little reason to marry. Yet despite these facts, it can be plausibly argued that the nuclear family still fulfills its central traditional functions. It remains a fair approximation—crude but essentially correct—to say that the nuclear family is universal.

HOWEVER constraining the biology of reproduction may be, and however general the emotional ties between parents and children, anthropologists have long insisted that these forces do not deliver uniform types of family or of marriage.

It must be admitted that anthropologists love to dwell on exceptional and exotic practices. They document societies where fathers may live apart from wives and children, sleeping in communal mens' houses. In matrilineal societies, adolescent children may live with their maternal uncles. There are a perhaps a handful of cases like the Nayar of old, where the family is marginalized to the point of disappearance.

They also cite some very peculiar forms of marriage. In addition to the plural marriage systems in which one man has several wives, or, very occasionally, a woman may have several husbands, there are African societies where a woman can marry another woman. Rich women take on male roles in some West African societies, and invest in wives and children. Woman-woman marriages may also permit a family to transmit an office through a woman to her son by means of a legal fiction. A woman may be legally married to a dead man, and her children may inherit his estate.

Anthropologists are fascinated by these extreme cases, and for good reason. They are of theoretical interest, since they test easy generalizations about the family and marriage. Yet the most striking thing is how few exceptions there are. Moreover, some of the most extreme cases represent short-lived adaptations to extreme circumstances. Other unusual institutions may be regarded as oddities even by those who use them. Where strange forms of marriage are practiced, these are regarded locally as a rare alternative to the established marriage forms.

More interesting anthropological arguments have to do with the ways in which the family is shaped by its relationship with other families, or accommodates to economic pressures or political demands. The Trobriand father is a friendly, undemanding figure because, in a matrilineal society, his son will not inherit his estate. It is the boy's uncle who must take social responsibility for his peccadilloes. The boundaries set by the incest taboo are also influenced by these broader factors. Among the Trobrianders, a cousin on the father's side is a man's preferred bride, while he may not marry a cousin on his mother's side—a rule obviously related to the matrilineal form of inheritance and succession in this society.

Sociologists have shown that even in a modern industrial society, family structure may vary considerably. Different relationships become more or less significant according to circumstance. Shortly after World War II, the sociologists Michael Young and Peter Willmott conducted research on family relationships in the East End of London. They discovered that the nuclear families were sustained by ties to the wife's mother, whose role in child-rearing and emotional guidance was crucial. Their later studies of middle-class families brought out the salience of ties between men, particularly in matters of employment and finance. A man often turned for economic help to his father or brothers, and also to a father-in-law or brother-in-law.

The degree of importance that family and kin assume in the lives of individuals is also very variable. There are great differences in the weight carried by kinship relationships in everyday affairs. To take a simple instance, immigrants will generally place more store on stable family relationships than do members of the home community. A new immigrant anywhere will look to an uncle or cousin for help more readily than he or she might do at home.

Patterns of marriage alliance suit the political and economic interests of parents. Young people are generally allowed to make their own choices only when little is at stake for others. If there is competition for husbands and wives with particular advantages, dowry and bride-wealth payments may allow the rationing of spouses. Where such payments are customary, the "price" of a husband or bride will vary depending on the advantages they bring with them—advantages that may be gauged less from the point of view of the young couple than from the perspective of their parents.

The very rate of family formation can be adjusted as the environment changes. Marriages may be postponed if resources are under pressure, and a proportion of the population may even remain celibate. A celebrated example is the response of small farmers in Ireland to the potato famine of 1845–1847. The introduction of the new crop, potatoes, from the Americas at the end of the sixteenth century had enriched the peasantry, allowing families to support increasing numbers of children on the same small farms. In the late eighteenth century legal reforms allowed new lands to be brought into production. The population soared. After the famine, farmers recognized the dangers of subdividing their small holdings. From that time on, only one son—usually the youngest—was granted the wherewithal to marry. He was given charge of the farm, but on the condition that he supported his parents. The dowry he received with his wife was given to one of his sisters, to allow her to marry. The other children had to migrate in search of new lives, or remain celibate. One in three or four adults remained unmarried; those marriages that did occur were contracted relatively late in life; and millions migrated. The population of Ireland went into precipitate decline, from just over five million in the mid-nineteenth century to just under three million a century later.

The number of children in a family is also open to manipulation. Although abortion techniques are known universally, the most common technique for restricting the number of children is to postpone marriage. Historical studies of pre-industrial Europe show clearly that the age at first marriage fluctuated with the fortunes of farming families, with a run of good harvests or increased employment opportunities leading to earlier marriage and thus to a rapid rise in population.

In short, the family may be universal but it is a flexible institution, its internal arrangements adapted to the structure of the broader society, its breeding policies responsive to economic signals. How variable, then, are the basic ingredients of family life: the relationships between husband and wife, parents and children? To what extent do these vary between societies? Are the roles of men, women, and children fixed by the biology of reproduction, or perhaps by the exigencies of family life? These are the central issues in another long-running research program in anthropology.

· 8 ·

MALE AND
FEMALE

In the summer of 1925, at the age of twenty-three, Margaret Mead stepped onto a train in Philadelphia on the first leg of her journey to Samoa. As she told it, she "had all the courage of almost complete ignorance. I had read everything that had been written about the Pacific island peoples who had become known to the western world through Captain Cook's voyages, and I was deeply interested in the processes of change. But I myself had never been abroad or on a ship, had never spoken a foreign language or stayed in a hotel by myself. In fact, I had never spent a day in my life alone."

She had, however, been educated at Columbia University by Franz Boas, the father figure of American anthropology. An immigrant German scholar, Boas established the first major school of anthropology in an American university. He himself had studied in Berlin under a leading anti-Darwinian physiologist, Rudolph Virchow, and in the Virchow tradition he was skeptical of bold evolutionist generalizations.

Boas's first target was a crude evolutionism that represented all cultures as staging posts on a highway stretching out west into the future. Against the simple evolutionists, Boas insisted on the complexity of local historical processes and the unpredictable but profound effects of environmental factors on cultural development. The cultural history of the Americas was driven by contacts and exchanges between native groups. There was no inevitable sequence of cultural development. Religious ideas, mythologies, kinship institutions, even political and economic systems were borrowed and adapted; and each had its own particular history in any population.

By the 1920s, Margaret Mead recalled in her autobiography, *Black-*

berry Winter, Boas began to sketch out a new program for research. "He felt that sufficient work had gone into demonstrating that peoples borrowed from one another, that no society evolved in isolation, but was continually influenced in its development by other peoples, other cultures, and other, differing, levels of technology. He decided that the time had come to tackle the set of problems that linked the development of individuals to what was distinctive in the culture in which they were reared." Some of Boas's students were already moving in this direction, increasingly persuaded that culture was a major determinant of behavior.

The old racist view was that biological differences determined differences in culture. Boas had demonstrated that race, culture, and language do not coincide, and his students took this for granted. Culture, not race, was the cause of significant differences between populations. The question that interested them was how, and how far, culture could modify behavior. Influenced by Freudian theory, the young Boasians believed that child-rearing practices form adult personality. However, such practices vary. Perhaps each community molds personalities in culturally specific ways, in accordance with particular local ideals. So how far can human beings—biologically everywhere the same—be trained to behave in different ways?

The question could be sharpened by considering the real biological differences that exist within populations, above all those between adults and children and between men and women. How much play is there in these basic roles? With these questions in mind, Boas directed Margaret Mead to investigate adolescence. And he had his eye on a particular heresy, a version of biological determinism that was ripe for attack.

In 1907 G. Stanley Hall, the founder of Clark University, had published a large book grandly entitled *Adolescence: Its Psychology and Its Relations to Physiology, Anthropology, Sociology, Sex, Crime, Religion and Education.* Hall was a follower of Haeckel, and he argued that the growing child recapitulates the stages of development of the human species. The play of the child recalled the work of savages. The adolescent was reliving the great break in human evolution: the move from savagery to civilization, from natural and spontaneous forms of behavior to the rule-bound, disciplined behavior of culti-

FRANZ BOAS (1858–1942), a German Jewish scientist who became the founding father of modern American cultural anthropology, was appointed to a position at Columbia University in 1899 and remained there for the rest of his career. He conducted ethnographic research in Baffin Island and subsequently among the native peoples of Vancouver Island and the coast of British Columbia. His austere devotion to science, and particularly to empirical research, was combined with a commitment to combating racism, and he was perhaps the most influential and original of the scholars who were to demonstrate that "race" has no connection with language, culture, or intelligence. His students, who included Edward Sapir, Alfred Kroeber, Robert Lowie, Ruth Benedict, and Margaret Mead, became the leading figures in American cultural anthropology.

vated people. "Adolescence," he wrote, "is a new birth for the higher and more completely human traits are now born . . . The child comes from and harks back to a remoter past; the adolescent is neo-atavistic, and in him the later acquisitions of the race become prepotent. Development is less gradual and more saltatory, suggestive of some ancient period of storm and stress when old moorings were broken and a higher level attained."

Boas had a personal reason for taking on Hall, since his first position in the United States had been in Hall's new university, and it had ended with a quarrel and Boas's resignation. But Hall represented a good theoretical target as well, with his thesis that the storm and stress of adolescence were something natural, programmed in the genes. Even if the recapitulation thesis had become discredited among biologists, it still had adherents among psychologists; and there were many other psychologists who believed more straightforwardly that the problems of adolescence were caused by biological changes at puberty. In the cities and suburbs of America, adolescents were often rebellious or sullenly submissive, and the general view was that glandular changes induced adolescent misbehavior.

Boas suggested that the nature of the adolescent experience in America might be culturally specific, that the recalcitrance of adolescents expressed a frustrated desire for independence. "I am not at all clear in my mind," he commented, "in how far similar conditions may occur in primitive society and in how far the desire for independence may be simply due to our modern conditions and to a more strongly developed individualism."

Accordingly, Boas wanted Margaret Mead to investigate the experience of adolescence in another culture, and specifically in one of the native cultures of North America which the Boasians had been studying for two decades. Mead really wanted to study culture change, but she was willing to take on the problem of adolescence. However, she was not prepared to make her study in North America. Her heart was set on going to Polynesia, for she had immersed herself in the ethnographic literature for the region. Boas gave in, but he insisted that she should choose an island where a ship called regularly. Thus Mead decided to work in Samoa, but she picked the isolated Manu'an islands for her intensive fieldwork. "Everyone agreed that the Manu'an islands were much more old-fashioned and were, therefore, much better for my purposes."

On Manu'a she made her base in an American naval dispensary, writing to Boas that she had decided not to live with a Samoan family because of "the loss of efficiency due to the food and the nervewracking conditions of living with half a dozen people in the same room in a house without walls, always sitting on the floor and sleeping in the constant expectation of having a pig or a chicken thrust itself upon one's notice."

This was a choice that would not be acceptable to a later, more purist generation of fieldworkers, but in her autobiography she pointed out some real advantages in her situation. "Living in the dispensary, I could do things that otherwise would have been wholly inappropriate. The adolescent girls, and later the smaller girls whom I found I had also to study, came and filled my screen-room day after day and night after night." She worked intensively with fifty subjects, and although this phase of her research was concentrated in a period of only four months, and even this was disrupted by a hurricane and by school terms, it provided the basis for her conclusions about adolescent Samoan girls.

Her findings on adolescence were published in 1928, and she chose to present them not in a scientific paper but in a book written for a popular audience, *Coming of Age in Samoa.* Her publisher insisted that she add a long final chapter addressing American educational practices, and she obligingly drove home the implications of the Samoan case study for the understanding of American adolescence.

According to Mead, Samoan women moved easily from childhood through adolescence to adulthood without suffering difficult adjustments or strains. The nuclear family was embedded in a close-knit local community, and a child could turn to a wide range of surrogate parents, running free in a warm, tolerant extended family. Children were indulged and enjoyed considerable license. When adolescence came it "represented no period of crisis or stress, but was instead an orderly developing of a set of slowly maturing interests and activities. The girls' minds were perplexed by no conflicts, troubled by no philosophical queries, beset by no remote ambitions. To live as a girl with many lovers as long as possible, and then to marry in one's own

MARGARET MEAD in dancing dress in Samoa. Only twenty-three years old when she went to Samoa in 1925, and looking even younger, Margaret Mead carried out her research mainly among teenage girls, and she was easily assimilated into their social circle. Shortly after her death, in 1978, a slashing critique was published of her apprentice Samoan study. Her more mature research in New Guinea and Bali, conducted in collaboration with her second and third husbands, Reo Fortune and Gregory Bateson, has also had its detractors. Although by modern standards her research was superficial, she had a powerful understanding of the relevance of what she saw to the life of her own contemporaries in America, and the great gift of being able to communicate complex and novel ideas in a popular way.

village, near one's own relatives, and to have many children, these were uniform and satisfying ambitions." Adults were calm, easy-going, without strong passions.

In the final chapter of her book, Margaret Mead drew the moral for Americans. The disturbed adolescence typical of America was caused by several factors: sexual inhibitions; what Mead described as "the evils inherent in the too intimate family organization"; and above all the unpreparedness of the American child, confronted with a bewildering array of life choices—between religions, political loyalties, moral standards, and career possibilities. "The principal causes of our adolescents' difficulty," she concluded, "are the presence of conflicting standards and the belief that every individual should make his or her own choices, coupled with a feeling that choice is an important matter." Americans should rather encourage tolerant sexual attitudes, loosen the grip of the nuclear family, and design an educational system that would equip a young person to make rational choices.

Coming of Age in Samoa became one of the great best-sellers of the generation, and it was as a famous author that Margaret Mead returned to the Pacific to carry out further field studies. She was now more independent of Boas and under the influence of her friend—and for a time her lover—Ruth Benedict.

Benedict had become Boas's assistant in the 1920s, but she moved on from the Boasian obsession with local histories toward a view of cultures as integrated wholes, each with its own style and values. According to Benedict, human potential is only partially realized in any particular culture, which selects and develops just one of a range of possibilities, to create a coherent but necessarily limited design for living. In the process, each culture also fosters a specific personality type. At the time Margaret Mead went back to the Pacific, Ruth Benedict was in the throes of writing a book, *Patterns of Culture*, which was finally published in 1934. The questions of cultural patterning and personality with which it dealt were to preoccupy Margaret Mead in the new series of field studies that she was about to undertake.

Mead had not only found a new theoretical inspiration; while in America she also divorced her husband. In 1928 she married another anthropologist, Reo Fortune, whom she met on a boat when she traveled back to America from Samoa. He was a New Zealander, edgy, aggressive, a chip on his shoulder, but a formidably talented field-worker.

In 1931 Reo Fortune and Margaret Mead began a series of field studies in New Guinea, working intensively in three different societies over a period of two years. Mead wanted to follow up Ruth Benedict's ideas about cultural patterns and the personality traits which they fostered, but she was particularly interested now in relationships between men and women. If the experience of childhood and adolescence varied between cultures, the forms taken by masculinity and femininity might also be culturally variable. Culture molded personality, but it might use different molds for men and for women; and these might take little account of biological differences. "What I planned," Mead wrote later, "was research on the way sex roles are stylized in different cultures, as a necessary prerequisite to any study of innate biological differences between the sexes."

Mead and Fortune set out on a long march to a study area inland from the northeast coast of New Guinea, across the Torricelli range. Their carriers deserted them halfway, stranding them in a mountain village, Alitoa, among a people whom they were to call the Mountain Arapesh. "So we found ourselves with an exceedingly simple culture, one in which the personality and roles of men and women alike were stylized as parental, cherishing and mildly sexed." Aggression was unacceptable. In terms of stereotyped American notions, Arapesh adults, men and women alike, were all supposed to behave in a rather feminine way. Margaret Mead found the Arapesh rather dull, but she approved of their arrangement of gender roles. Reo Fortune, however, found the men appallingly unmanly.

In 1932 Mead and Fortune moved on to the Mundugumor, a people living on the Yuat River, who had only been under firm government control for some three years. Reputed to be cannibals, certainly very fierce, the Mundugumor "preyed on their miserable swamp-dwelling neighbours and carried off their women to swell the households of the leading men." Like the Arapesh, the Mundugumor did not believe that men and women should behave in different ways, but the contrast between the two societies could hardly have been more sharp.

"The Mundugumor contrasted with the Arapesh in every conceivable way. Fierce possessive men and women were the preferred type; warm and cherishing men and women were culturally disallowed." (Fortune found himself in sympathy with these fierce people; Mead was repelled by their callous treatment of each other, and especially of their children. She was also dismayed to find that Fortune was very hard on her when she fell ill.)

In 1933 they moved to the Sepik river, and here they found an English anthropologist, Gregory Bateson, already at work. Bateson was the scion of a famous scientific family; his father, William Bateson, was the man who had rediscovered the work of Mendel. Indeed, Gregory was named after the great Silesian monk. He had studied anthropology at Cambridge with one of the pioneers of British field anthropology, A. C. Haddon. Reo Fortune had been a fellow student. They were already rivals. ("Haddon is very kind to me," Fortune once reported to Mead, "but he gave Gregory Bateson his mosquito net.")

Bateson explained that in the community he was studying, the Iatmul, sex roles *were* differentiated. Moreover, the contrasts between men and women were the subject of reflection and ritual play. He was investigating a ceremony, *naven,* which involved transvestism and other sex role reversals. Each man exchanged clothes with his father's sister, the men donning filthy workaday clothes, the women preening themselves in the finest ceremonial dress of the men; and they played at other inversions of normal behavior, including incest and homosexuality.

Generously, Bateson introduced Fortune and Mead to a neighboring community, the Tchambuli, who seemed to resemble the Iatmul in many ways. Mead and Fortune established themselves on the beautiful Chambri Lake, and found that here, as among the Iatmul, male and female roles were markedly different from each other. But for an American, the pattern of these roles was unexpected, reversing the American stereotypes of what men and women should be like. The women were brisk, businesslike managers, working in cooperative groups to run the affairs of the community. They were also sexually assertive. As for the men, they had long ago abandoned warfare, and although they were formally in charge of the households, "in fact the women managed all the valuables, dressed up the men and children, and went about their business unadorned, business-like and competent. Meanwhile, down by the lake shore in the ceremonial houses, the men carved and painted, gossiped and had temper tantrums, and played out their rivalries."

The villages in which the three scholars worked were within walking distance, and when the manuscript of Ruth Benedict's *Patterns of Culture* came into Mead's hands it stimulated a long, creative discussion. They had been studying how gender roles varied, but now an even more fundamental issue presented itself. The question, Mead recalled in her autobiography, was whether "there were other kinds of innate differences—differences as important as those between the sexes, but that cut across sex lines."

The debate soon developed a personal edge, as the two men played out their rivalry. The emotional triangle became very intense. "Gregory and I were falling in love," Mead later recalled, "but this was kept firmly under control while all three of us tried to translate the intensity of our feelings into better and more perceptive fieldwork." Even this emotional experience taught a theoretical lesson: "Gregory and I were close together in temperament—represented, in fact, a male and a female version of a temperamental type that was in strong contrast with the one represented by Reo." When she finally left Fortune for Bateson, she gave as one reason that only married people had a chance to finish their conversations.

The more academic conclusion of their theoretical debate was that there existed a limited repertoire of innate temperaments. Each culture selects some of these natural possibilities to construct its ideal types, and quite often a culture will fit two contrasting temperamental types to the male-female opposition. Mead published these conclusions in a semi-popular book, *Sex and Temperament*, which appeared in 1935.

Margaret Mead and Gregory Bateson traveled together to Bali, where they studied mother-child relations. When war threatened they returned together to the United States, and during the Second World War they collaborated in war work, attempting to apply anthropological ideas to the study of allies and enemies.

Mead and Bateson also had a child, and characteristically Mead insisted on feeding her daughter on demand, like a mother in New

Guinea. She arranged for the birth to be filmed, and applied her professional expertise with her accustomed vigor to the question of raising a child. Her pediatrician was Benjamin Spock, and she persuaded him to abandon the strict feeding schedules that American doctors imposed on mothers. Spock was later to write the most influential book ever published on the care of babies, and Mead's theories came to influence the American way of bringing up children.

After the war, Margaret Mead switched from ethnographic fieldwork to public affairs, becoming one of the great American gurus of the century. Incredibly active—"almost a principle of pure energy," Bateson commented—she counted even a night's sleep wasted if she didn't have an interesting dream. She was on every possible national committee, writing in every magazine, appearing on every radio program. For the American public she became the personification of anthropology. Her reputation reached such a point that a joke circulated in which she was introduced to the Oracle of Delphi and demanded, "Hello, isn't there something *you'd* like to know?"

The message for which Mead proselytized was a popular version of what was called cultural relativism. Human beings were malleable, formed by their cultures, though not with total efficiency. Every culture produced misfits, some of whom might turn out to be the most creative members of the community: artists, prophets, healers, even occasionally the inventors of new cultural practices. Cultural variation was certainly not connected with racial differences, and even sex and age differences were modified significantly by custom. Upbringing was more crucial than heredity in shaping the human adult. In Mead's work, the power of culture was very great, the force of biological constraints less evident.

M ARGARET MEAD died in 1978. Although she had become far and away the most famous anthropologist in the world, her professional reputation was never entirely secure. That she was a shrewd and dedicated fieldworker nobody could doubt, even if her linguistic skills were called into question. "Reo had a better ear than I have and Gregory had a much better ear," she commented, "but neither of them ever knew whose pig was dead. I always knew whose pig was dead." Nevertheless, her Samoan study and her three "sex and temperament" ethnographic vignettes are based on fieldwork that is, by modern standards, superficial. She was well aware that many colleagues were skeptical about her results, and in her autobiography she quotes Gregory Bateson to the effect that "anthropologists who had read my work but did not know me tended to doubt my conclusions because they could not allow for the speed with which I worked." More to the point, they missed the detail, the ethnographic underpinnings, which buttress the authority of most ethnographies, and they distrusted her airy generalizations about national characters.

It was only after Margaret Mead's death, however, that a direct attack was made on her reputation as an ethnographer. The challenge was addressed to her first field study, of Samoan adolescents, and it was mounted by Derek Freeman, a retired professor at the Australian National University at Canberra.

Freeman had first done fieldwork in 1940 in Western Samoa, where he spent two years, eventually coming to the conclusion that things were not as Mead had described them. "By the time I left Samoa in November 1943," he has recorded, "I knew that I would one day face the responsibility of writing a refutation of Mead's Samoan findings." He wrote once to Mead, to alert her to his criticism, but he delayed until some years after her death before publishing his book, *Margaret Mead and Samoa: The Making and Unmaking of an Anthropological Myth,* which appeared in 1983.

One part of Freeman's critique deals with Mead's general picture of Samoa (or at least of Manu'a, that Samoan backwater, as it had been in the twenties) as a tolerant, relaxed, traditional society. Records of the American courts in Samoa suggested that the crime rate in the twenties compared unfavorably with that of Chicago (and, Freeman suggested, with London in the early years of the century, citing a rather antiquated study of delinquent adolescents by none other than Cyril Burt). This compilation of crime figures had apparently held Freeman up for a decade, but crime rates are notoriously unreliable indicators of violence, and it is not at all clear how many cases of violent crime from the remoter parts of Samoa came to the attention of the courts.

But Freeman's main concern was Mead's representation of childhood and family life in Samoa. According to Mead, a child's relationship with its parents was not as fraught with emotion as it is in a typical American family. Parenting was shared by a wide circle of adults in the extended family; children could turn for comfort to surrogate parents. Freeman insisted to the contrary that the basic family relationships in Samoa were much as elsewhere. Mother-child bonding was crucial, adoptive relationships rare. Strong attachment to biological parents was the norm.

Mead maintained that children were indulged and enjoyed great freedom, but according to Freeman parental discipline in Samoa is strict and frequently violent. Children are conditioned to accept authority without question. They may react with anger to this strict discipline, but they are cowed by the threat of even more severe punishments. In consequence there is considerable covert hostility to parents.

According to Mead, Samoan adults are calm, without strong passions, "easy, balanced human beings." In Freeman's view, the adult Samoan hides his feelings behind elaborate etiquette, but is liable to outbreaks of rage and periods of sullen sulking which are called *musu* in Samoan, glossed by Robert Louis Stevenson (who was a resident there for some time) as meaning "literally cross, but always in the sense of stubbornness and resistance." Suicide and hysterical illness are common.

A vital part of Mead's argument (and an important element in its popular appeal) was her observation that the Samoans did not suffer from sexual frustration. The one snake in the grass in this Pacific Eden was the *moetotolo,* or sleep crawler. "The *moetotolo* is the only sex activity which presents a definitely abnormal picture," she wrote. "Ever since the first contact with white civilization, rape in the form of violent assault has occurred occasionally in Samoa. It is far less congenial, however, to the Samoan attitude than *moetotolo,* in which a man stealthily appropriates the favours which are meant for another."

Freeman was scornful. Samoans greatly value virginity, and when a girl marries her virginity is publicly tested in a defloration ceremony, in which her husband breaks her hymen with his finger. Virginity is

normal until marriage. Freeman even claimed, somewhat mysteri-
ously, that he and his wife had conducted a virgin census in one
village. All this puts the activity of the sleep crawler in a very different
light. He is not simply filching the prerogatives of an established
lover, he is raping a virgin. The girl is left with no alternative but to
marry her rapist, which is precisely his object.

Margaret Mead's *Coming of Age in Samoa* was based upon an apprentice study by a young scholar in her early twenties, carried out
at a stage when ethnographic fieldwork methods were still being
pioneered. Her reputation as an ethnographer was never assured
in professional circles, and by the 1980s few anthropologists were
surprised to learn that her first field study was unreliable.

Yet while Freeman's ethnographic criticism is not disputed on most
points (though its scabrous tone was widely deplored), the conclusions that he drew from his restudy are a different matter. Freeman
claims that by discrediting Margaret Mead's Samoan findings he has
kicked away the essential crutch of cultural relativism. The claim
has only to be formulated in this way for its absurdity to be apparent.
By the late twentieth century, a relativist could draw upon many more
substantial studies than Mead's. Some of her colleagues accepted
Freeman's critique of Mead's Samoan ethnography but believed
Mead's real theoretical error was that she had not been relativist
enough.

In any case, Freeman's critique suffered because he did no more
than sketch, in the vaguest terms, an alternative to the cultural
relativism for which he castigated Mead. He seemed to lean toward
the biological party, which posits a bed-rock of "human nature," even
of "nature," that is shared by all human beings, perhaps all primates.
Freeman had worked briefly with Konrad Lorenz and had also trained
as a psychoanalyst, and in 1979 he had written to his university
authorities repudiating his discipline of social anthropology and asking for his chair to be redesignated in the field of human ethology.
Yet while in his book he hints somewhat coyly at general propositions
about human nature, he is cagey about whether he expects these to
be of the sort proposed by Lorenz, by E. O. Wilson, or even by Freud.
His general conclusion is simply banal: "The time is now conspicuously due, in both anthropology and biology, for a synthesis in which

there will be, in the study of human behavior, recognition of the radical importance of both the genetic and the exogenetic and their interaction, both in the past history of the human species and in our problematic future." Even Margaret Mead could have said amen to that.

Because Freeman did not suggest an alternative theory or even provide a full alternative ethnography of Samoa, he has ultimately done no more than discredit a particular ethnography. Ironically, Mead's main theoretical conclusion nevertheless still stands. Freeman himself cites, without demur, an authoritative study which concluded that "research on ordinary adolescents has generally failed to substantiate claims of the inevitability and universality of adolescent stress."

B Y the time Freeman's book appeared, however, the biological party was promoting a more coherent theory to counter the exponents of cultural relativism, one that was particularly concerned with questions of gender.

Darwin had suggested that the different selective pressures operating on men and on women favored larger, stronger, and more aggressive males, and females who attract male interest and have strong maternal feelings. In industrial societies, these pressures have abated; but after eons of evolution we are left with characteristic types of male and female, bred for their historic functions. Starting from the axiom of modern evolutionary theory, that fitness is measured by success in procreation, the biological party now preferred to argue that women are defined above all by their maternal roles, and that men have a natural interest in their offspring, the bearers of their genes.

A view of human history was becoming current that represented the division of labor between the sexes as stable and of very long standing. In most places, for most of human history (so went the argument), young women could not be risked in hazardous operations. They would normally either be pregnant or nursing young children. While women nurtured children and kept the home fires burning, men fought and hunted. The primary attachment of women was to their children, while men bonded with other men to form cooperative teams to protect the group, and competed among themselves for access to the women.

In 1969 Lionel Tiger published a book, *Men in Groups,* that gave a powerful account of this thesis. The conclusion was that there have always been fixed gender roles, and for good reason. They constitute the most effective adaptation to the sexual functions of males and females.

The main opposition to the resurgent biological party came from feminist theorists, who were reluctant to concede that family arrangements and gender roles were given by nature. "Freud's ideas on feminine psychology," complained Eva Figes, "all spring from the tenet that woman's role in life is to stay at home, be passive in relation to man, bear and raise children." She went on to make the remarkable claim that "of all the factors that have served to perpetuate a male-oriented society, that have hindered the free development of women as human beings in the Western world today, the emergence of Freudian psychoanalysis has been the most serious." Others, however, took an equally dim view of ethology and sociobiology, which also assumed that families provide a necessary framework for human reproduction, and that a woman's destiny is to be played out as a wife and mother.

The feminist response was that women might bear the children, but that the family was a male construction, a cultural artifact. While granting, even celebrating, woman's role as procreatrix, they represented fathers as parasites upon the natural unit of mother and child, who could do perfectly well without them if only society were better ordered. It was the patriarchal system that limited the potential of women, not female nature.

The new pacemakers of the cultural party were not down-the-line successors of Margaret Mead. Mead had denied that gender roles were a straightforward expression of sexual differences; witness the variety of forms they took in different cultures. Feminist anthropologists agreed that gender roles were not ineluctably shaped by the biology of sex. Yet some, at least, denied that gender roles were as picturesquely various as Margaret Mead liked to suggest. The position of women was everywhere the same, at least in essence: for women everywhere were subordinated by men.

Feminism came into its own in the 1970s. This was a time when Marxist ideas were enjoying a revival among Western intellectuals. The idea of a patriarchal domination of women was not in itself a novel one, and some feminists rediscovered the ideas about the family and the oppression of women that had been developed nearly a century earlier by Marx's collaborator, Friedrich Engels.

Engels represented the family as an instrument for male ascendancy. He seized upon the theories of some Victorian anthropologists, who imagined an original condition of life in which fatherhood was socially unimportant. Family groups did not exist in early society. Women banded together, forming promiscuous and temporary attachment to males. Then came the rise of patriarchal power. For most Victorian anthropologists, this represented a great step forward. Engels, however, wrote:

> The overthrow of mother right was *the world historical defeat of the female sex.* The man took command in the home also; the woman was degraded and reduced to servitude; she became the slave of his lust and a mere instrument for the production of children. This degraded position of the woman . . . has gradually been palliated and glossed over, and sometimes clothed in a milder form; in no sense has it been abolished.

Within the modern family, he continued, the husband "is the bourgeois, and the wife represents the proletariat." The equality of women would be won only when the family in its present form was overthrown.

Engels, it had to be admitted, was the prisoner of some very old anthropological illusions. Matriarchy had not universally preceded patriarchy. In fact one could not talk about matriarchy or patriarchy without radical qualifications. Men were in charge of public affairs almost everywhere. Nor was the family the invention of the modern bourgeoisie. Nevertheless, some feminist writers were convinced that Engels was right on the essentials: the family system suppressed women.

How then had men established their almost universal ascendancy over women? Either through the abuse of brute physical strength, or, according to a more complex theory, because their initial specialization as hunters gave them a monopoly on weapons, and also the chance to explore new opportunities for trade and thus for the accumulation of resources. This argument was in the traditional Marxist mold, even if the more imaginative flourishes of Engels had been abandoned. The classical Marxist position was that the ruling class controlled the means of production, and this monopoly was the basis of their power. All else was mere technique, although Marx had allowed ideology a role in the machinery of domination. Religion, he remarked, was the opium of the workers, and it was dispensed by a cynical elite. But this was all secondary: what really mattered was who controlled the factories, the banks, what Lenin called the commanding heights of the economy.

In the 1970s, other kinds of Marxist argument became influential. These paid more attention to the ways in which hearts and minds were controlled. One of the most fashionable writers in this period was the Italian communist Antonio Gramsci. Imprisoned by Mussolini, Gramsci had evolved a new doctrine of what he called "hegemony." He argued that class domination depended above all on making people believe that the ruling class enjoyed a moral or spiritual ascendancy, which was more important than the brute control of material resources. The ruling class maintained its grip because it controlled the educational system and the media.

Ideological accounts of domination became standard, and sociologists began to concentrate their attention on the work of the media in shaping public opinion. Michel Foucault, another theorist who was very fashionable in the seventies and eighties, initiated a new stream of research, developing a series of brilliant analyses of the ways in which systems of knowledge acted as mechanisms of political control. As industrial society became more complex, so new professional specialists were created—psychiatrists, criminologists, teachers—who wielded the power of an apparently neutral expertise to rule a segment of society, or to tighten the grip of the system on deviants.

A parallel thesis was developed within symbolic anthropology to account for the apparent male victory in the battle of the sexes. In an influential essay published in 1974, the American anthropologist

Sherry Ortner accepted that "the secondary status of woman in society is one of the true universals, a pan-cultural fact." Yet while this was generally and unhappily the "true universal" fact, the cause was not biological but cultural. Men had imposed this subordination on women by means of a gigantic lie, a cultural trick of staggering proportions. Ortner's view was that the subordination of women requires the elaboration of myths and symbolic representations. These disguise the fact that women are potentially capable of performing any masculine task, fulfilling any male role. Women can even carry out their feminine role of procreation perfectly well without being burdened with husbands. Women are the victims of culture, not nature.

There are several ironies in this thesis. For generations, the argument over the position of women had been waged between the proponents of a universal nature and a variable culture. Ortner's innovation was to treat this opposition between nature and culture as an artifact, an ideological statement. But unlike most cultural inventions, this one was to be found in virtually every culture, and everywhere it took the same basic form. Women were associated with nature, men with culture; and since culture was always valued above nature, women were regarded as lesser beings than men.

The association of women with nature followed from a view of women that emphasized their reproductive functions. The essence of womanhood was to give birth, to feed and nurture. But as natural beings in a cultural world, women were also regarded as a threatening presence. Their reproductive activities were treated as dangerous and polluting. Childbirth and menstruation were typically hedged with taboos. Men, on the contrary, were associated particularly with technology and with public affairs, and thus with culture and the control of nature—including women. The upshot was that women were not subordinate because the nature of men and women so dictated; they were culturally defined as natural and so as inferior creatures.

There was another twist to this ideological trick. The place of women—their natural vocation—was in the home. This left the public domain to the men, giving them opportunities to manipulate political and economic resources in their own interest. The public identity of women derived from their menfolk. There was (wrote Ortner and Harriet Whitehead in 1981) a general "tendency for the image of women to be refracted through different modes of attachment to men." A woman was in the first place a wife or a sister of a particular man, and that fixed her position in the community.

Whatever their other differences, the feminist theorists generally agreed on a radical and fundamental premise: they shared the belief that the subjugation of women is universal, but caused by cultural processes rather than by biological determinants. Mead would certainly have been astonished at this assumption, and perhaps not without reason, for it has proved to be vulnerable to a relativist challenge. This challenge was a weighty one, since contemporary relativists have more sophisticated tools at their disposal than the impressionistic monographs of a Margaret Mead.

Ethnographic studies in a variety of societies show that women are seldom a homogeneous group, and that other roles may be more important in shaping their life-chances than those which follow from their gender. Women may be defined as mothers, wives, sisters, and daughters, but a woman may also be treated as in the first place an adolescent or an adult, a fellow-villager or a stranger, a noble or a commoner. Any one of these attributes may be more significant for her status than the fact that she is female.

Nor is work necessarily gender-specific, though almost everywhere women are primarily responsible for child care, housekeeping, and cooking, while men hunt, wage war, and make weapons and many tools. (Gender specialization in the making of pottery and clothing is less predictable.) Some types of economy do tend to be associated with a specific division of labor by sex. Women in foraging societies seldom hunt, but they often provide the bulk of the meals, by gathering wild foods (though men also participate in gathering). In pastoral societies, there is often sharp sexual segregation. Women are often relatively unproductive, and are subject to strict control by fathers and husbands. In other types of economic systems, the division of labor by sex may be less marked. The strongest predictor of what will be considered women's work is the compatibility of such work with child care, but this varies by age, wealth, and status.

The division of labor affects social status. Where women contribute significantly to production, or trade freely, there may be little if any discrimination against their participation in other activities. Though there are no societies in which the fact of being a woman is actually an advantage in achieving influence and authority (except in very restricted contexts), it is not universally true that men control women. Quite commonly, women enjoy considerable autonomy in their domestic affairs. There are also many societies in which women monopolize some economic activities, and in most societies they are more or less equal partners in the business of sustaining the family. Public affairs are more usually in the hands of men, but women— particularly older women—are often influential, especially in ritual matters. In hunter-gatherer societies, some women become band leaders. Moreover, as many anthropologists have remarked, there is a distinction between the realities of power and their formal representation. Women are often more autonomous and powerful than they may seem.

I N the early 1980s, half a century after Mead and her husband Reo Fortune had studied the Tchambuli, two American anthropologists, Deborah Gewertz and her husband Frederick Errington, returned to these people (whom they called, using the modern orthography, the Chambri). Deborah Gewertz's mother had owned a copy of Mead's *Male and Female,* a popular book in which the Tchambuli figured as a mirror image of the Americans. Here apparently was a society in which women managed the business of the community, tolerating the vanities of their preening, artistic, impractical menfolk. This image of the Tchambuli had inspired women like Gewertz's mother to foster what Americans had once deprecated as "masculine" qualities in their daughters.

Coming to the Chambri, Gewertz expected to feel comfortable with local notions of proper female behavior. To her mortification, she almost immediately found that she was shut out of a session about secret ritual knowledge between a key informant and her husband. The other women of the household accepted their exclusion without complaint. Evidently matters were more complicated than Mead had led Deborah Gewertz to expect.

The trouble, as Gewertz and Errington diagnosed it, was that "Mead underestimated the extent to which cultures differ from each other." Margaret Mead certainly repudiated the American belief that men were naturally practical, dominant, public-minded, and women the reverse; but when she saw that the Chambri women were very active in the economy on their own account, sexually adventurous, and assertive, she assumed that they were like American males. Because Chambri males went in for self-decoration and other vanities, Mead saw them as being rather like American females. Among the Chambri, however, men and women live separate lives, each concerned with their own affairs. The independence of women, their autonomy in certain economic pursuits, does not give them control over men. The Chambri women are playing different games from both American men and American women.

Mead's American perspective also made her misread the motives of the Chambri, as in her interpretation of why they are so troubled by the position of young widows. The Chambri pay a bride-price, but this is variable and open to negotiation. Men are obsessed by these negotiations, but women pay them little heed. According to Margaret Mead, this was because the women are too down-to-earth and impatient with shilly-shallying to tolerate the delicate diplomatic maneuvers involved. Errington and Gewertz disagreed with this interpretation. In their view, the Chambri women ignore the bridewealth game because they know that their own position will not be greatly affected by the negotiations.

If a woman is already set on marrying a particular man, he cannot be charged a high price. Thinking in American terms, Margaret Mead suggested that Chambri men knew and feared the sexual independence of women, and this made them worry particularly about young widows. They believed that given half a chance the widow would simply go out and find a man for herself, putting at risk the investment which her late husband's family had made in her. Accordingly, they did their best to arrange a quick remarriage to another man in the family.

Again, Gewertz and Errington disagreed. The concern that a widow arouses has less to do with a nervous recognition of her sexual independence than with a dread of what she might do with the secret

knowledge she will have acquired. A married woman learns the totemic names of her husband's family, and this gives her a hold over
them. The men of the family are terrified that she will impart the
secret names to a lover. That was why Deborah Gewertz had been
excluded from the secret knowledge into which her husband had
been initiated early in their field study.

A N impatient reader may by now be wondering when, if ever, the
question will be resolved. Are gender roles very diverse or are
they not? To what extent can culture reshape nature?

Yet an equally interesting lesson can be learned from the very
difficulty that anthropologists have in resolving these apparently
straightforward questions. The facts do not always speak for themselves, and sometimes they refuse to talk straight at all.

Derek Freeman has a rather simple faith in the power of facts, and
in a recent documentary film he has tried to prove his contention
that Margaret Mead was systematically misled by her Samoan informants. The high point of the film is the appearance of an eighty-
year-old Samoan lady. She is identified as one of Margaret Mead's
informants from 1925, and a voice-over tells us that "her account
will settle once and for all the controversy." She then speaks, in
Samoan, and we are given a translation: Yes, she says, we lied to
Margaret Mead. We lied and lied.

Proof positive? Hardly. The film was made sixty years after the
event, and witnesses are not always able to recall precisely what
happened so long ago. Moreover, it is possible that she was put
under some pressure, since Samoa is now dominated by puritanical
Christians, who are appalled by the image of Samoan women given
by Mead. Finally, of course, how can one believe somebody who tells
one she is a liar? This is the famous paradox of Epimenides the
Cretan, who said that all Cretans are liars. If that is true, he is lying.
If he is telling the truth, then what he says is false.

For many anthropologists, the most interesting aspect of the
Freeman-Mead controversy, and indeed of the less controversial but
more sophisticated ethnographic critiques like that of Gewertz and

Errington, is that they put on the agenda the question of how far any ethnographer can understand another culture.

Franz Boas, the foremost ethnographer of his generation, had relied largely on texts dictated by informants, from which he put together compilations of oral history and folklore. He did not often draw on his own direct observation. Consequently, his documentation of certain aspects of culture was highly reliable, but his ethnographic writings give little sense of how people actually behave.

Margaret Mead preferred direct observation, but her methods were rough and ready, her command of languages was inadequate, and by modern standards she spent too brief a period in any community. More thorough fieldwork procedures had been pioneered, however, by the time she went to Samoa. Bronislaw Malinowski spent two years between 1915 and 1918 in the Trobriand Islands. Working in the vernacular, he developed there the methods that became standard in modern ethnographic research—methods designed to allow the ethnographer to penetrate beyond the official version of how things are done to the realities of life as it is lived.

Malinowski insisted that the observer had to understand the native language and appreciate the actor's point of view in order to assess what he was told, to grasp the difference between what people said and what they did. Actions had meaning, and they had to be interpreted in the light of actors' intentions. People guessed at each other's motives and adjusted their own behavior accordingly in order to achieve goals that might be hidden, contradictory, culturally specific, and situationally variable. The observer had to "come off the verandah" (as Malinowski said, in what became a famous phrase), because the detachment of a Boas, diligently recording rules, myths, and historical accounts, lent only the illusion of objectivity, and actually inhibited a genuine understanding of what was going on.

Ethnographic fieldwork on the Malinowski model became one of the main research strategies in the human sciences. But despite its successes, it is evident that the move from the neutral, precise, and systematic methods of Boas and his generation to the personal, messy, homemade methods of Malinowski and Margaret Mead had its costs.

MALINOWSKI in the Trobriand Islands. Bronislaw Malinowski (1884–1942) was a Polish scholar who became the leading social anthropologist in Britain. Between 1915 and 1918 he conducted field research in the Trobriand Islands off New Guinea, carrying ethnographic research to a new level of professional sophistication. Previous ethnographers had generally been content with informants' reports and with the collection of texts; Malinowski insisted on the importance of direct observation, and he demonstrated the systematic difference between what people say and what they do, indicating a tension between rules and practice that was to be a central theme of his monographs. In this photograph he poses opposite a Trobriand man, who is wearing a wig.

If the observer has to participate in social life in order to get a true sense of what is going on, then appeals to the authority of personal experience and to unique insights become uncomfortably prominent. Consequently, it is not easy to correct for observer bias, or to choose between two accounts of a culture.

By the 1960s, other anthropologists and psychologists had made studies in Samoa. One, Lowell Holmes, had gone to Mead's Samoan village thirty years after her study, specifically in order to reassess her work. He concluded that it was substantially correct, but Margaret Mead recognized that the accounts of Holmes and of other scholars diverged from her own on several points. According to Freeman, she had simply got it all wrong, because she had been duped by playful Samoan girls; but Mead herself suggested two other plausible explanations for discrepancies between her account and those of others.

First, it was possible that she had happened upon an island that differed from mainstream Samoan culture. Freeman rejected this argument, but it is quite likely that at least some of the divergences between her studies and his might be explained in this way, since she had been working in another part of Samoa (under a different colonial regime, with different missionary influences and with a different economic base) twenty years—and a world war—before Freeman's fieldwork.

The second possibility raised by Mead is that she had inadvertently adopted the perspective of the girls with whom she had spent most of her time. It is certainly possible that Samoans had two conflicting theories about adolescence, one propounded by adults, the other an unofficial, underground ideology of the young people themselves. Freeman, an authoritarian New Zealander who gloried in his honorary title as chief, may be presenting the point of view of respectable elders, while Mead (who went into the field a diminutive twenty-three-year-old, and who participated mainly in the activities of adolescent girls) may be generalizing from what was an informal subculture. She may also well have given a reliable account of what the girls were up to behind the backs of their elders.

According to one body of opinion within anthropology, uncertainties of this kind are inevitable, and it is virtually impossible to choose between conflicting accounts of another culture. Each ethnographer is the prisoner of his or her native culture, and will be restricted by his or her age, gender, and personal qualities. The more one believes that cultures really are very different, and the more one accepts that they influence personality, perceptions, and values, the more likely it is that any account of another culture must be treated as itself the product of a specific, culturally conditioned point of view.

In short, driven far enough, cultural relativism undermines the authority of its own witnesses. We cannot trust the Samoan lady who says that all Samoan girls are liars; but nor should we put too much faith in the objectivity of a cultural anthropologist who tells us that nothing can be seen except through particular cultural spectacles.

Even if one takes a less extreme position, and grants the reliability of the observations made by a good ethnographer—a Malinowski, perhaps, rather than a Mead—the interpretation of observations remains problematic. Chambri men worry about young widows; on that Mead, Gewertz, and Errington agreed. But what motivates their concern? That was a matter of interpretation. Mead assumed that the answer was evident, for any man would naturally worry about valuable assets getting out of his control; but according to Gewertz and Errington, she failed to recognize the more profound anxieties Chambri men had about the power of the secret family knowledge that wives acquired.

These are, broadly speaking, problems of translation. The ethnographer divines the meaning of behavior and then translates it into our language, but tries not to lose the nuances, the values and ideas that give the behavior its meaning in context. This is obviously more difficult than simply describing what one sees; but it is essential if one wants to understand the meaning of behavior.

No translation is definitive, however. Clifford Geertz, the leading relativist in contemporary anthropology, defines a culture as a symbolic system, a web of meanings. The anthropologist is trying to understand and communicate from one web to another. This is a personal, probably ultimately impossible, though worthwhile endeavor, comparable to the attempt to translate a Japanese haiku into English. Except at the most elementary level, such an enterprise cannot be judged to be correct or incorrect; but equally there can be no definitive translation.

If there is so much uncertainty involved in the process of apprehending another culture, then cross-cultural comparisons will inevitably be very tricky indeed: perhaps quite intractable. Is the position of a Chambri widow, bonded by bride-price, comparable to the position of a widow in societies without bride-price? How can one compare the degree of sexual freedom allowed to a Chambri woman and a Samoan woman?

These methodological problems are deeply disturbing, since they raise questions about the nature of our common humanity. Cultural relativism presents awkward ethical issues. Margaret Mead was acutely aware of this. She believed that cultures could shape people to behave in a variety of ways: to be more cooperative or more competitive, more caring or more violent, to value individual variation or to stamp on deviance. But in each culture one also finds a specific hierarchy of values. Is there any way of judging the practices of another culture without simply denying that their values, their judgments are as valid as your own? Can one find a general human reason for condemning—or condoning—debt slavery, or the excision of the clitoris in female initiation, or the stoning to death of adulterers?

Some writers have suggested that there are universally acknowledged, bedrock values; but it is hard to find any ethical principles that command assent in all cultural traditions. Others might prefer to seek, with Robin Fox, an ethic based on our real human nature; but it is hard to be sure what ingredients make up that common, underlying nature, and even if they could be identified they might be worth modifying if we can do so.

Of all the issues raised by cross-cultural studies, the most sensitive have to do with human rights, since the very concept makes no sense unless the rights in question should be enjoyed by all human beings, regardless of where they happen to live. Since Aristotle at least, Western philosophers have therefore tried to specify the fundamental moral basis of political association. This quest for a universal basis of civility is the subject of the next chapter.

· 9 ·

THE ORIGIN OF
SOCIETY

Reflecting on the essential conditions of social existence, the philosophers of the European Enlightenment found it helpful to imagine what human life might have been like without government or society. They thought that before people came together to form civil societies, they must have lived in what they termed a state of nature. Individuals in the state of nature were free, independent, and equal, but they were also insecure and uncultivated. Granted the capacity to reason, they would have been willing to exchange their rude independence for security and civilization. Yet this choice was not free of risk. Once native freedom was compromised, it might be totally extinguished by a powerful government. Born free, in a state of nature, the individual might end up in chains, in an unjust society.

Conservative writers thought that governments should be strong, and accordingly they tended to emphasize the horrors of life in a state of nature. "In such condition," wrote Thomas Hobbes in 1651, sheltering in exile as the regicide Oliver Cromwell prepared to take power at home, "there is . . . no knowledge of the face of the earth; no account of time; no arts; no letters; no society; and which is worst of all, continual fear, and danger of violent death; and the life of man, solitary, poor, nasty, brutish, and short." Since the state of nature was a state of war, Hobbes argued that strong government was required to provide order. In return for that great good, people would be prepared to surrender their liberty.

Liberal and radical writers, concerned to promote individual liberty, were more inclined to celebrate the advantages of life in the state of nature. Jean-Jacques Rousseau suffused the natural human condition in a pastoral glow. Writing in 1762, he described natural man as "an animal weaker than some, and less agile than others; but, taking him all around, the most advantageously-organized of any. I see him slaking his thirst at the first brook, finding his bed at the foot of the tree which afforded him a repast; and, with that, all his wants supplied." Above all, he celebrated the individual's enjoyment of freedom and—necessarily—equality in a natural state.

Although Rousseau presented the most persuasive view of the advantages of the state of nature, he extolled the cultural benefits offered by society in a famous passage.

> And although in civil society man surrenders some of the advantages that belong to the state of nature, he gains in return far greater ones; his faculties are so exercised and developed, his mind is so enlarged, his sentiments so ennobled, and his whole spirit so elevated that . . . he should constantly bless the happy hour that lifted him for ever from the state of nature and from a narrow, stupid animal made a creature of intelligence and a man.

Whatever their political differences, the philosophers of the Enlightenment agreed that rational individuals had rightly elected to enter society, because membership paid off for them. But once the step was taken, they had to submit to a government. Since a government was instituted by a social contract, a pact between free and equal individuals, acting for their own advantage, the philosophers concluded that legitimate government derives its authority from the consent of its subjects. But equally, once the pact has been sealed the individual is subject to the authority of the state. The balance to be struck between individual and state was the central issue in political debate.

The state of nature, the rationalist alternative to Eden, was a fantasy, a thought experiment. Nevertheless, writers in the Enlightenment tradition more or less seriously imagined that in the course of their voyages European explorers might stumble upon some people still living in that aboriginal condition. "Thus in the beginning," John Locke wrote in 1690, "all the world was *America*." A party of native Americans might still be enjoying the freedoms of our most ancient ancestors.

For a Darwinian, it was simply absurd to think that some early humans had engineered a historic break with an aboriginal state of nature. Early human society was not the product of reason. On the contrary, the earliest human societies must have resembled the societies of other apes. Therefore, some natural social bond must have provided the initial basis of a broader sociability. And this primordial bond, the early anthropologists agreed, could only have been blood relationship. "The history of political ideas," wrote an English law professor, Henry Maine, in 1861, "begins, in fact, with the assumption that kinship in blood is the sole possible ground of community in political functions."

The alternative to blood loyalties was local patriotism, but this, they thought, had evolved much later. It was taken for granted that early humans were nomadic. Territorially based associations had become significant only at a late stage in human history. According to Maine, a great revolution occurred, perhaps the greatest revolutionary moment in the political history of our species, when territorial loyalties became more important than kinship ties. Kinship and territory, blood and soil, were antithetical principles of association.

However, as reliable studies began to be made of simple, small-scale human societies, it became evident that these principles could be combined. Ethnographers reported that territory, local rootedness, was by no means unimportant even among foragers and pastoralists. Even nomadic groups had a local identity. According to the ethologists, moreover, "territoriality" was based on an instinct shared with other species. Nevertheless, it was generally agreed that in small-scale, technologically simple communities, descent—Maine's blood relationships—was ideologically more important than local loyalties. And such societies, it was thought, provided clues to the conditions of life of early human communities.

The type-case of small-scale societies, living from hunting and gathering, was, as ever, taken to be the Australian aborigines. The British anthropologist A. R. Radcliffe-Brown characterized the social structure of these societies in an influential monograph in 1931. Reviewing two generations of field research, he concluded that the basic unit of Australian society was the "band." The Australians had two kinds of descent groups, matrilineal and patrilineal, but it was the patrilineal grouping that formed a local band. Bands were therefore made up of groups of men related in the male line, with their wives and children. Each band was also associated with a particular territory, and this territory was sacred, being identified with totemic spirits.

This model was generalized by the American scholars Julian Steward and Elman Service. In an article published in 1936, Steward argued that the most common form of band society was ordered by patrilineal descent: descent traced through males only to a common ancestor. Each band was made up of a single patrilineal lineage (that is, all the descendants in the male line of one ancestor). Such patrilineal bands were "politically autonomous, communally land owning, exogamous, patrilocal, patrilineal in land inheritance, and consisting theoretically or actually of a single lineage, which, however, comprises several house-holds or elemental bilateral families." The implication was that early human societies had been patrilineal bands associated with specific territories.

How, then, were more complex societies ordered? In the first half of the twentieth century, ethnographers produced fascinating accounts of African societies in which hundreds of thousands of people were organized into political communities, yet without any centralized authority. Pastoralists or agriculturalists rather than hunters and gatherers, these people nevertheless managed to engage in long-term economic projects without the benefit of government or courts of law. Moreover, even these large-scale societies were apparently constructed on the same primordial principle of blood relationship. As among hunter-gatherers, the basic unit was a patrilineal group. In the more complex societies, local patrilineal bands were joined together in a sort of federation.

The most famous of these studies of headless federations was carried out in the 1930s by the leading British ethnographer of his generation, E. E. Evans-Pritchard, working among the Nuer people of the Southern Sudan. The Nuer occupied small settlements strung along the lower Nile, moving between agricultural settlements on the banks of the river to cattle camps on the uplands as the season demanded. They made a living from their large and highly valued herds of cattle, and also from agriculture and fishing, but their lives were regulated particularly by the demands of their herds.

According to the constitutional theory of the Nuer, each tier of

EVANS-PRITCHARD in the Sudan, with friends. Edward Evan Evans-Pritchard (1902–1973) was perhaps the greatest ethnographer in the tradition established by Malinowski. His field researches in East Africa resulted in the publication of some of the finest (and most stylish) monographs ever written on the social life and religious practices of African peoples. A sophisticated and unorthodox man, he had a complex and somewhat ambiguous relationship to the colonial regimes in the region (as this photograph may suggest), but he published a devastating critique of the colonial history of Libya. Like most of the best ethnographers, his reportage broke through the constraints of his analytic framework, allowing later scholars to recast his observations and to draw upon them to criticize his theoretical formulations.

political association was built around a patrilineal descent group. Most men in any one village or district could trace a common ancestry. In the tribe itself, the majority could claim a (possibly fictive) descent from a founding ancestor who was supposed to have lived many generations ago.

No political authority ordered relations between these camps and villages. If a young man in one village stole an ox—or a wife—from another, then the two villages would mobilize their fighting men and confront each other, perhaps actually fighting until the debt was repaid, or compensation extracted for the loss. They did so because every man recognized that he had to support his close kinsmen against more distant relatives. When conflict arose with a still more distant village, then the previous quarrel would be abandoned and all would combine against the outsiders. Neighboring villages would contribute fighting men to take on the men of the other district, and in such a battle lives might be lost. The local units, therefore, united and divided depending on what they were up against. "Fission and fusion," Evans-Pritchard remarked, were the principles of political action. The calculus for alliance and opposition was provided by genealogies: people allied with close patrilineal kin against more distantly related lineages. Fission and fusion yielded an automatic balance of power, in a system of ordered anarchy.

Further research, however, tended to undermine the view that simple political systems were based on patrilineal blood ties. Although members of small-scale hunter-gatherer communities were as a rule related in some way to one another, it was not necessary to trace unilineal descent back to a founding ancestor in order to be accepted as a band member. Relatives did enjoy privileged access to band membership, and people generally felt a moral duty to help even quite distant kin, but the band was not just a patriarchal family writ large. There were various routes to becoming a band member. A claim through a mother or father, a husband or wife, a brother or sister would serve. Even an unrelated exchange partner of a band member could usually be accommodated.

Often a person would be a member of several bands during a lifetime. Some individuals lived a peripatetic existence. And while crucial resources—a fountain, a grove of fruit trees—might be claimed by a band, the band members did not have a monopoly on the resources of a clearly defined territory. In sum, it was not the case that the small-scale communities of hunter-gatherers were generally organized into patrilineal bands.

The lineage model also provided an inadequate guide to the operation of larger headless political systems. The everyday organization of real-life Nuer communities was not, as it turned out, neatly governed by rules of descent. Local communities, even among the Nuer, were actually constituted rather like real-life hunter-gatherer bands. They included a wide variety of relatives. Individuals lived with mother's or father's kin, husband's or wife's, as it suited them. Many cattle camps and villages included several families unrelated to each other. The patrilineal principle apparently operated as an ideology, rather than as a law governing everyday choices.

Evans-Pritchard did not deny this, but he argued that the lineage system nevertheless provided the constitutional basis for the society. There was flexibility in practice, but "it is the clear, consistent, and deeply rooted lineage structure of the Nuer which permits persons and families to move about and attach themselves so freely, for shorter or longer periods, to whatever community they choose by whatever cognatic or affinal tie they find it convenient to emphasize."

Yet even at the level of ideology, the Nuer were not down-the-line practitioners of blood-tie politics. Evans-Pritchard himself provided evidence which indicated that the Nuer paid more attention to local interests than to abstract ideas about lineages. When pressed, a Nuer would explain politics in terms of local loyalties rather than genealogies. In a revealing passage, Evans-Pritchard admitted:

> A Nuer rarely talks about his lineage as distinct from his community, and in contrast to other lineages which form part of it, outside a ceremonial context. I have watched a Nuer who knew precisely what I wanted, trying on my behalf to discover from a stranger the name of his lineage. He often found great initial difficulty in making the man understand the information required of him, for Nuer think generally in terms of local divisions and of the relationships between them.

Attempts to apply the lineage model to tribes without rulers in other parts of the world also tripped over discrepancies between the elegant model of the anthropologists and the messy realities.

Ethnographers working in the New Guinea Highlands tested out the model with particular thoroughness. One summary account listed their doubts: "We find that people are more mobile than any rules of descent and residence should warrant, that genealogies are too short to be helpful . . . that local and descent groups are fragmented and change their alignments." In New Guinea, local communities are based on a complex mix of ideas about locality and kinship. Some New Guineans believe that if people eat crops grown in one territory they become kin, for their bodies are formed by the same substances. Authority is not based on genealogical claims, but has more to do with entrepreneurial talents and skills in oratory and mediation.

To sum up, Maine's thesis—indeed, the apparently commonsense view of most Victorians—was that the political community must have emerged in the first place from natural kinship relationships. This assumption was built into the more elaborate models of the first field anthropologists. To a Darwinian, it seemed natural that blood ties would motivate respect for social institutions and inspire political loyalties. Yet these confident assumptions eventually dissipated in the light of ethnographic reports. Societies without government are not ordered simply on the basis of kinship or descent. Kinship is important in all sorts of ways, but no human community has ever been discovered that is based on kinship groupings alone, or even ordered primarily by kinship principles. The roots of sociality would have to be sought elsewhere.

ANOTHER candidate for that original organizing principle of so-cial life was suggested by a classic philosophical source. Writing during the English civil war, Hobbes had reasoned that the lives of people living in ancient human communities were dominated by concerns about war and peace, violence and security. The state of nature was a state of war. The inference was therefore that civil society had been established to secure order and guarantee the means of livelihood.

This struck a chord with Darwinians. All nature was engaged in a struggle for survival. Early humans must have been obliged to fight off predators and to compete with each other for scarce resources.

The most convinced Hobbesians among modern human scientists were the ethologists, who tended to interpret animal behavior in terms of status competition and the aggressive defense of resources. In their view, the fundamental political mechanism was an instinctive drive to defend a territory. If anything, this drive was yet stronger among humans than among other primates. Konrad Lorenz had suggested that only among humans did the territorial imperative result in acts of murderous aggression even against members of the same species. Society was a fighting machine, territory the prize.

But primatologists reported that murderous violence against members of one's own species is by no means a human monopoly. What is perhaps most intriguing, the closest primate relatives of humanity, the chimpanzees, go in for murderous attacks on their neighbors. On the other hand, it turns out that organized violence is in fact rare among contemporary hunter-gatherer communities. Indeed, these people often profess an ethic of non-violence and cooperation. Attempts to dominate others are strongly censured. There are seldom strong leaders who can boss others around; decisions generally follow extended debate that eventually produces a consensus. Violent attacks upon neighboring communities rarely occur.

Violence is more usual within the band, and in sudden bursts of anger people kill rivals in love or even lash out in a wild, random homicidal frenzy. The conditions of close living and interdependence seem to stoke up destructive anger: but the violent individual is isolated, rejected even by close relatives, finally expelled from the community.

According to the American anthropologist Bruce Knauft, who has investigated this issue, the style of inter-group aggression found among the chimpanzees is absent among the egalitarian hunter-gatherers. Systematic feuding and warfare are characteristic rather of more complex societies. As technology develops; as communities settle down, tied to their investments in particular landscapes; as, perhaps in consequence, population density increases, so systematic hostility between groups becomes more common. The Nuer feuding relationships are therefore characteristic of relatively populous societies, with valuable resources like the cattle of the Nuer themselves, the camels of the Bedouin, or the horses of the Native American Plains Indians.

Some small-scale societies in the Amazon forests or the Highlands of New Guinea are extremely warlike. They tend to practice a mix of horticulture and foraging in conditions of shortage, and competition for land is one common reason for conflict. In contrast, contemporary communities of foragers tend to live in remarkable harmony, and there is no reason to suppose that this was not true of many early human communities as well. Inter-group violence seems to grow with the sophistication of economic and political arrangements. Hobbes, it seems, was quite wrong: if human beings organized themselves into strong political communities in order to avoid war, even civil war, they were making a very bad mistake.

BUT Hobbes himself had suggested that there was another basis for social relationships: people might make a bet on the principle of reciprocity. He identified the principle of fair exchange as one of his Laws of Nature. Every rational person was bound to agree: "*That a man which receiveth Benefit from another of meer Grace, Endeavour that he which giveth it, have no reasonable cause to repent him of his good will.*" One good turn deserves another. Or as Hobbes himself saw it, rational people accepted the biblical principle that one should do unto others as one would wish to be done by.

The greatest theorist of the market, Adam Smith (1723–1790), professor of moral philosophy at Glasgow University, suggested that a system of exchange based on the principle of reciprocity could bind naturally selfish and amoral individuals into harmonious communities. "It is not from the benevolence of the butcher, the brewer, or the baker that we expect our dinner, but from their regard to their own interest. We address ourselves, not to their humanity but to their self-love, and never talk to them of our own necessities but of their advantages."

Smith pointed out that a market stimulates specialization and the division of labor. After markets had been established, it was no longer profitable for every person to make everything that he needed for himself. It was more efficient to concentrate, to produce one thing that was needed by others, and to enter into exchanges in the market to supply one's wants. The market therefore fostered and rewarded individual enterprise, but in doing so it bound individuals together in a system of exchanges. The hidden hand of the market aggregates a myriad of individual selfish actions and magically redirects them to serve public ends.

Adam Smith's market is made up of hard-headed business people making canny deals about goods and services. He suggested that society itself may be constituted on similar principles: "Society may subsist among different men, as among different merchants, from a sense of its utility, without any mutual love or affection; and though no man in it should owe any obligation, or be bound in gratitude to any other, it may still be upheld by a mercenary exchange of good offices according to an agreed valuation."

Smith also speculated about the division of labor and forms of exchange in hunter-gatherer and pastoralist societies, and he suggested that even in the absence of the market there would be a natural tendency to make exchanges. From practical experience, people would come to appreciate the benefits of reciprocity and the consequent necessity of mutual dependence.

This was much the same conclusion that Bronislaw Malinowski reached in his classic ethnographic study of the Trobriand Islanders. Far from being passive slaves of custom, the Trobrianders, according to Malinowski, were calculating individualists who recognized an unconditional loyalty only to their families. "Love of tradition, conformism and the sway of custom," he reported, "account but to a very partial extent for obedience to rules." Whenever a person could "evade his obligations without the loss of prestige, or without the prospective loss of gain, he does so, exactly as a civilized business man would do." What then kept the wheels of society oiled? The Trobrianders recognized a simple and universal premise: to receive, it is necessary first to give. Persistent miscreants were excluded from exchange relationships; that was tantamount to expulsion from society.

The Trobrianders engage in a great deal of trade, some of it utilitarian (yams for fish, for example), some of it not obviously economic at all. Most spectacular was the *Kula* exchange system, described by Malinowski in the first of his famous Trobriand monographs, *Argonauts of the Western Pacific*, published in 1922. Partners from a chain of islands visited one another in festive and often dangerous canoe journeys, and exchanged ceremonial tokens: necklaces and bracelets. These had no ulterior value, and could not be exchanged again for anything of obvious utility. The most famous necklaces and bracelets were nevertheless much prized, and their possession brought prestige. But one could not hang on to the precious trophy that one had wheedled from an exchange partner. The temporary owner was obliged to pass it along fairly quickly to another *Kula* player. This was, in the end, a system of exchange that operated for its own sake—a game of social life, whose payoff, if any, was perhaps the stimulus it gave to foreign social contacts, which might ultimately serve useful purposes. The *Kula*, however, dramatically brought out—ritualized even—the basis of Trobriand society. The rule of reciprocal exchange was the elementary social rule.

The most important modern contribution to the theory of reciprocity was made by a French sociologist, Marcel Mauss. In direct opposition to Adam Smith, Mauss argued that reciprocity was not to be confused with the operations of entrepreneurs in a market. Indeed, with money and markets the ancient principle of reciprocity had been fatally diluted. It was, in origin, a moral idea, not simply an accounting principle; and it could be seen most clearly in operation in societies that were not dependent on market exchanges.

Mauss challenged Malinowski's image of the Trobriander as a sort of antipodean businessman. Malinowski had represented the *Kula* as a mixture of calculated deal-making and ritualized, irrational tradition. To Mauss, however, the *Kula* was an instance of the ancient form of gift exchange. In a study published in 1925, *Essay on the Gift*, Mauss argued that traditional societies were based on relationships of give-and-take from which the profit motive was absent. In ancient times every gift was charged with the personality of the giver, and gift exchanges were the currency of social relationships, creating and sustaining them. Nor were exchanges truly voluntary; there was no escape from the twin obligations to give and to receive. The sanctions against those who did not play the game could culminate in the last resort in exclusion from society, or, between communities, in warfare.

Mauss also emphasized that the exchanges that shaped social relations were not exclusively or even predominantly exchanges of goods and wealth. "In the systems of the past," Mauss wrote, "they exchanged rather courtesies, entertainments, ritual, military assistance, women, children, dances and feasts."

Perhaps Mauss's most potent suggestion was that the exchange of women between groups was one of the basic forms of exchange. This was the central premise of Lévi-Strauss's "alliance theory." For Lévi-Strauss, following Mauss, exchange was the basis of all social relationships, and the exchange of women in marriage was the foundation of the social order. The incest taboo had been instituted in order to enforce this exchange: it marked the foundation of human society because it inaugurated relationships of marriage alliance. The super-gift, women and children, defined the social relationships between families.

Mauss believed that in modern, market societies, these collective exchange relationships had been undermined by the individual, impersonal, profit-seeking deals of capitalism. The market, and money, had broken down traditional structures of reciprocity and threatened to replace them with moral anarchy, or at best with the dog-eat-dog society of capitalism. Where they still operated, traditional systems of reciprocity were very different from markets. And even in the most thoroughgoing industrial system there were still islands of traditional, non-market reciprocity. The family, the club, the church congregation, the regiment are all collectivities based on a notion of exchange which is not governed by a profit and loss account. Christmas may be seen as a celebration of this ancient moral economy based on the gift, even in the commercial society in which we live.

FIELD studies of hunter-gatherer peoples have yielded the richest accounts of the importance of reciprocity in social life. One of the most humane of these ethnographies was produced by an American family, the Marshalls. Laurence Marshall retired in 1950 from a successful career in engineering and business, during which he had

participated in the development of radar and pioneered the micro-
wave oven. He and his family then undertook a new, collective project:
the study of the !Kung Bushmen in the Kalahari desert. They made
eight expeditions to the Kalahari between 1950 and 1961. Laurence
made a photographic record; his son John produced one of the finest
ethnographic films, *The Hunters;* his daughter Elizabeth wrote a best-
selling account of the Bushmen, *The Harmless People;* and Lorna
Marshall, a graduate in English literature, published systematic ethnographic reports that were finally collected in her book, *The !Kung
of Nyae Nyae,* published in 1976. In these papers she described
the great importance of exchange relationships and the principle of
reciprocity in !Kung daily life.

The !Kung bands, containing anywhere from ten to thirty members,
were open and fluid groupings. Larger gatherings might form in the
winter, when surface water was available, allowing a more expansive
social life. This was the time for trance dances, for initiation ceremonies, for the exchange of goods and for wooing. It was the holiday
period of !Kung life, which everyone looked forward to.

Although there were occasional violent eruptions of jealousy or
anger within the band, cooperation was the norm. The band had no
permanent leaders, and even skilled hunters might take a rest rather
than appear to dominate others by virtue of their talents. The key
resources were available to anyone accepted into the band. The conditions of band membership were flexible, and virtually any connection through a kinsman or affine would serve as an entry ticket.
Equally, a quarrel could be settled by the migration of one party to
join another community, an easy enough option in this very mobile society.

"Occasions when tempers have got out of control are remembered
with awe," Lorna Marshall reported of the !Kung Bushmen.

> The deadly poisoned arrows are always at hand. Men have killed each
> other with them in quarrels—though rarely—and the !Kung fear fighting
> with a conscious and active fear. They speak about it often. Any expres-
> sion of discord ("bad words") makes them uneasy. Their desire to avoid
> both hostility and rejection leads them to conform in high degree to the
> unspoken social laws. I think that most !Kung cannot bear the sense of
> rejection that even mild disapproval makes them feel. If they do deviate,

LORNA MARSHALL among the !Kung. The Marshall family's involvement with the !Kung of southwest Africa combined ethnography, filmmaking, and popular reportage. Beginning her fieldwork without a professional training, Lorna Marshall became a distinguished African ethnographer; her articles on the social life of the !Kung are now classics.

they usually yield readily to expressed group opinion and reform their ways.

Richard Lee corrected this slightly idealized picture, recording that fights were in fact not uncommon. On some measures, the !Kung homicide rate compares unfavorably with that in the worst American urban areas (though for such tiny communities these comparisons are not necessarily significant, since the homicide rate must be extrapolated from a very small number of cases). Lee noted that a high proportion of homicides were crimes of passion, and remarked that !Kung fighting seems to be "a kind of temporary insanity or running amok rather than . . . an instrumental act in a means-end framework."

He agreed with Lorna Marshall that the !Kung fear violence, and that they have developed a variety of mechanisms to defuse quarrels and to control the expression of aggression. One means is talking, and the !Kung are great talkers. They are "the most loquacious people I know," reported Lorna Marshall. "The San do not fight much," Richard Lee agreed, "but they do talk a great deal." The !Kung are great singers too, and Lorna Marshall wrote that "a song composed specifically about someone's behaviour and sung to express disapproval, perhaps from the deepest shadow of the encampment at night, is a very effective means of bringing people who deviate back into the pattern of approved behaviour." Direct criticism was even more common, and it characteristically sparked off an intense debate in the camp.

Above all else, however, social peace is achieved among the !Kung through sharing and giving. Meat is always shared, with everyone in the camp, if possible, getting a share. Other possessions are claimed and passed on in a continuous cycle, from weapons to items of clothing and decoration. The main topic of their constant conversation, Lorna Marshall reported, is food; but perhaps next most common is talk about gift-giving:

Men and women speak of the persons to whom they have given or propose to give gifts. They express satisfaction or dissatisfaction with what they have received. If someone has delayed unexpectedly long in making a return gift, the people discuss this. One man was excused by his friends because his wife, they said, had got things into her hands and made him poor, so that he now had nothing suitable to give. Sometimes, on the other hand, people were blamed for being ungenerous ("far-hearted") or not very capable in managing their lives, and no one defended them for these defects or asked others to have patience with them.

Gifts are not only exchanged with neighbors and close relatives; they are traded between partners over a distance of hundreds of miles. Many adults have a number of partners, sometimes dozens spread over a great area. !Kung adults spend a great deal of time and energy traveling across the desert to visit relatives and exchange-partners, depending on their hospitality and exchanging gifts with them.

Exchange is clearly at the heart of their social being, and they recognize this very well. As a !Kung informant told Lorna Marshall: "The worst thing is not giving presents. If people do not like each other but one gives a gift and the other must accept, this brings a peace between them. We give to one another always. We give what we have. This is the way we live together."

This obsession with giving and reciprocity is characteristic especially of small-scale societies—today, mostly people who live largely by foraging. The Israeli anthropologist Nurit Bird-David has pointed out that such people also often have a theory about their relationship with the natural environment and with the spirit world that assumes the same principles of sharing and reciprocity.

A French ethnographer, Philippe Descola, has provided two fascinating, contrasting instances from the Amazon region. Among the people of the Tukano linguistic family, wives are exchanged between groups. Specialist goods are also traded between rival bands. Relationships between bands are therefore ordered on principles of reciprocal exchange. These people believe that similar principles rule the relationships between human beings and animals, and govern their relationship with the rulers of the natural world. After death, the souls of human beings go to the underground storehouses of gods. The souls of the animals of the forest and the fish of the rivers are stored in the same places. A shaman, in a drug-induced state of trance, regularly visits the Master of Animals and negotiates for the release of some animals into the forest, where his people will hunt them. However, compensation must be offered: the soul of a person, which will be transformed into an animal to replace the animal that has been hunted. In short, concludes Descola, "the Tukano social domain is entirely ruled by a logic of reciprocity."

Among the Jivaro tribes of the Upper Amazon, however, reciprocity is differently ordered. They do not imagine that humans and animals are linked in an ecological system regulated by exchanges. In their system there are only a limited number of human souls available, but a community can augment its numbers by capturing another soul. This is done through head-hunting and cannibalism. "Head-hunting," remarks Descola, "is a predatory process of accumulation which deliberately excludes reciprocity. However, the compensation for a head is always exacted forcefully in the long term, since the laws of revenge require that a killing never be left unpunished. The benefit brought by the taking of a head is always temporary, and the captured identity is later redistributed in an endless dialectic of violence." Similarly, when a man is killed in these feuds, his wife and children are normally abducted: so even marriage is often predatory—but once again the act of abduction invites reciprocation, initiating a fresh cycle of revenge. There is thus a sort of reciprocity in the feud itself, though now it takes a negative form.

What might be called the principle of negative reciprocity underlies very widespread ideas of justice. In most societies there are two sorts of crime: one is against the individual, the other against the society. The more powerful the central authority, the more likely it is that offenses against the law will be treated as offenses against authority, and punished by fines, beatings, mutilations, imprisonment, exile, or even execution. Most societies, however, insist rather on reciprocal loss. "And thine eye shall not pity," the Book of Deuteronomy instructs us, "but life shall go for life, eye for eye, tooth for tooth, hand for hand, foot for foot." This is also the rule that governs the feud, though in practice a payment may be accepted in settlement of a blood debt. Among the Nuer, for instance, compensation for a life may be made by a transfer of cattle that is equivalent to a bride-wealth payment.

It is a chilling thought, perhaps, but the same logic governs the friendly, ceremonial exchange of the *Kula* cycle and the relentless exchanges of the feud. Both are driven by the principle of reciprocity, which is the nearest thing to a universally recognized canon of justice. One has a right to even the score, to *get even.*

Yet our lives are not governed just by considerations of reciprocal exchange. Mauss thought that the moral basis of reciprocity was eroded by the development of money and markets, but it seems that its place has been taken by the development of powerful central authorities which play by different rules, and which are more concerned with control and power than with the personal satisfactions of balanced reciprocity. Relations between rulers and ruled are governed by unequal exchanges. Between communities too, relative power tends to be more important than ideas about fair exchange.

This suggests that it is somewhat naive to base a sociology on a calculus of individual choice. The fact is that governments bind individuals to them. Even in societies without government, individual relations of reciprocity may be subordinated to the claims of the group.

A DAM Smith began with the individual, and explained what bound him to society. Societies were associations of individuals, and their selfish interests meshed to create workable associations. In his view, governments should interfere as little as possible in the self-regulating work of the market. Individuals would behave themselves because they recognized the logic of enlightened self-interest.

But according to another tradition of social thought, it makes little sense to argue about why individuals live in groups. There are no pre-social individuals who have to be tempted into the group. Human beings are essentially social, and each society creates the individuals it requires. Individual consciousness is a product of social forces. Not all individuals everywhere behave like Adam Smith's butcher, brewer, and baker, whose commercial habits were formed by the Calvinism of Glasgow and Edinburgh.

According to the collectivists, simple, small-scale societies, in particular, were happily totalitarian. Once again, the classic account of such a society was based on reports about the Australian aborigines. This was *The Elementary Forms of the Religious Life,* published in 1912 by the founding father of French sociology, Emile Durkheim.

Citing descriptions of Australian aboriginal ritual, Durkheim suggested that each community came together from time to time to worship a god that was, in effect, a projection of the group itself into the heavens. The rituals whipped up feelings of loyalty and inspired every individual to subordinate his or her wishes to the community. More subtly, the very concepts that people unconsciously used— ideas about space or time or causality—were derived from social experience. The camp-site, with its sacred and profane sites, its customary layout, served also as a map of the world, giving a socially relevant meaning to topography and even to the planetary system. The individual literally did not think to act except as a member of a group.

Despite the relatively impoverished ethnographic reports available to him, Durkheim's view has worn well. Later reports have brought out the complex way in which initiation rituals, marriage arrangements, and gift exchanges combined to weave a social fabric that guided individual activity and ultimately maintained the extraordinary conservatism of Australian aboriginal technology and social arrangements.

But it is too simple to oppose traditional, collective societies and modern societies based on an individualist ethic. This was apparent to the pioneer sociologists around Durkheim, and his nephew Marcel Mauss had explored this issue in 1906 in an essay entitled *Seasonal Variations of the Eskimo*. Mauss pointed out that among the Eskimo (or Inuit, as they generally prefer to be called today) the year was divided into two seasons of economic and social activity. In their small summer camps the Eskimo lived in individual family groups, and pursued individual economic strategies. In the winter, however, they came together in large communities, and it was here that the ceremonies and exchanges of a more social existence flourished. "In the dense concentrations of the winter, a genuine community of ideas and material interests is formed. Its strong moral, mental and religious unity contrasts sharply with the isolation, social fragmentation and dearth of moral and religious life that occurs when everyone has scattered during the summer."

This insight has been confirmed by later studies among societies such as the Kalahari Bushmen and the Australian aborigines. Even among the most apparently collectivist societies, there are seasons of individualism. And even among ourselves, living as we do in societies that stress individual achievement and competition, there are times when we celebrate a more collective ethic, based on reciprocity. Thanksgiving and Christmas are festivals of solidarity, when we exchange gifts, eat and drink together, care for the needy, and turn our backs on the business of the market.

Individualism is a peculiarly Western ideology. It takes for granted a specific notion of the "person." The idea of a self-conscious personality, formed by a unique psychic history, living by his or her own rules—the "character" of a novel or a film, or the hero of a history, or the subject of psychoanalysis—is both modern and culturally specific. (It is also, incidentally, under recurrent attack from avant-garde novelists, who question the continuity of individual identities, and from sociologists who believe that the social role has precedence over the individual.)

Extreme individualists take our conventions for granted. The individual is not only real, but the only realistic point of reference for social analysis. The community has a shadowy presence in their accounts; it may even be regarded as an illusion.

"There is no such thing as society," Margaret Thatcher once observed robustly (adding, with fidelity to her particular intellectual tradition, "there are only individual men and women, and families"). But even in modern capitalist societies, extreme individualism is an inadequate basis for political theory. Conservative individualists find that they have to combine their basic tenet with a patriotic call to serve the national cause. There is a similar contradiction in the ideas of thinkers on the left, who would like to argue the case both for social solidarity and for inviolable individual rights. It is hard to be unwaveringly individualist or consistently collectivist in politics.

Similarly, the extreme sociological standpoints are unconvincing. There are no pre-social individuals, but equally there are no—or mercifully few—totalitarian communities that consume all individual choice. The most ancient societies were perhaps not much more, or less, individualistic than our own. They seem to have been open, transient, fragile associations. Yet they may well have constituted powerful moral communities, shaping individual goals, constraining choices, imbuing actions with particular meanings. The best guess is that early societies, like all those we know today, had somehow to accommodate the divergent pressures generated by common interests and individual goals, communal institutions and entrepreneurial strategies.

There is no simple, natural, universal primal constitution of human society, no single motive for sociality. The family was probably the universal basis of domestic organization, and the principle of reciprocity always had a greater or lesser role in regulating relationships; but ancient forms of social life were surely very various. A great many mechanisms have been developed that persuade individuals, generally speaking, to behave as good citizens. We are unlikely ever to discover through empirical research the first—or fundamental—form of citizenship.

Nor has it proved possible to identify a principle of legitimate authority that is accepted across the spectrum of cultural traditions. We cannot specify a universally accepted human right. In any case, even if all hitherto-known societies recognized a particular law, we might nevertheless decide not to abide by it any longer. What laws should prevail will not be settled by empirical research; it is a matter for political debate. Nor is there any inevitable progression in the forms of government. The future is a different story.

⋅ 10 ⋅

THE SECOND
MILLENNIUM

A story need not begin at the very beginning. Human destiny does not unfold straightforwardly from what we know of human origins, and anyway our understanding of early humans is still contested, the meager data open to conflicting readings. If we could only know the end, that would be a perfect place to start, putting everything in its proper perspective.

The Bible is the great model for Genesis narratives, and it also provides ample precedents for eschatological and millenarian accounts of human destiny. The key source of the Christian millenarian tradition is Revelation 19–22, ascribed to St. John but composed when Christians were suffering severe persecution under the emperor Domitian, who ruled Rome with great cruelty from A.D. 81 to 96.

The Book of Daniel and some of the Hebrew prophets had foretold the end of the world in a great holocaust. The Gospels predicted a second coming, in which Jesus would return to judge the world. The Book of Revelation, which brought together these two great visions of the end of things, tells of a final war between Gog and Magog, at the end of which Satan will be bound in a bottomless pit for a thousand years, while the martyrs of the Church will live and reign with Christ. Satan would then briefly be let loose once more, before the final establishment of the kingdom of the saints on earth.

The interpretation of this mystical text has always been contentious. One of the most perplexing questions—and potentially the most practically relevant—concerned the dating of the millennium (from the Latin for 1,000 years). From the third century onward the general view was that the millennium would come 1,000 years after the birth of Christ, rather than 1,000 years after Satan's confinement;

but once the first millennium had passed without a cosmic revolution, fresh debates raged about the timing of the end of days. According to one common view, the millennium would come only 2,000 years after Christ. If so, we should expect it at the end of the present decade.

This may seem an exotic, even quaint way to think about the future in an increasingly secular world, but secular thinking is sometimes disconcertingly reminiscent of theological models, despite the adoption of a rationalist, even scientific idiom. There is today a widespread secular millenarian belief in an imminent technological catastrophe that will put an end to human history—and so, retrospectively, define it.

In this version of the apocalypse Satan is played by Frankenstein's machine turned monster. The machines that we built to meet our needs have needs of their own. Perhaps they will become our masters rather than our servants. We programmed them to tame nature, but they will destroy our natural environment.

In the aftermath of Hiroshima and Nagasaki many serious people predicted that a nuclear war would wipe out the human species and perhaps destroy the world. With the end of the Cold War this fear has receded, but it has been replaced by concerns about ecological devastation. The population will grow beyond the point where we can feed ourselves; we will exhaust the fossil fuels on which we have come to depend; our technology will poison the atmosphere and cause calamitous climatic changes.

For the Christian millenarians the nature of man is to be sinful, sin is bound to bring retribution, and all sinners will be consumed at the end of days. The secular millenarians predict a collective catastrophe, brought upon us by a collective sin. Civilization has sinned against nature, culture against biology.

THE original and most enduring theme of the modern millenarians has to do with the relationship between human population and resources. Its classical statement is the *Essay on Population*, published in 1798 by a Church of England clergyman, Robert Malthus. The book had its origin in a friendly argument that Malthus, a diffident thirty-two-year-old bachelor still living at home, had with his father. The elder Malthus, a friend of both Jean-Jacques Rousseau and David Hume, had welcomed the French Revolution. The application of human reason would now at last lead to the improvement of political institutions and the greater welfare of humanity.

His son rejected this secular vision of a new Jerusalem. The prospects for humanity were gloomy, he felt, not because of original sin but by reason of another "great cause intimately united with the very nature of man." This was "the constant tendency in all animated life to increase beyond the nourishment prepared for it." The moralists had always warned that sexual indulgence caused misery and disease. Malthus wrote a Rake's Progress for humanity itself. The instinct to propagate was the root of human woes.

The rate of natural increase for human beings was such that in theory population could almost double every decade. In practice, the Four Horsemen of the Apocalypse culled the increase with grim efficiency. However, in the most favored circumstances, population still grew rapidly. "In the northern states of America," noted Malthus, "where the means of subsistence have been more ample, the manners of the people more pure, and the checks to early marriages fewer, than in any of the modern states of Europe, the population was found to double itself for some successive periods every twenty-five years." This Malthus took to be the effective top rate of population expansion. Unchecked by misfortune, population doubled every twenty-five years—but then it redoubled over the following twenty-five years, and so on.

What could such burgeoning populations find to eat? Agricultural resources were not yet fully exploited, Malthus conceded. New lands could be brought under production in many parts of the world, which is why colonial populations often experienced such rapid growth. Backward populations could slowly be educated to higher levels of productivity. Even in Europe, farming practices could be improved. In time, however, extra efforts would tend to yield diminishing returns, as the best land lost fertility and increasingly marginal lands were brought into production. On the most optimistic view, increases in agricultural production would lag further and further behind the potential growth of population.

Malthus was prepared to formulate a mathematical law: population might increase geometrically (doubling and redoubling itself), but food production could grow only arithmetically, by cumulative additions. If the present population of the world were 1 billion, he wrote, "the human species would increase as the numbers 1, 2, 4, 8, 16, 32, 64, 128, 256, and subsistence as 1, 2, 3, 4, 5, 6, 7, 8, 9. In two centuries the population would be to the means of subsistence as 256 to 9; in three centuries as 4096 to 13; and in two thousand years the difference would be almost incalculable."

Malthus lived during a period of very rapid population growth. Between 1750 and 1850 the population of Europe rose from about 120 million to 210 million, and the world population from some 750 million to perhaps 1.2 billion. Since then growth has continued, by Malthusian leaps. By the 1950s, the world population was some 2.5 billion. By the nineties, it was estimated at 5 billion. By 2025 it may have risen to between 7.5 and 9 billion.

According to Malthus, population explosions could not be sustained. Eventually the Four Horsemen would ride in to redress the balance between population and resources. What he called misery and vice would cut back any sudden rise in population. By "misery" he meant famine and disease; by "vice" he meant war and also promiscuity and the practice of abortion, both of which, he believed, went against nature and caused sterility.

It was a dismal scenario, and Malthusian economics was soon known as the dismal science. But some contemporaries refused to accept the implication of Malthus's view, that humans were like animals, the playthings of instincts and natural forces beyond their control. In the second edition of his *Essay* Malthus granted a place to moral—or cultural—factors. Human beings might come to understand their perilous situation and sensibly opt for sexual abstinence, or at least the postponement of marriage.

Something of the sort has happened, though not, as Malthus imagined, through the development of stricter sexual codes. Malthus believed that we had an instinct to propagate, but it is more realistic to assume that human beings raise children because they need them. In pre-industrial economies children were cheap to raise, and could be productive at an early age. But as economic well-being has come to depend more and more on investment, and especially investment in human capital, so parents have been inclined to limit the number of children. The demand for children changes as economic circumstances alter. An ironic consequence is that the richer parts of the world are experiencing less rapid population increases than the poorer parts, so that by 2025 Nigeria and Brazil will have larger populations than the United States, and the Western European countries will be fat minnows in a sea pullulating with hungry whales.

What is called the "demographic transition"—the shift among richer populations to lower birth rates—has so far occurred in only a small part of the world. In gross terms, the population history of the world since Malthus's day bears out his worst fears. War and famine have also taken an increased toll, as he predicted. But Malthus's essentially biological scenario left out another cultural factor, which was perhaps even more crucial than sexual morality: technical innovation.

The agricultural revolution had already been under way for a century when Malthus was born, in 1766. Enclosures of land, better plows, new crops, and the more intensive use of arable land through crop rotation were steadily raising the output of English farmers throughout the eighteenth century. Indeed, this agricultural revolution was the precondition for the Industrial Revolution, for which it released capital and labor. And as industrialization stimulated further technical development, so agriculture was transformed again. After 1850 mechanization spread rapidly. Reapers, steam-powered steel plows, and new fertilizers revolutionized productivity, incidentally providing the tools for the settlers who surged at the same time into the American West. In the twentieth century there followed an even more radical revolution in agriculture. Mechanization transformed agricultural practices; pest and disease controls reduced losses; new storage and transportation methods stimulated a great expansion of world trade in agricultural products. The rich began to overproduce food—and also, incidentally, to eat too much.

And yet it is perhaps premature to dismiss the fears of Malthus. In the richer countries, technology has apparently freed us from a Malthusian fate, but Malthus may still rule, if only in the South. Indeed, the poorer countries may find themselves in a peculiarly horrible Malthusian trap. Better public health policies will result in continued rapid population growth, but there is no guarantee that a lower death rate will bring a lower birth rate in its wake.

In any case, a population that has experienced a phase of rapid increase will continue to grow for some time, even if the birth rate declines. The earlier spurt of population increase would have resulted in a larger population, with more young women. Even if they have fewer children on average than their mothers, the absolute number of people in the population will still increase in the next generation. Even while the birth rate falls, population may well reach an unsustainable level.

Nor can we count upon a sustained rise in productivity. The technologies that have served the agriculture of Europe and North America may be positively deleterious in the tropics. Forests will be chopped down, dams built, and new lands brought into use, but these may provide only short-term solutions, bringing in their train further environmental deterioration and greater catastrophe in the longer run.

The quintessential Malthusian image which confronts the world at the end of the twentieth century is that of drought and famine in Africa. On the most apocalyptic reading of these tragic events, they are the inevitable consequence of the highest population growth rates in the world (over 3 percent per year, and still rising); environmental degradation, the desert creeping inexorably across the farmlands and ranges bordering the Sahara; and drought conditions, perhaps the harbinger of even more destabilizing global climatic changes.

The misery can hardly be overstated, but this does not mean that things can only get worse until populations fall back again to the level that the resources can sustain—a level that may itself be dropping, as these resources are depleted. At an early stage of the AIDS epidemic in Africa some writers saw it as a cruelly apt Malthusian check on population growth, caused, as Malthus had predicted, by promiscuity. But it is now evident that even in the worst-affected areas, deaths from AIDS will not significantly check the rate of population growth. Things are very tough, but the end is not at hand, even in Africa.

To begin with, it is not at all certain that the objective conditions are getting worse. Climatic records are poor in Africa, so it is not easy to assess long-term changes, but the recent drought was not a freak, and it may not signal the start of a long-term climatic shift. Africa has always been subject to great fluctuations in rainfall, and traditional farmers were geared to cope. The two decades of drought that ravaged the West African Sahel in the 1970s and 1980s may have been the longest of the century, but there was an even more severe drought between 1910 and 1915. In that drought, absolute mortality was even higher, although in 1968 the population was nearly three times as great as it had been in the early decades of the century.

The drought, moreover, cannot fully explain the famines. Some countries managed to feed the hungry, despite drought conditions; others suffered excruciating famines even though they escaped the drought. The famines represent human failures.

Bradford Morse, director of the United Nations Office for Emergency Operation in Africa, is emphatic that "drought itself is not the fundamental problem in sub-Saharan Africa. After all, drought prevails in many parts of the world and, in affluent societies, need be no more than a nuisance. The real problem in Africa is poverty— the lack of development—the seeds of which lie in Africa's colonial past and in unwise policy choices made in the early days of independence by national governments and external aid donors."

Certainly African governments were poorly placed to cope with the drought conditions that afflicted many parts of the continent over the past two decades. Theirs was a crippling legacy. Most tropical African countries were in the hands of European colonial powers until the 1950s and 1960s. Decolonization was swift and largely unprepared, leaving the new states with stunted economies, weak political institutions, and small, young, and untried elites. In the early seventies they faced a great double shock. There were huge oil price increases in 1973. Then, as the world economy faltered, African countries were hit by a sharp deterioration in the prices commanded by their own natural resources and by the cotton, coffee, and cocoa crops that they grew for export. Struggling to cope, they fell into debt to the rich countries, incurring a burden that threatens to impoverish the next generation.

But the new governments in Africa often themselves made the

largest contributions to the woes of their people. The African states generally chose to invest in industry, and their investments were often unwise or poorly managed. The capital came largely from the agricultural sector, and thus the inefficient industries of the seventies and eighties were built on the backs of the poor farmers. Food prices were kept artificially low to subsidize the growing populations of the cities, to whom investment flowed. These city dwellers sucked in imports without paying their own way, but their clamoring presence in the main population centers granted them political priority. Governments were fragile, inefficient, often corrupt: foreign investors were discouraged, local entrepreneurs restricted and bullied.

The farmers were also put under pressure to switch from food crops to export crops, in order to finance imports of consumer goods for the people in the cities. Export crops had to be marketed through inefficient and often corrupt parastatal companies, and when world prices fell—as they did right through the eighties—the farmers themselves could not buy enough food to sustain their families. At the best of times, food imports are now needed to cover a fifth of African consumption.

The African famine of the late twentieth century is not the first or the worst to be caused by mismanagement. The collectivization of peasant farms by Stalin caused a famine that claimed many millions of lives. China was a byword for famine from the late nineteenth century to the mid-twentieth century, and the 1876–1879 famine in north China cost some ten million lives. The last, and worst, famine was the direct result of the disruption of agricultural production caused by Chairman Mao's most reckless exercise in social engineering, the Great Leap Forward. Between 1959 and 1961 some thirty million people perished from hunger. India was also notorious for famine conditions for much of the twentieth century, not least when it was under British rule.

There is some consolation to be drawn from the fact that Russia, China, and India seem to have escaped from the shadow of famine. After the catastrophic Bengal Famine of 1943, India's food distribution services were improved, and despite severe droughts in the sixties and seventies there have been no more famines, though there is still great hardship. The success of the Green Revolution made

India self-sufficient in food, and a net exporter of rice. In China, farming was increasingly privatized after a great policy change in 1978. Prices were largely freed, and output grew spectacularly.

Contrary to Malthus, the Scandinavian economist Ester Boserup has argued that population pressure may itself stimulate an increase in production. People do not simply curl up and die: they are forced, in adversity, to think up new and better ways of doing things, and to work harder. She suggests that a population explosion—caused, perhaps, by climatic changes, or by fortunate changes in the vectors of disease—actually sparked the development of the first agricultural economies. Agriculture was a harder, more labor-intensive way of life than hunting or herding, and people took it up only under the pressure of population on resources. Later intensifications of agriculture were the result of further periods of population growth. A more densely concentrated population can also organize public works, like deforestation or irrigation, and will stimulate investment in transportation and trade.

Since the days of Malthus, the rich countries have been able to multiply agricultural output while sharply cutting back the number of people working the land. Capital costs slowed the modernization of agriculture in the poorer countries, but the Green Revolution, based on new strains of rice, brought high yield levels to some of the poorest, most overpopulated countries in the 1970s, and genetic engineers promise a new generation of crops for the tropics. Zealous agronomists are confident that even a world population of 10 billion could be comfortably fed if agricultural resources were used more effectively.

In most of the world today, the immediate problems of agricultural production have been solved. The real story concerns the management of economic growth, and that is a story of industry, cities, and natural resources.

I N pre-industrial England, according to the economic historian Phyllis Deane, "the ordinary man saw little evidence of economic growth within his own lifetime and no improvement that could not be eliminated within a single year by the incidence of a bad harvest or a war or an epidemic." This was the world according to Malthus, but it was being transformed during his own lifetime, although Malthus, cloistered in his quiet rural curacy, did not realize the implications of the great changes under way in London and the industrial cities to the north.

The Industrial Revolution began in England. It was preceded by a transformation in agriculture and a rapid growth in trade between Britain and the rest of the world. Labor shifted from agricultural work to the cities, where new industries were sited. Profits from agriculture and trade were made available for investment in manufacture. And Britain had huge resources of coal, the fuel of the new machines.

Between 1801 and 1851 the country's income from industrial enterprises trebled, and Britain became the first great industrial nation. In the process it broke with the world of Malthusian economics. Population grew rapidly, but so did the average standard of living. "One of the features that distinguishes the modern industrial (or industrializing) economy from its predecessors," Phyllis Deane concludes, "is that it involves sustained long-term growth in *both* population *and* output."

One great effect of the Industrial Revolution was the transfer of work and wealth from farm to factory, and thus of populations from the countryside to the cities. During the lifetime of Malthus, London became the second city (after Peking) with a population of 1 million, a total reached in 1810. By 1850 its population had doubled, and by 1900 it had reached 5 million.

In 1899 an observer wrote that "the most remarkable social phenomenon of the present century is the concentration of population in cities." By then a majority of the population of Britain was urbanized. Many were horrified by the unnatural life of the cities, but Darwin, who hated London, wrote: "Life in the crowded condition of cities has many unattractive features, but in the long run these may be overcome, not so much by altering them, but simply by changing the human race into liking them."

At the start of the twentieth century there were some dozen cities in the world with a population of a million or more. By 1990 there were 226 cities in this class, a fifth of them in China alone. Even in

Africa there were 21 cities with a population of over a million. Six cities have populations of over 10 million. Thus, near the end of the twentieth century, London is no longer one of the world's largest cities, and New York is not even one of the largest cities of the Americas. São Paulo's population is projected to be 24 million by the year 2000, Mexico City's 31 million.

These gigantic urban populations have been produced by immigration rather than by natural growth. There has been a great, international movement from the countryside to the cities. This shift occurred first in the richer countries, as agricultural productivity increased. In the middle of this century, half of the population in the richer countries already lived in cities, but this was true of only perhaps 15 percent of the population of the poorer countries of the world. By 1980, 70 percent of the rich world lived in cities, and 30 percent of the poor. Two-thirds of the population of Latin America now live in towns and cities, and it is predicted that within the next forty years half the population of Asia and of Africa will be urbanized. In these poor countries, the urban population increased 250 percent in the period between 1950 and 1980, while the rural population increased by only 60 percent. Soon more than half the population of the world will live in cities, and early in the third millennium the whole world may well be as urbanized as the richest countries are today.

Urbanization and industrialization are the most evident twin features of modernity. Today, according to one authority, "an undeveloped country may be defined as a country with 80 per cent of its people in agriculture and a developed country as one with 15 per cent of its employment in agriculture." In the rich countries today, less than 10 percent of the population works the land, but this small work-force produces a surplus of food for the country as a whole.

The modern cities began as centers of manufacture and trade, and it is tempting to imagine Shanghai, Bombay, or São Paulo following the path of London or New York in the nineteenth century. Shanty-towns, on this comforting view, are temporary road-stations on the route to modernity.

The theory behind this view is that Britain was simply the first country to find the way from traditional forms of production to the modern, industrial system. One by one, other countries followed (some, indeed, outstripping the pioneer). Eventually, even the poorest country in the world can expect to pass through what the economist Walter Rostow called the "stages of growth." Rostow's theory postulated an evolutionary process powered by technological change. Every country would recapitulate the movement made by the rich countries from agriculture to industry, and industrial development would follow the same route everywhere. This optimistic vision encouraged formerly colonial states to invest in industry at the expense of agriculture, in an attempt to force the pace of history.

What Rostow's theory left out was the connection between economies. According to another view, northern European countries were able to industrialize only because they could exploit tropical colonies, stripping them of their resources, exploiting their labor, and forcing them to consume the commodities produced in the metropolis. The poor countries are kept poor because that profits the rich. The world economy is a single system.

"World-system theory" borrowed a Marxist idiom, casting the poor countries as the international proletariat and the great multinational companies as the new capitalists, irresistibly increasing their profits and further impoverishing the poor. At its simplest, this theory postulated a dichotomous world, split between the few rich countries and a multitude of impoverished and exploited states on the periphery of the capitalist system. This was a powerfully simplifying view of the world, but too crude to cope with the complexity of real history. There were too many anomalous cases. How, for instance, could one account for the history of Britain's North American colonies?

World-system theorists therefore invented a third category, intermediate between the two poles of their system (perhaps even serving as middlemen between the rich and the poor). In this third category they dumped their difficult cases—but these turned out to be frustratingly diverse. Some of the misfits had once been rich imperial powers, for instance Turkey, Portugal, or Spain. Others had once been flourishing industrial states, like Argentina. Then, almost impossible to classify, there was Japan. And following the example of Japan, in the decades after World War II other Asian economies began to emerge from colonial torpor into a phase of unprecedented industrial development—Hong Kong, Singapore and Taiwan, South Korea and Thailand, now China and India. These countries grew so rapidly in the eighties that the economies of the Pacific Basin became a genuine counterweight to the Atlantic economies of the old world system.

Although world-system theory ignored a great deal, it had one great advantage over the Rostow "stages of growth" view of economic change: it took for granted the interdependence of economic systems in the industrial age. It is apparent that the economies of the third millennium will be integrated in a way never before known. Today Korean industrialists build factories in Canada to evade American tariffs, and computer programmers in Bombay process the records of a London-based life insurance company. A new theory will have to be developed to make sense of the new economic conditions.

It is already evident that the cities that make the world's goods also effect great cultural changes. The modern city mixes together people of various ethnic groups and nationalities, speaking different languages and worshipping different gods, or none. Whereas New York was celebrated as the melting pot of the United States, the new world cities are forging a cosmopolitan international community. Even the oldest cities have become atypical of their home countries. Of the 6.6 million people who lived in London in 1981, 1.2 million were born outside the United Kingdom. The impact of such cities on their own countries is hard to guess, but they may burst the bounds of the nation-states that harbor them, anticipating the cultural forms of a cross-national order.

I N the richer countries the goal is no longer simply to sustain population at the minimal level necessary for survival. People expect a constant increase in the standard of living. A period of sustained stagnation would be regarded as little short of a catastrophe. The problem in these countries is not population growth—population is generally stable—but economic improvement. The danger is that we may be outstripping—or even destroying—the resources needed to sustain economic growth. There are perhaps limits to growth, as the famous slogan of the Club of Rome suggested.

Yet a less self-punishing, more optimistic view is not unrealistic. Perhaps energy sources are finite, as some maintain, but the limits have not yet been approached. In 1968, proven recoverable oil reserves were put at 50 billion metric tons. Then prices rose, stimulating exploration. New technologies made offshore drilling a practical proposition. In 1988 there were thought to be 124 billion metric tons of recoverable oil reserves. World coal resources—proven, recoverable resources—represent over two hundred years of consumption at present rates. Nuclear power is still expensive and hazardous, but its potential is enormous. The record suggests that other substitutes for fossil fuels will continually be found—or invented—as scarcity and rising cost begin to limit the use of any particular resource.

Prices provide a warning of future shortages, but the energy cost of production has been falling for many decades. The cost of energy used to produce goods and services in the United States fell, at constant prices, by one-half between 1850 and 1900. It continued to fall in the twentieth century, and even after the oil shock of the early 1970s—when OPEC engineered a huge price rise—energy costs in the United States were a third down in real terms compared to those that prevailed at the beginning of the century. Moreover, the oil shock stimulated richer countries to conserve energy, and in the 1980s and 1990s the real cost of energy went down again.

Industrial growth does have potentially terrible ecological costs, but these are still poorly understood, and even unchecked they may not impose great changes in human adaptation. Optimists argue that there are technical solutions to be found even to global warming and the greenhouse effect. The record suggests that culture will provide the means for us to cope.

We have adapted well to the new world we have created, certainly on the classic Darwinian measures. We can expect to live longer than our forebears. Our population has grown exponentially. There are today billions of people living where once, just ten thousand years ago, only as many millions lived. These billions of lives bear witness to the success of cultural innovations, most obviously in agriculture, trade and industry, and public health programs. This hardly suggests that we are fitted only to be Pleistocene hunters, or that human nature has been betrayed by technology. This changing, growing, converging world we now live in is the long-term product of the cumulative and accelerating development of culture, which began only some forty millennia ago. Perhaps, with Rousseau, we should bless the happy hour that made us creatures of intelligence.

And yet it is not easy to be sanguine about our future. Human beings have been their own worst enemies. The calamities of the twentieth century were caused by human agency. Technological gains have given our political leaders the power to cause more devastation than any of their predecessors could. The horrors that have marked the twentieth century will not suddenly come to an end. There will surely be more suffering, more injustices, more tragic accidents. It is callous to be easily hopeful, foolish to put our faith in dangerous technologies, naive to expect ready political solutions to the great economic and environmental problems of our age; but it is not too optimistic to believe that we have the means to survive, and perhaps to make things better. Even at the end of the second millennium, there is still time.

FURTHER READING
AND NOTES

INDEX

FURTHER READING
AND NOTES

1. ALL DARWINIANS NOW?

FURTHER READING

The Origin of Species (London: John Murray, 1859) and *The Descent of Man* (London: John Murray, 1871) both went through several major revisions in Darwin's lifetime. In this book I cite the second edition of *The Descent of Man* (London: John Murray, 1874), and the Penguin edition of *The Origin of Species* (first published in 1968 and based on the first edition). Both texts are available in a number of modern editions.

Darwin's *Autobiography*, largely written in 1876, was first published (in part) after his death in *Life and Letters of Charles Darwin*, edited by Francis Darwin (London: John Murray, 1887). A convenient edition of the text, together with T. H. Huxley's autobiography, was published by Oxford University Press in 1974.

There are a number of biographies of Darwin. The most recent, *Darwin*, by Adrian Desmond and James Moore (London: Michael Joseph, 1991; Penguin Books, 1992) is a huge, readable, and scholarly account of Darwin's life and work, which places his ideas in their broader intellectual and political context. A good brief introduction is *Darwin* by Jonathan Howard (Oxford: Oxford University Press, 1982). Stephen Jay Gould has written many fine essays on aspects of Darwinism. See, for example, *Ever Since Darwin* (Harmondsworth: Penguin Books, 1977).

Ernst Mayr's *The Growth of Biological Thought: Diversity, Evolution, and Inheritance* (Cambridge, Mass.: Harvard University Press, 1982) is the standard modern scholarly account of the development of Darwinian and neo-Darwinian theory in biology. A more accessible book is his *One Long Argument: Charles Darwin and the Genesis of Modern Evolutionary Thought* (Cambridge, Mass.: Harvard University Press, 1991).

NOTES TO THE TEXT

1 "Origin of man now proved": "Darwin's Early and Unpublished Note-books," transcribed and annotated by Paul H. Barrett, in Howard E.

Gruber, *Darwin on Man: A Psychological Study of Scientific Creativity* (London: Wildwood House, 1974), p. 281.

2 "I am almost convinced": Desmond and Moore, *Darwin*, p. 314.

2 "Probably all the organic beings": *The Origin of Species*, p. 455.

3 "Now I am quite sure": Quoted in Adrian Desmond, *Archetypes and Ancestors: Palaeontology in Victorian London 1850–1875* (Chicago: University of Chicago Press, 1984), p. 75.

3 "Hurrah the Monkey Book has come!": Cited in Desmond and Moore, *Darwin*, p. 516.

3 "descended from some lowly organised form": Darwin, *The Descent of Man*, p. 946.

3 "descended from a hairy, tailed quadruped": Ibid., p. 930.

4 "high standard of our intellectual powers": Ibid., p. 931.

5 Desmond Morris had a great success with a book entitled *The Naked Ape* (London: Jonathan Cape, 1967). Jared Diamond's *The Third Chimpanzee* (New York: Harper Collins) appeared in 1991.

7 "individuals, originally belonging to one species": Lamarck (1809), quoted in Mayr, *The Growth of Biological Thought*, p. 346.

8 "faculty of continuing to improve": Quoted in Mayr, ibid., p. 528.

8 "veritable rubbish": Quoted in Mayr, ibid., p. 358.

8 "Heaven forfend me": Quoted in L. J. Jordanova, *Lamarck* (Oxford: Oxford University Press, 1984), p. 106.

10 "provisional hypothesis of pangenesis": This is the title of Chapter XXVII of Darwin's *Variation of Animals and Plants under Domestication* (London: John Murray, 1868).

11 "This preservation of favourable variations": *Origin of Species*, p. 131.

12 "happened to read for amusement": Darwin, *Autobiography*, p. 71.

12 "two fair criticisms": Francis Crick, *What Mad Pursuit: A Personal View of Scientific Discovery* (London: Weidenfeld and Nicolson, 1989), pp. 30–31.

14 "It must not be forgotten": *The Descent of Man*, p. 203.

15 "Man, after he had partially acquired": *The Descent of Man*, p. 195.

16 "Apart from being mediated": Peter Medawar, "Unnatural Science," in *Pluto's Republic* (Oxford: Oxford University Press, 1982), p. 173. This essay was first published in 1977.

17 "make plain that competition": Desmond and Moore, *Darwin*, p. xxi.

2. TO BEGIN AT THE BEGINNING

FURTHER READING

An excellent modern textbook that covers the topics discussed in this chapter is Richard G. Klein, *The Human Career: Human Biological and Cultural Origins*

(Chicago: University of Chicago Press, 1989). Two valuable works of reference are the *Encyclopedia of Human Evolution and Prehistory*, edited by Ian Tattersall, Eric Delson, and John Van Couvering (New York and London: Garland, 1988), and the more popular and also more wide-ranging *Cambridge Encyclopedia of Human Evolution*, edited by Steve Jones, Robert Martin, and David Pilbeam (Cambridge: Cambridge University Press, 1992). A recent reader, *The Human Evolution Source Book*, edited by Russell L. Ciochon and John G. Fleagle (Englewood Cliffs, N.J.: Prentice-Hall, 1993), republishes both classic and modern sources.

There are also two excellent popular accounts of paleoanthropology: Roger Lewin's *Bones of Contention: Controversies in the Search for Human Origins* (New York: Simon and Schuster, 1987) and John Reader's *Missing Links: The Hunt for Earliest Man* (2nd ed., Penguin, 1988). An exciting popular account by one of the major participants is Donald Johanson's *Lucy* (New York: Simon and Schuster, 1981).

On the Piltdown affair, Frank Spencer has recently published a major work: *Piltdown: A Scientific Forgery* (London, Oxford, and New York: Natural History Museum Publications, Oxford University Press, 1990); and for do-it-yourself sleuths he has published a companion volume that gives all the clues and theories: Frank Spencer, ed., *The Piltdown Papers: 1908–1955* (London, Oxford, and New York: Oxford University Press, 1990).

NOTES TO THE TEXT

19 The quotations from Linnaeus are drawn from J. S. Slotkin, ed., *Readings in Early Anthropology* (London: Methuen, 1965), pp. 179–180.

21 "As the various mental faculties": *The Descent of Man*, p. 81.

24 Le Gros Clark's views were published in *The Fossil Evidence for Human Evolution* (2nd ed., Chicago: University of Chicago Press, 1964).

24 "anterior extremity": Ernst Mayr's argument was published in a landmark paper, "Taxonomic Categories in Fossil Hominids," *Cold Spring Harbor Symposia on Quantitative Biology*, 15 (1950): 109–118.

25 "undoubtedly had some sort of communication system": Jeffrey Laitman, "The Anatomy of Human Speech," *Natural History*, 92 (1984): 27.

25 "would be greatly eased": Bernard Wood, "Origins and Evolution of the Genus *Homo*," *Nature*, 355 (1992): 787.

26 "The fossil man game": Quoted in John Reader, *Missing Links: The Hunt for Earliest Man* (Harmondsworth: Penguin Books, 1988), p. 207.

29 "It is therefore probable": Darwin, *The Descent of Man*, p. 240.

30 "a strange blend of man and ape": Arthur Keith, *The Antiquity of Man* (2nd ed., London: Williams and Norgate, 1925), p. 503.

32 "It was not the adoption": Quoted in Phillip Tobias, "Piltdown, an Ap-

praisal of the Case against Sir Arthur Keith," *Current Anthropology*, 33 (1992): 281.

36 "What was so unexpected": Phillip Tobias, *Dart, Taung, and the "Missing Link"* (Johannesburg: Witwatersrand University Press, 1984), p. 47.

37 "Professor Dart was right": Arthur Keith, "Australopithecine or Dartians," *Nature*, 159 (1947): 377.

37 "Thinking it all over again": J. S. Weiner, *The Piltdown Forgery* (Chicago: University of Chicago Press, 1980; first published 1955), p. 27.

37 "the idea was repellent indeed": Ibid., p. 30.

38 "It is now clear": J. S. Weiner, K. P. Oakley, and W. E. Le Gros Clark, "The Solution to the Piltdown Problem," *Bulletin of the British Museum of Natural History* (Geol.), 2 (1953): 145.

38 "a most awkward and perplexing": Ibid., p. 146.

41 "suspense account": P. G. H. Boswell, "Human Remains from Kanem and Kanjera, Kenya Colony," *Nature*, 135 (1935): 371.

45 "We have proved I was right": Roger Lewin, *Bones of Contention* (New York: Simon and Schuster, 1987), p. 156.

45 "There was a tape recorder": Donald Johanson, *Lucy: The Beginnings of Humankind* (New York: Simon and Schuster, 1981), p. 18.

47 "It was an uncanny experience": Ibid., p. 256.

49 "social qualities": Darwin, *The Descent of Man*, p. 96.

3. A HUMAN WAY OF LIFE

FURTHER READING

The Cambridge Encyclopedia of Human Evolution, edited by Steve Jones, Robert Martin, and David Pilbeam (Cambridge: Cambridge University Press, 1992) is once again a valuable reference book for some of the topics covered here. A controversial, feminist account of the story told in this chapter can be found in Donna Haraway, *Primate Visions: Gender, Race and Nature in the World of Modern Science* (New York and London: Routledge, 1989).

Sherwood Washburn is a major presence in this chapter. For Washburn's memoirs see Sherwood L. Washburn, "Evolution of a Teacher," *Annual Review of Anthropology* (1983): 1–24. See also the interview of Washburn by Irven DeVore, *Current Anthropology*, 33 (1992): 411–423.

NOTES TO THE TEXT

55 "The Pleistocene way of life": S. L. Washburn and C. S. Lancaster, "The Evolution of Hunting," in *Man the Hunter*, ed. Richard B. Lee and Irven DeVore (New York: Aldine, 1968), p. 296, note.

55   "a very good Protestant": Remark in an interview with Irven DeVore, *Current Anthropology*, 33 (1992): 413.

57   "He chose me": Irven DeVore, personal communication, 1993.

59   "Baboon groups are closed social systems": Irven DeVore and K. R. L. Hall, "Baboon Ecology," in *Primate Behavior*, ed. Irven DeVore (New York: Holt, Rinehart and Winston, 1965), p. 38.

59   "is organized around the dominance hierarchy": K. R. L. Hall and I. DeVore, "Baboon Social Behavior," in *Primate Behavior*, ed. DeVore, p. 54.

60   "usually ensures stability": Ibid., p. 71.

61   Reporting on mountain gorillas in Zaire: George B. Schaller, "The Behavior of the Mountain Gorilla," in *Primate Behavior*, ed. DeVore.

61   "during one of these occasions": Jane Goodall, "Chimpanzees of the Gombe Stream Reserve," in *Primate Behavior*, ed. DeVore, p. 451.

61   "On the other occasions": Ibid., p. 445.

62   "The astonishment which I felt": *The Descent of Man* (first edition), pp. 919–920.

62   "In the early 1960s": R. B. Lee, Introduction to *Kalahari Hunter-Gatherers: Studies of the !Kung San and Their Neighbors*, ed. Richard B. Lee and Irven DeVore (Cambridge, Mass.: Harvard University Press, 1976), p. 10.

63   "My hunch was that research": R. B. Lee, *The !Kung San: Men, Women, and Work in a Foraging Society* (Cambridge: Cambridge University Press, 1979), p. 9.

67   "Some foods are adversely affected": Ibid., p. 438.

68   Richard B. Lee and Irven DeVore, eds., *Man the Hunter* (New York: Aldine, 1968).

69   "the original affluent society": Marshall Sahlins's intervention in *Man the Hunter*, pp. 85–89.

69   S. Washburn and C. S. Lancaster, "The Evolution of Hunting," in *Man the Hunter*.

69   "general characteristics of man": Ibid., p. 293.

69   "When males hunt and females gather": Ibid., p. 301.

70   On the carrying-bag: A. L. Zihlman, "Women as Shapers of Human Evolution," in *Woman the Gatherer*, ed. F. Dahlberg (New Haven: Yale University Press, 1981.)

71   Glynn Isaac, "The Food-sharing Behavior of Proto-human Hominids," *Scientific American*, 238 (1978): 90–108.

71   Lionel Tiger, *Men in Groups* (New York: Random House, 1969).

71   See, for example, Lewis Binford, "Human Ancestors: Changing Views of Their Behavior," *Journal of Anthropological Archaeology*, 4 (1985): 292–327.

72   Misia Landau, *Narratives of Human Evolution: The Hero Story* (New Haven: Yale University Press, 1991).

72   "I now see": Washburn, "Evolution of a Teacher," p. 15.

72   "devolved descendants": Claude Lévi-Strauss, "The Concept of Primitiveness," in *Man the Hunter*, ed. Lee and DeVore, p. 350.

73   Edwin Wilmsen, *Land Filled with Flies: A Political Economy of the Kalahari* (Chicago: University of Chicago Press, 1989); George Silberbauer, *Hunter and Habitat in the Central Kalahari Desert* (Cambridge: Cambridge University Press, 1981); Alan Barnard, *Hunters and Herders of Southern Africa: A Comparative Ethnography of the Khoisan Peoples* (Cambridge: Cambridge University Press, 1992).

73   John Yellen, "The Present and Future of Hunter-Gatherer Studies" in *Archaeological Thought in America*, ed. C. C. Lamberg-Karlovsky (Cambridge: Cambridge University Press, 1989).

74   Barbara B. Smuts, Dorothy L. Cheney, Robert M. Seyfarth, Richard W. Wrangham, and Thomas T. Struhsaker, *Primate Societies* (Chicago: University of Chicago Press, 1987).

77   Lars Rodseth, Richard W. Wrangham, Alisa M. Harrigan, and Barbara B. Smuts, "The Human Community as a Primate Society," *Current Anthropology*, 32 (1991): 221–254.

77   "In fact, with the possible exceptions": Ibid., p. 229.

78   "the capacity to sustain relationships in absentia": Ibid., p. 240.

78   "social evolution as a *human* affair": Ibid.

4. THE EVOLUTION OF CULTURE

FURTHER READING

Richard G. Klein's *The Human Career* (Chicago: University of Chicago Press, 1989) is again recommended as a textbook on human biological evolution. Robert J. Wenke's *Patterns in Prehistory: Humankind's First Three Million Years* (3rd ed., New York: Oxford University Press, 1990) is a good introduction to the archaeological debates. On the evolution of modern humans see E. Trinkaus, ed., *The Emergence of Modern Humans: Biocultural Adaptations in the Later Pleistocene* (Cambridge: Cambridge University Press, 1989) and Paul Mellars and Chris Stringer, eds., *The Human Revolution: Behavioural and Biological Perspectives on the Origins of Modern Humans* (Edinburgh: Edinburgh University Press, 1990), and for a useful summary see Paul Mellars, "The Origins and Dispersal of Modern Humans," *Current Anthropology*, 30 (1989): 349–385. On the Neanderthals, see Christopher Stringer and Clive Gamble, *In Search of the Neanderthals: Solving the Puzzle of Human Origins*

(London: Thames and Hudson, 1993) and Erik Trinkaus and Pat Shipman, *The Neandertals: Changing the Image of Mankind* (New York: Knopf, 1993).

NOTES TO THE TEXT

79 "Prior to the emergence of modern people": Klein, *The Human Career*, p. 344.

79 "there is no basis for arguing": Ibid., p. 262.

80 "paleoculture . . . differed significantly": Philip G. Chase and Harold L. Dibble, "Middle Paleolithic Symbolism: A Review of Current Evidence and Interpretations," *Journal of Anthropological Archaeology*, 6 (1987): 285.

82 "Among the remarkable changes": Lewis Binford, "Isolating the Transition to Cultural Adaptations," in *The Emergence of Modern Humans*, ed. E. Trinkaus (Cambridge: Cambridge University Press, 1989), pp. 35–36.

82 On Neanderthal speech see Philip Lieberman, *Uniquely Human: The Evolution of Speech, Thought, and Selfless Behavior* (Cambridge, Mass.: Harvard University Press, 1991). Cf. his note "On Neanderthal Speech," *Current Anthropology*, 33 (1992): 409–410.

83 "signals the most fundamental change": Klein, *The Human Career*, p. 358.

83 J. M. Lindly and G. A. Clark, "Symbolism and Modern Human Origins," *Current Anthropology*, 31 (1990): 233–261.

84 "cave Neanderthals came to a relatively quick end": W. W. Howells, *Mankind in the Making* (Garden City, N.Y: Doubleday, 1967), p. 305.

85 For a vivid, popular, but well-referenced account of the debate on the African Eve, see Michael H. Brown, *The Search for Eve* (New York: Harper and Row, 1990).

88 Chris Stringer, "Secrets of the Pit of the Bones," *Nature*, 362 (1993): 501–502, reporting on Juan-Luis Arsuaga et al., "Three New Human Skulls from the Sima de los Huesos Middle Pleistocene Site in Sierra de Atapuerca, Spain," *Nature*, 362 (1993): 534–537.

88 "The Neanderthal lineage": Stringer, "Secrets of the Pit," p. 502.

92 See Ferdinand Braudel, *On History* (Chicago: University of Chicago Press, 1980).

93 "the Neolithic has been perceived": Marek Zvelebil, "Fear of Flying, or How to Save Your Own Paradigm," *Antiquity*, 66 (1992): 811–814.

98 Marvin Harris, *Cows, Pigs, Wars, and Witches: The Riddles of Culture* (New York: Random House, 1978).

100 "come to be at odds": Roy A. Rappaport, *Pigs for the Ancestors* (2nd ed., Ann Arbor: University of Michigan Press, 1984), p. 444.

5. CULTIVATING THE SPECIES

FURTHER READING

A fine history of eugenics is Daniel J. Kevles, *In the Name of Eugenics: Genetics and the Uses of Human Heredity* (New York: Knopf, 1985). For the Nazi program of eugenics, and the role of scientists in its development, see Benno Müller-Hill, *Murderous Science: Elimination by Scientific Selection of Jews, Gypsies and Others, Germany 1933–1945* (Oxford: Oxford University Press, 1988). A lively history of the study of intelligence is Stephen Jay Gould's *The Mismeasure of Man* (New York: W. W. Norton, 1981).

D. W. Forrest's biography, *Francis Galton: The Life and Work of a Victorian Genius* (London: Paul Elek, 1974) is useful, but it is still worth reading Galton's own *Memories of My Life* (London: Methuen, 1908).

The Burt affair, discussed in this chapter, is still the subject of controversy. See L. S. Hearnshaw, *Cyril Burt: Psychologist* (London: Hodder and Stoughton, 1979) for the major statement of the case against Burt. For a defense see R. B. Joynson, *The Burt Affair* (London: Routledge, 1989). Hearnshaw responded to Joynson in "The Burt Affair—a Rejoinder," *The Psychologist: Bulletin of the British Psychological Association*, 2 (1990): 61–64.

NOTES TO THE TEXT

102 Quoted in Adrian Desmond and James Moore, *Darwin* (London: Michael Joseph, 1991; Penguin Books, 1992), pp. 601–602.

103 "the destruction of Slavery": Ibid., p. 521.

103 "leads to the inevitable extinction": Ibid., p. 521.

105 "three good genera": Ibid., p. 428.

105 "eminently *domesticated* animal": Ibid., p. 554.

105 "Man scans with scrupulous care": *The Descent of Man*, p. 944.

106 "Vaccination has preserved thousands": Ibid., p. 206.

107 "The careless, squalid, unaspiring Irishman": William Greg, quoted by Darwin, Ibid., p. 213.

107 "the intemperate suffer": Ibid., p. 206.

107 "Of the high importance": Ibid., p. 196.

108 "in the rudest state of society": Ibid.

109 "There is a prevalent belief": Francis Galton, *Hereditary Genius* (London: Macmillan, 1869), pp. 331–332.

109 "I have no great quickness": Darwin, *Autobiography*, p. 84.

111 "superior to the common run": Ibid., p. 85.

111 "You have made a convert": Desmond and Moore, *Darwin*, p. 572.

111 "Mr. Gladstone was amusingly insistent": Galton, *Memories of My Life*, pp. 249–250.

114 "it would be quite practical": Galton, "Studies in National Eugenics," in *Essays in Eugenics* (London: The Eugenic Society, 1909), p. 66.

115 "The children of successful and cultured parents": L. M. Terman, *The Measurement of Intelligence* (Boston: Houghton Mifflin, 1916), p. 115.

116 "a superstitious thrill": Cyril Burt, "Cyril Burt," in *A History of Psychology in Autobiography*, ed. E. G. Boring, H. S. Langfeld, H. Wener, and R. Yerkes (New York: Russell and Russell, 1952), p. 59.

116 Burt's writings on intelligence are reviewed in chapter 4 of Hearnshaw, *Cyril Burt*.

118 Margaret Mead, "Intelligence Tests of Italian and American Children," unpublished master's essay, Barnard College, 1924.

119 "It is better for all the world": Oliver Wendell Holmes, Supreme Court decision in *Buck v. Bell*, 1927.

119 "many of the deeds": Quoted in Kelves, *In the Name of Eugenics*, p. 123.

119 "ancestor worship, anti-Semitism": Ibid., p. 127.

120 "the Germans are beating us": Ibid., p. 116.

120 "Permission to marry": Müller-Hill, *Murderous Science*, p. 9.

120 "for the prevention of progeny": Ibid., p. 28.

121 "about 85 percent": Marcus Feldman, "Population Genetics," in *The Social Science Encyclopedia*, ed. Adam Kuper and Jessica Kuper (London and New York: Routledge, 1985), p. 627.

124 "the numbers left behind by Professor Burt": Leon J. Kamin, *The Science and Politics of IQ* (Potomac, Md.: Lawrence Erlbaum, 1974), p. 47.

124 "It seemed highly likely": Oliver Gillie, "Burt: The Scandal and the Cover-up," *A Balance Sheet on Burt*, Supplement to the *Bulletin of the British Psychological Society* (1980): 33.

124 "In the context of what I already knew": Ibid., p. 10.

125 "The verdict must be": Hearnshaw, *Cyril Burt*, p. 259.

125 "regressive reactivation of behaviour patterns": Ibid., p. 290.

126 "IQ tests assess such different components": P. V. Tobias, "IQ and the Nature-Nurture Controversy," *Journal of Behavioral Science*, 2 (1974): 9.

127 "This is a sizeable effect": Matt McGue, "Nature-Nurture and Intelligence," *Nature*, 340 (1989): 507.

128 "in the current environments": Thomas J. Bouchard, David T. Lykken, Matthew McGue, Nancy L. Segal, and A. Tellegen, "Sources of Human Psychological Differences: The Minnesota Study of Twins Reared Apart," *Science*, 250 (1990): 224–228.

129 "The moral faculties": *The Descent of Man*, p. 935.

6. THE COMMON HERITAGE

FURTHER READING

The field of sociobiology is still so full of sound and fury that no introductory overview can be recommended as providing a cool account of the twists and turns of the various arguments. The basic source is E. O. Wilson, *Sociobiology: The New Synthesis* (Cambridge, Mass.: Harvard University Press, 1975). A lively polemical attack on sociobiology and other forms of genetic determinism, by leading scientists, is to be found in *Not in Our Genes: Biology, Ideology, and Human Nature* by Richard Lewontin, Steven Rose, and Leon Kamin (New York: Pantheon Books, 1984). An interesting survey of the views of anthropologists on sociobiology can be found in Leonard Lieberman's "A Discipline Divided," *Current Anthropology*, 30 (1989): 676–682. In addition to the texts cited below, I would recommend Christopher Wills, *The Wisdom of the Genes: New Pathways in Evolution* (Oxford: Oxford University Press, 1989), for an introduction to genetics and evolution.

NOTES TO THE TEXT

132 "There is no doubt": Konrad Lorenz, *Civilized Man's Eight Deadly Sins* (New York: Harcourt Brace Jovanovich, 1973), p. 59.

132 "I hoped that National Socialism": Cited by Benno Müller-Hill, *Murderous Science: Elimination by Scientific Selection of Jews, Gypsies and Others, Germany 1933–1945* (Oxford: Oxford University Press, 1988), p. 183.

132 "Fortunately, the elimination of such elements": Ibid., p. 14.

132 "one of the greatest joys": Ibid., p. 184.

133 "all sanctimonious manipulators": Robin Fox, *The Search for Society: Quest for a Biosocial Science and Morality* (New Brunswick, N.J.: Rutgers University Press, 1989), p. 43.

134 "all 'history' is": Ibid., p. 218.

134 "would state that all human action": Ibid., p. 49.

134 "Since man evolved": Ibid., p. 127.

134 "the problem is not violence": Ibid., p. 135.

134 "the violence in man": Ibid., p. 133.

135 "It could only be remarkably poor judgment": Peter Medawar and Jean Medawar, *Aristotle to Zoos: A Philosophical Dictionary of Biology* (Cambridge, Mass.: Harvard University Press, 1983), p. 189.

136 "What is the direct evidence": Stephen Jay Gould, *Ever Since Darwin* (New York: Viking Penguin, 1977), p. 254.

136 "A single gene": François Jacob, *The Possible and the Actual* (New York: Pantheon Books, 1982), p. 19.

137 "human beings are guided": E. O. Wilson, *On Human Nature* (Cambridge, Mass: Harvard University Press, 1978), p. 38.

137 "profitable to the individual": *The Origin of Species,* p. 255.

138 "is lessened, or . . . disappears": Ibid., p. 258.

139 W. D. Hamilton, "The Genetical Theory of Social Behaviour," *Journal of Theoretical Biology,* 12 (1964): 12–45.

139 Robert Trivers, "The Evolution of Reciprocal Altruism," *Quarterly Review of Biology,* 46 (1971): 35–57.

139 "has resulted in the introduction": James King, "The Genetics of Sociobiology," in *Sociobiology Examined,* ed. Ashley Montagu (New York: Oxford University Press, 1980), p. 99.

140 "the organism is only DNA's way": Wilson, *Sociobiology,* p. 3.

140 "The genes march on": Richard Dawkins, *The Selfish Gene* (Oxford: Oxford University Press, 1976), p. 37.

141 Wilson's view on territoriality among humans can be found in *Sociobiology,* pp. 546–565, and in *On Human Nature,* pp. 107–111.

141 H.-J. Heinz, "Territoriality among the Bushmen in General and the !Ko in Particular," *Anthropos,* 67 (1972): 405–416.

141 Cf. Alan Barnard on !Xo territoriality: *Hunters and Herders of Southern Africa: A Comparative Ethnography of the Khoisan Peoples* (Cambridge: Cambridge University Press, 1992), pp. 66–67. On Bushman territoriality in general, see his chapter 12.

142 Bruce M. Knauft, "Reconsidering Violence in Simple Human Societies: Homicide among the Gebusi of New Guinea," *Current Anthropology,* 28 (1987): 457–500.

144 On Yanomami violence, see Napoleon Chagnon, *Yanomamo: The Fierce People* (3rd ed., New York: Holt, Rinehart and Winston, 1983), and his paper "Life Histories, Blood Revenge, and Warfare in a Tribal Population," *Science,* 239 (1988): 985–992. For criticisms see Bruce Albert, "Yanomami 'Violence': Inclusive Fitness or Ethnographer's Representation?" *Current Anthropology,* 30 (1989): 637–640. See further Napoleon A. Chagnon, "On Yanomamo Violence: Reply to Albert," *Current Anthropology,* 31 (1990): 49–53, and Bruce Albert, "On Yanomami Warfare: A Rejoinder," *Current Anthropology,* 31 (1990): 558–563.

145 For the Cheyenne case see John H. Moore, "The Reproductive Success of Cheyenne War Chiefs: A Contrary Case to Chagnon's Yanomamo," *Current Anthropology,* 31 (1990): 322–330.

146 "the profound differences in social behavior": Ernst Mayr, *The Growth of Biological Thought* (Cambridge, Mass.: Harvard University Press, 1982), p. 599.

146 "Moderately high heritability": E. O. Wilson, *Sociobiology,* p. 550.

147 "While in lower organisms": Jacob, *The Possible and the Actual,* p. 61.

148　*"Human ethology might be defined":* Sherwood Washburn, "Human and Animal Behavior," in *Sociobiology Examined,* ed. Ashley Montagu (New York and London: Oxford University Press, 1980), p. 273.

148　"simplistic notions of geneticism": Medawar and Medawar, *Aristotle to Zoos,* p. 241.

148　"a project so ambitious": L. L. Cavalli-Sforza, "Genes, Peoples and Language," *Scientific American* (November 1991), p. 72.

149　L. L. Cavalli-Sforza, A. Piazza, P. Menozzi, and J. Mountain, "Reconstruction of Human Evolution: Bringing Together Genetic, Archaeological, and Linguistic Data," *Proceedings of the National Academy of Science of the USA,* 85 (1988): 6002–6006. For a clear account see S. J. Gould, "Grimm's Greatest Tale," *Natural History,* 2 (1989): 20–28. For a criticism see Richard Bateman, Ives Goddard, Richard O'Grady, V. A. Funk, Rich Mooi, W. John Kress, and Peter Cannell, "Speaking of Forked Tongues: The Feasibility of Reconciling Human Phylogeny and the History of Language," *Current Anthropology,* 31 (1990): 1–24.

151　Boyd and Richerson on altruism: *Culture and the Evolutionary Process* (Chicago: University of Chicago Press, 1985), chap. 7.

151　"It might be argued that individuals co-operate": Ibid., p. 229.

152　"Cultural transmission is analogous": Dawkins, *The Selfish Gene,* p. 203.

153　"we have in cultural transmission": L. L. Cavalli-Sforza and Marcus Feldman, *Cultural Transmission and Evolution* (Princeton: Princeton University Press, 1981), p. 10.

153　"The main reason": Boyd and Richerson, *Culture and the Evolutionary Process,* p. 31.

7. FIRST FAMILY

FURTHER READING

My book entitled *The Invention of Primitive Society* (London and New York: Routledge, 1988) is a history of anthropological theories of kinship and the family. On incest see W. Arens, *The Original Sin: Incest and Its Meaning* (Oxford: Oxford University Press, 1986), and Robin Fox, *The Red Lamp of Incest* (New York: E. P. Dutton, 1980). See also David H. Spain, "The Westermarck-Freud Incest-Theory Debate," *Current Anthropology,* 28 (1987): 623–645. Other sources are given in the notes that follow.

NOTES TO THE TEXT

154　"As braves and hunters were required": J. F. McLennan, *Primitive Marriage: An Inquiry into the Origin of the Form of Capture in Marriage Ceremonies* (Edinburgh: Black, 1865), p. 132.

155 "The licentiousness of many savages": *The Descent of Man*, p. 896.

155 "expressed to me the strongest opinion": Ibid., p. 897.

156 "Therefore, looking far enough back": Ibid., p. 901.

158 "Human marriage appears": Edward Westermarck, *The Origin and Development of the Moral Ideas* (London: Macmillan, 1908), vol. 2, p. 364.

158 "The younger males": *The Descent of Man*, p. 901.

159 Yonina Talmon, "Mate Selection in Collective Settlements," *American Sociological Review*, 29 (1964): 491–508.

159 Joseph Shepher, *Incest: A Biosocial View* (New York: Academic Press, 1983).

160 Arthur Wolf and Chieh-Shan Huang, *Marriage and Adoption in China* (Stanford: Stanford University Press, 1980).

161 "when the young male grows up": Darwin, quoting a Dr. Savage, in *The Descent of Man*, p. 901.

161 "ontogeny recapitulates phylogeny": For a characteristically lucid and entertaining account of the theory, see Stephen Jay Gould, *Ontogeny and Phylogeny* (Cambridge, Mass: Harvard University Press, 1977).

164 "Among tribes of low culture": E. B. Tylor, "On a Method of Investigating the Development of Institutions: Applied to Laws of Marriage and Descent," *Journal of the Anthropological Institute*, 18 (1889): 267.

164 Claude Lévi-Strauss, *The Elementary Structures of Kinship* (Boston: Beacon Press, 1969; original French edition, 1949).

167 For his views on the Trobriand family and incest, see Bronislaw Malinowski, *Sex and Repression in Savage Society* (London: Routledge, 1927), and *The Sexual Life of Savages in North-Western Melanesia* (London: Routledge, 1929).

168 On the Nayar case, see C. J. Fuller, *The Nayar Today* (Cambridge: Cambridge University Press, 1976).

168 "hold it to be a great honour": Ibid., pp. 2–3.

168 "are not married": Ibid., p. 3.

169 "In Europe, soldiers are forbidden": Ibid., p. 5.

170 Herbert Gutman, *The Black Family in Slavery and Freedom* (New York: Pantheon, 1976).

170 Robert Lowie, *Primitive Society* (New York: Liveright, 1920), pp. 74–75.

172 "far from being the basis": E. R. Leach, *A Runaway World* (London: BBC, 1967), p. 44.

172 "authoritarian family": Wilhelm Reich, *The Mass Psychology of Fascism* (New York: Farrar, Straus and Giroux, 1970), p. 30.

172 "the time of the Grand Climacteric": Peter Laslett, "Marriage's Ups and Downs," *Times Literary Supplement* (August 4, 1989), p. 843.

174 See P. Laslett and R. Wall, eds., *Household and Family in Past Time* (Cambridge: Cambridge University Press, 1972).

177　Michael Young and Peter Wilmott, *Family and Kinship in East London* (London: Routledge, 1957).

8. MALE AND FEMALE

FURTHER READING

There is a huge modern literature on gender studies in anthropology, much of it published in the past twenty years. An overview is available in Henrietta Moore, *Feminism and Anthropology* (Minneapolis: University of Minnesota Press, 1988). See also Shirley Ardener, ed., *Defining Females: The Nature of Women in Society* (New York: Halstead, 1978), and Michaela Di Leonardo, ed., *Gender at the Crossroads of Knowledge* (Berkeley: University of California Press, 1991).

NOTES TO THE TEXT

179　"had all the courage": Margaret Mead, *Letters from the Field 1925–1975* (New York: Harper and Row, 1977), p. 19.

180　"He felt that sufficient work": Margaret Mead, *Blackberry Winter* (New York: William Morrow, 1972), p. 126.

182　"Adolescence is a new birth": G. Stanley Hall, *Adolescence* (New York: D. Appleton, 1907), p. xiii.

182　"I am not at all clear in my mind": Boas to Mead, quoted in *Blackberry Winter: My Earlier Years*, p. 138.

182　"Everyone agreed that the Manu'an islands": Ibid., p. 150.

183　"Living in the dispensary": Ibid., p. 151.

183　"represented no period of crisis": Margaret Mead, *Coming of Age in Samoa* (New York: William Morrow, 1928), p. 157.

186　"the evils inherent": Ibid., p. 173.

186　"The principal causes of our adolescents' difficulty": Ibid., p. 235.

186　Ruth Benedict, *Patterns of Culture* (New York: William Morrow, 1935).

187　"What I planned": Mead, *Letters from the Field*, p. 101.

187　"So we found ourselves": Ibid.

187　"preyed on their miserable swamp-dwelling neighbours": Mead, *Blackberry Winter,* p. 204.

188　"The Mundugumor contrasted with the Arapesh": Ibid., p. 205.

188　"Haddon is very kind to me": Quoted in David Lipset, *Gregory Bateson: Legacy of a Scientist* (Boston: Little Brown, 1982), p. 135.

188　Gregory Bateson, *Naven* (Cambridge: Cambridge University Press, 1936).

188　"in fact the women managed all the valuables": Mead, *Blackberry Winter,* p. 215.

189　"there were other kinds of innate differences": Ibid., p. 216.

189 "Gregory and I were falling in love": Quoted in Lipset, *Gregory Bateson,* p. 138.

189 "Gregory and I were close together in temperament": Mead, *Blackberry Winter,* p. 216.

190 "almost a principle of pure energy": Bateson on Mead, in Jane Howard, *Margaret Mead: A Life* (New York: Simon and Schuster, 1984), p. 253.

190 "Reo had a better ear": Howard, *Margaret Mead,* p. 163.

191 "By the time I left Samoa": Derek Freeman, *Margaret Mead and Samoa: The Making and Unmaking of an Anthropological Myth* (Cambridge, Mass.: Harvard University Press, 1983), p. xiv.

192 "The *moetotolo* is the only sex activity": Mead, *Coming of Age,* p. 93.

193 "The time is now conspicuously due": Freeman, *Margaret Mead and Samoa,* p. 302.

194 "research on ordinary adolescents": Cited by Freeman, ibid., p. 255.

195 "Freud's ideas": Eva Figes, quoted in Juliet Mitchell, *Psychoanalysis and Feminism* (Harmondsworth: Penguin, 1974), p. 335.

196 "The overthrow of mother right": Friedrich Engels, *The Origin of the Family, Private Property and the State* (London: Lawrence and Wishart, 1972; first German edition, 1884), chap. 2, part iii.

198 "the secondary status of woman in society": Sherry Ortner, quoted in *Woman, Culture and Society,* ed. Michelle Rosaldo and Louise Lamphere (Stanford: Stanford University Press, 1974), p. 67.

199 "tendency for the image of women": Sherry B. Ortner and Harriet Whitehead, "Accounting for Sexual Meanings," in *Sexual Meanings: The Cultural Construction of Gender and Sexuality,* ed. Sherry B. Ortner and Harriet Whitehead (Cambridge: Cambridge University Press, 1981), p. 8.

201 "Mead underestimated the extent": Frederick Errington and Deborah Gewertz, *Cultural Alternatives and a Feminist Anthropology* (Cambridge: Cambridge University Press, 1987), p. 9.

202 The film, produced by Frank Heimans in 1988, was entitled *Margaret Mead and Samoa.*

205 Lowell Holmes, *Quest for the Real Samoa: The Mead/Freeman Controversy and Beyond* (South Hedley, Mass.: Bergin and Garvey, 1987).

206 Clifford Geertz, *The Interpretation of Cultures* (New York: Basic Books).

9. THE ORIGIN OF SOCIETY

FURTHER READING

In addition to the sources noted below, my *Invention of Primitive Society* (London and New York: Routledge, 1988) reviews some of the debates covered in this chapter.

NOTES TO THE TEXT

208 "In such condition": Thomas Hobbes, *Leviathan* (1651), chap. 13.

209 "an animal weaker than some": Jean-Jacques Rousseau, *A Discourse on Inequality* (1755), second paragraph of the text.

209 "And although in civil society": Jean-Jacques Rousseau, *The Social Contract* (1762), book 1, chap. 8.

209 "Thus in the beginning": John Locke, *Second Treatise on Government* (1690), chap. 5, par. 49.

210 "The history of political ideas": Henry Maine, *Ancient Law* (London: John Murray, 1861), p. 165.

210 A. R. Radcliffe-Brown, *The Social Organization of Australian Tribes* (Sydney: Oceania Monographs No. 1, 1931).

211 "politically autonomous": Julian Steward, 1936, "The Economic and Social Basis of Primitive Bands," in *Essays in Anthropology in Honor of Alfred Louis Kroeber* (Berkeley: University of California Press, 1936), p. 311. Cf. E. R. Service, *Primitive Social Organization: An Evolutionary Perspective* (New York: Random House, 1962).

211 E. E. Evans-Pritchard, *The Nuer: A Description of the Modes of Livelihood and Political Institutions of a Nilotic People* (Oxford: Clarendon Press, 1940).

214 "it is the clear, consistent, and deeply rooted lineage structure": Ibid., p. 28.

214 "A Nuer rarely talks about his lineage": Ibid., p. 203.

215 "We find that people are more mobile": Paula Brown, "Non-Agnates among the Patrilineal Chimbu," *Journal of the Polynesian Society*, 71 (1962): 57.

216 Bruce Knauft, "Violence and Sociality in Human Evolution," *Current Anthropology*, 32 (1991): 391–428.

217 "*That a man which receiveth Benefit*": Thomas Hobbes, *Leviathan* (1651), part 1, chap. 15.

217 "It is not from the benevolence": Adam Smith, *An Enquiry into the Wealth of Nations* (London: Strahan, 1776), vol. 1, chap. 2.

218 "Society may subsist": Ibid.

218 "Love of tradition": Bronislaw Malinowski, *Crime and Custom in Savage Society* (London: Routledge, 1926), p. 30.

219 On the *Kula* see Bronislaw Malinowski, *Argonauts of the Western Pacific* (London: Routledge, 1922).

220 "In the systems of the past": Marcel Mauss, *Essay on the Gift* (London: Routledge, 1954; first French edition, 1925), p. 3.

220 Claude Lévi-Strauss, *The Elementary Structures of Kinship* (Boston: Beacon Press, 1969; first French edition, 1949).

221 "Occasions when tempers have got out of control": Lorna Marshall,

"Sharing, Talking, and Giving: Relief of Social Tensions among the !Kung," in *Kalahari Hunter-Gatherers: Studies of the !Kung San and Their Neighbours*, ed. Richard B. Lee and Irven DeVore (Cambridge, Mass: Harvard University Press, 1976; essay originally published in 1961).

223 "a kind of temporary insanity": Richard Lee, *The !Kung San* (Cambridge: Cambridge University Press, 1979), p. 397.

223 "the most loquacious people": Marshall, "Sharing, Talking, and Giving," p. 351.

223 "The San do not fight much": Lee, *The !Kung San*, p. 372.

223 "a song composed": Marshall, "Sharing, Talking, and Giving," p. 351.

223 "Men and women speak": Ibid., p. 352.

224 "The worst thing is not giving presents": Ibid., p. 370.

225 "the Tukano social domain": Philippe Descola, "Societies of Nature and the Nature of Society," in *Conceptualizing Society*, ed. Adam Kuper (London and New York: Routledge, 1992), p. 118.

225 "Head-hunting is a predatory process": Ibid., p. 119.

226 Emile Durkheim, *The Elementary Forms of the Religious Life* (London: Allen and Unwin, 1915; first French edition, 1912).

227 "In the dense concentrations": Marcel Mauss with Henri Beuchat, *Seasonal Variations of the Eskimo* (London: Routledge, 1979; French edition, 1950), p. 76.

228 "There is no such thing as society": Margaret Thatcher in an interview in the magazine *Women's Own*, October 31, 1987.

10. THE SECOND MILLENNIUM

FURTHER READING

There is a large and mainly pessimistic literature in futurology, but by its very nature it dates quickly. As good as any is R. J. Johnston and P. J. Taylor, eds., *A World in Crisis?* (Oxford: Basil Blackwell, 1986).

NOTES TO THE TEXT

231 T. R. Malthus, *An Essay on the Principle of Population*, ed. Donald Winch, based on the text of the 1803 edition, prepared by Patricia James in 1990 (Cambridge: Cambridge University Press, 1992).

232 "great cause intimately united": Ibid., book 1, chap. 1, p. 13.

232 "In the northern states of America": Ibid., p. 16.

233 "the human species would increase": Ibid., p. 19.

236 "drought itself is not the fundamental problem": Bradford Morse, Foreword to *Drought and Hunger in Africa: Denying Famine a Future*, ed.

Michael H. Glantz (Cambridge: Cambridge University Press, 1988), p. xiv.

238 Ester Boserup, *Conditions of Agricultural Growth* (Chicago: Aldine, 1965).

238 "the ordinary man saw little evidence": Phyllis Deane, *The First Industrial Revolution,* 2nd ed., (Cambridge: Cambridge University Press, 1980), p. 12.

239 "One of the features": Ibid., p. 20.

239 "Life in the crowded conditions of cities": Quoted in Robert J. Wenke, *Patterns in Prehistory: Humankind's First Three Million Years* (New York: Oxford University Press, 1990), p. 603.

240 "an undeveloped country may be defined": H. Singer, "The Concept of Economic Growth in Economic Development," in *Economic Growth,* ed. E. Nelson (London, 1960), p. 73.

241 Walter Rostow, *The Stages of Economic Growth* (Cambridge: Cambridge University Press, 1960).

241 I. Wallerstein, *The Capitalist World-Economy* (Cambridge: Cambridge University Press, 1979).

INDEX